Dimensions of

Also available from Continuum

Philosophy of Education, Richard Pring
Vocational and Professional Capability, Gerard Lum
Perspectives of Quality in Adult Learning, Peter Boshier
Work Based Knowledge, Carol Costley and Pauline Armsby

Dimensions of Expertise
A Conceptual Exploration of Vocational Knowledge

Christopher Winch

continuum

Continuum International Publishing Group

The Tower Building	80 Maiden Lane
11 York Road	Suite 704
London SE1 7NX	New York NY 10038

www.continuumbooks.com

© Christopher Winch 2010

First published 2010
Paperback edition first published 2012

British Library Cataloguing-in-Publication Data
A catalogue record for this book is available from the British Library.

ISBN: 978-1-8470-6268-0 (hardcover)
ISBN: 978-1-4411-0021-4 (paperback)

Library of Congress Cataloging-in-Publication Data
Winch, Christopher.
  Dimensions of expertise: a conceptual exploration of vocational
knowledge/Christopher Winch.
     p. cm.
  Includes bibliographical references.
  ISBN 978-1-4411-0021-4 (pbk.) – ISBN 978-1-4411-8906-6 (ebook) (pdf) –
ISBN 978-1-4411-8067-4 (ebook) (epub) 1. Vocational education–Philosophy.
2. Expertise–Philosophy. 3. Knowledge, Theory of. I. Title.

  LC1042.5.W55 2011
  370.113–dc23   2011031617

Typeset by Newgen Imaging Systems Pvt Ltd, Chennai, India
Printed and bound in Great Britain

To all the members of my family.

Contents

Acknowledgements

I have profited in the writing of this book from the thoughts and comments of more people than can be mentioned here. I would, however, like to express a special thanks for inspiration from Linda Clarke, Michaela Brockmann, Paul Hager, Gerard Lum, Theodore Lewis, John Gingell, Richard Pring, Ewart Keep, Lorraine Foreman-Peck, Leesa Wheelahan, Geoff Hinchliffe, Mili, Rohit Dhankar, Padma Sarangapani, Dietrich Benner, Ewart Keep, Geoff Hayward, Lorna Unwin and Michael Young.

Preface

A detailed philosophical debate on the nature of expertise has been long overdue. This volume is a modest attempt to start that debate. The focus is twofold. First, I attempt to explain and defend a particular account of know-how, or practical knowledge, derived primarily but not exclusively from the pioneering work of Gilbert Ryle. The book takes account of the debate that Ryle's work has engendered over the 64 years since he first published on this issue. Second, I try to relate this epistemological debate to various discussions concerning the nature of expertise that have arisen in vocational and professional education over the past 25 years, including attempts to provide a theory of expertise.

This book argues against the possibility of a general theory of expertise on the grounds that the activities to which the term 'expertise' is applied are too diverse for a theory to be possible. This is not to say, however, that there is nothing useful that can be said about expertise. One of my aims has been to chart the various dimensions of expertise that might need to be taken account of in trying to provide a description of expertise in any particular area. In this sense, the book can be said to offer guidance to those who wish to explore the character of expertise in the particular area in which they work.

Chapter 1

The Two Faces of Expertise

Introduction

This book attempts two interrelated tasks. The first is to arrive at an understanding of practical knowledge and how expertise is related to it. The second is to show how such an understanding informs the various educational tasks of developing expertise. 'Practical knowledge' is understood in a broad sense of 'knowing how' rather than 'knowing that', as set out by Ryle[1] and includes consideration of the moral aspect of knowing how to act, as well as what is known as practical judgement in the broader sense of being able to act rationally in practical contexts and includes consideration of 'competence', 'skill' and related terms. Declarative knowledge and knowledge by acquaintance are not the main concern, although, as will be seen, the relationships between these and practical knowledge will be a continuing thread in the discussion, particularly declarative knowledge. Indeed, in order to understand these relationships it will be necessary to devote some attention to some important distinctions within these two areas of knowledge, namely the distinction between organized knowledge and singular knowledge on the one hand and between aspectual and non-aspectual acquaintance on the other hand.

There are two related aspects to the concept of expertise. On the one hand, an expert can be thought of as a *subject expert*, someone who is extremely knowledgeable concerning an academic subject area. An important feature of subject expertise is the ability to acquire fresh knowledge within the subject, such as a scientist or scholar might accomplish. On the other hand, the concept of expertise is related to *practical activity* such as carpentry, medicine, engineering, painting or fishing, which involves mastery of an occupation, profession or activity. We tend to think of the first kind of expertise as related to declarative or propositional knowledge and the second related to practical knowledge, ability or skill. Although I shall be concerned primarily with the practical kind of expertise, one of the central arguments of this book is that there is often an intimate relationship between the two and that they cannot really be understood except in terms of each other. Thus, the kinds of mastery involved in subject expertise involve practical knowledge, while most kinds of practical expertise involve some, and sometimes a considerable degree of, propositional knowledge. In order to understand either kind of expertise, we need to be able to understand each kind of knowledge and how each relates to the other, while not losing sight of acquaintance knowledge.

There is a growing contemporary philosophical literature on the nature of practical knowledge, which was largely restarted by Ryle and which has come to life in recent years. Ryle's celebrated distinction between two kinds of knowledge, *knowing how* and *knowing that* has become hotly contested, with some commentators arguing for an assimilation of practical to propositional knowledge, while others have sought to distinguish skill from practical knowledge. Others again have tried to defend Ryle's initial distinction. Work carried out by David Carr in the early 1980s was taken up by Jason Stanley and Timothy Williamson in 2001 and the debate has continued with contributions from Ian Rumfitt, John Koethe, Paul Snowdon and Tobias Rosefeldt among others. Although relevant to the interest in skill and expertise in vocational education, the mainstream philosophical debate has not so far touched on an issue that was not treated in a satisfactory way by Ryle, namely the relationship between practical and propositional knowledge in action and judgement. However, it is a question not only of considerable epistemological interest in its own right but also one of great relevance to our full understanding of expertise.

Chapter 2 will deal with the debate initiated by Ryle. It is, however, worth reflecting on why the debate has educational significance; this will be the main task of the current chapter. In its concerns with teaching and learning Philosophy of Education has, in the main, focused on the learning of propositional knowledge in formal educational contexts. One must, of course, be careful not to overstate this case. Aristotle's work practical knowledge and the development of the virtues and Rousseau and his successors' claim that learning takes place in practical ways, should give the lie to the idea that Philosophy of Education is unconcerned with practical knowledge or its acquisition in a variety of contexts. It is, however, arguable that it has not received the detailed attention that it deserves in comparison with the attention paid to the teaching and learning of propositional knowledge. It is even more plausible to argue that the relationship between the ways in which propositional and practical knowledge are related in action has received comparatively little attention. Yet this is a matter of the greatest interest to those who are concerned, as I am, with the development of professional judgement, action and expertise.

What are the Issues?

Ryle argued that knowing how could not be subsumed to knowing that. The latter should be considered as a distinct epistemic category. In Chapter 2, his arguments will be considered. It is, however, worth noting that although Ryle's distinction is widely employed and recognized in everyday contexts, his arguments for that distinction are by no means universally accepted. In the main, those who reject them also reject Ryle's claim that knowing how is a distinct category from knowing that. For such commentators, any instances of knowing how are, in fact, instances of knowing that. I will call this Thesis 1.

What hangs on this dispute? Those who resist Ryle's distinction claim, on the whole, that knowing how is a species of knowing that. In other words knowing that or propositional knowledge is a more basic epistemic category than knowing how and that, despite some appearances to the contrary, in its fundamentals knowing how is a form of knowing that. If this claim is true then one important proposition follows:

1. Anything that can intelligibly be said about a case of *knowing that* can be intelligibly said about a case of *knowing how*.

What applies to a whole conceptual field must also apply to its parts. Of course, the converse does not follow, that what can be intelligibly said about knowing how cannot necessarily be intelligibly said about knowing that. If the critics of Ryle are correct, then nothing that can intelligibly said about knowing that cannot be intelligibly said about knowing how. This has the potential to pose problems for those who hold Thesis 1. It is relevant to our understanding of practical knowledge in educational contexts as well, since a faulty account of the relationship between knowing that and knowing how threatens to pose difficulties for the development of useful pedagogies and curricula in areas, such as vocational education, that are engaged in the development of practical knowledge.

On the face of it, 1 is problematic. To keep matters simple, let us use examples of knowing that where a knower knows one proposition and of knowing how where an agent knows how to do one action. Then

2. *A knows that* p

where *p* is a proposition, does not look like

3. *A knows how to F*

where F is an action.
It does not look as if

4. *A knows how to* p*

makes any sense, thus violating 1 above.

This is not, however, a fatal flaw in Thesis 1 as it can be maintained that, in order to lay bare the conceptual relationship between knowing how and knowing that, one must do a little 'unpacking'; a procedure not unknown to Ryle himself. This can be done by showing that the best way to read

A knows how to F

is as

5. *A knows that* w *is a way to F*

Where *w* is a procedure, and if

w *is a way to F*

is abbreviated as *p.*
Then it can be shown that

A knows how to F

can be understood as

A knows that p

and 1 is not violated.

But another problem threatens. It makes sense to say something like

6. *A knows how to F better than B does.*

But not apparently

7. *A knows that* p *better than B does.**

This is the *Degree Problem* that holders of Thesis 1 need to solve for their preferred account of knowing how to work. The Degree Problem is that one can have knowledge how in degrees, but not knowledge that, and if this is so, then Thesis 1, that everything that can intelligibly be said about knowing how can be said about knowing that, is violated.

As A. R. White points out, one can make sense of the above issue in some interpretations, but although one can usually make sense of 6 in terms of a single action, one cannot make sense of 7 in terms of a simple proposition.[2] This means that the earlier construal of knowing how as a species of knowing that through constructions like 5 will not work for constructions like 6.

This is not to say that there are no solutions to such problems for holders of Thesis 1 and we will examine them in Chapter 2. At this point, however, I will suggest that the *Degree Problem* needs to be solved as it is based on a fundamental feature of practical knowledge which is not present in the same way in propositional knowledge. Practical knowledge is something that one can improve on by, for example, becoming more skilful at a particular activity. It is possible to compare the abilities of more than one individual. It is also possible to *appraise* an instance of practical knowledge by drawing attention to those features of it that merit admiration or disapprobation. Ryle uses the term 'intelligence epithets' for these primarily adverbially expressed intelligence concepts and maintains that they apply to the actions to which they are ascribed, not to any mental acts that may be supposed to accompany them.[3] Since vocational and professional education are largely concerned with the development of practical knowledge so that, in the course of time, novices progress to competence, on to proficiency and, finally, to expertise, our ability to intelligibly employ such intelligence concepts in such normative activities as instructing, training, encouraging, explaining, demonstrating and assessing is essential to the possibility of vocational education in this sense. Any epistemological account of practical knowledge that fails to account for the possibility of such practices must be fatally flawed.

In the meantime, however, it is necessary to look more closely at knowing that. Although as has been argued, knowledge how is rightly considered to be the special province of vocational and professional education, it would be a grave mistake to think that knowledge that has no role to play in it. It has, and the relationship between knowledge how and knowledge that in vocational and professional education will be one of the central concerns of this book.

One Face of Expertise: Subject Knowledge

A possible riposte to the Degree Problem would be to say that it is non-existent. Just as it makes sense to say that A knows how to do F better than B, so it makes sense to say that A knows how to do F well or badly, so it also makes sense to say that A knows French History better than B, and one can also, for example, know French History well or badly.[4] Indeed, to take another example, it does not make sense to say that one knows how to spell 'illiterate' well or badly, one either knows how to or not.[5] This response is incorrect and furthermore does not deal with the issue raised by Ryle, since his formulation of the Degree Problem is not concerned primarily with whether or not one can partly know that p, but with the application of intelligence concepts, which cannot be done in the case of knowing that when applied to single propositions. It is incorrect because it is not the case that one can simply spell 'illiterate' without any evaluative qualification.[6] Thus one can spell 'illiterate' neatly, quickly, accurately, and so on, but one cannot apply an intelligence concept to

A knows that Napoleon went to Elba in 1815.

It is, of course, perfectly true that one can know French History well or badly, and it is worth looking more closely at why this is the case. If French History is taken to be the set of all relevant facts concerning that country's past, then it is clear that A could know French History better than B and it is also clear that A could, for example, have a thorough or deep knowledge of French History in this sense. A could simply know a lot of true propositions about France's past or know more of them than B.

However, most historians would rightly complain that this was a superficial way of understanding the history of France and that, although a good grasp of French History does indeed require the knowledge of many facts about France's past, it is by no means a sufficient condition for such a grasp. We would require, as a minimum, that A would be able to make sense of French History, by showing how events can be considered in terms of reasons and causes, of responses and reactions organized in a coherent narrative. And for this to be the case, A would need to know *why* events occurred, not merely *whether* they did. In other words, he would need to be able to offer *explanations* as well as facts. The cohering of A's knowledge into bodies of plausible, defensible and, possibly, compelling explanations of sequences of events or of processes, is what would lead us to ascribe a good grasp of a historical period to him. We might well want to use 'intelligence concepts' in Ryle's sense to characterize this grasp. For example, A might show a *subtle* understanding of the personality of Napoleon or Ney, or be able to *discriminate* between the motives of a Mirabeau or a Robespierre. He might be able to *incisively* recount the factors that led to the Thermidor counter-revolution or be able to weave together the complexities of the interactions between domestic and foreign policies between 1793 and 1812 into a coherent narrative. Obviously all this knowledge would depend on a range of abilities which would involve, although not be exhausted by his knowledge of many relevant facts. In this sense, his good grasp of French History will be informed by organizational and explanatory ability as well as by raw propositional knowledge. The example, if anything tends against those who try to dismiss the Degree Problem, because it shows how ability, in the sense of *knowing how*, is a central ingredient of the grasp of a subject like History, or indeed of many others.

However, we have not gone far enough either in characterizing what we mean by subject knowledge nor what we mean by subject expertise. A's good grasp of French History described above might be expected of an able upper secondary school student. Of a professional historian we would expect far more, including the ability to *evaluate* historical claims and to *generate* historical knowledge. It would also be reasonable to expect certain virtues, not the least of which would be a love of the truth (Weil 1949, pp. 53–7).[7] In order to understand this properly, we need to make a distinction between subjects as *collections of facts* and subjects as *modes of acquiring and maintaining knowledge*. This distinction has been made, in various forms by, for example, Michael Oakeshott with his 'Modes of Experience', by Paul Hirst with his 'Forms of Knowledge' and by Philip Phenix with his 'Realms of Meaning'.[8] The basic idea of a *form of knowledge* (I will use Hirst's term) is that it is not merely a collection of facts but a historically evolved and conceptually organized way of acquiring, testing and transmitting knowledge. To avoid confusion, I will use the term 'subject' to talk of groupings of organized knowledge of this kind, while bearing in mind the following provisos:

1. There is a fluidity about subject boundaries which is, to an extent, purpose relative.
2. Subject boundaries are not immutable.
3. Knowledge can be organized by drawing from the knowledge otherwise located in already existent subjects.

A subject in this sense thus involves: central organizing concepts; central facts; characteristic modes of inference which use the central organizing concepts and central facts as the basis of inferential warrants within the subject.[9] In addition, there are characteristic activities of investigation, discovery, validation, inference and teaching which ensure that the subject protects its relationship to the truth and augments and strengthens the knowledge that it lays claim to. A subject in this sense is a form of life organized around a set of concerns which have been so organized both because they suit human purposes but also because they have been found to constitute effective ways of organizing knowledge. Within such a form of life the whole gamut of engagement can be found from the dabbler and the dilettante, to the novice, to the expert and the devotee. Each of these does not merely possess a store of knowledge to varying degrees but has a range of abilities connected with the central activities that constitute the core of a subject. In this sense, traditional subjects depend heavily on human know-how as well as on extensive knowledge that.

As is well-known, such schemes for surveying the conceptual map of subject knowledge classify the field in different and sometimes mutually inconsistent ways. In addition, it is arguable that some of them are incomplete. For example, Hirst's Forms of Knowledge scheme admits and later drops Religious Knowledge as a distinct epistemic category, while knowledge of foreign languages is not admitted into the scheme at all. For our purposes, the precise details of such classificatory schemes do not matter too much. It is arguable that different schemes are suitable for different purposes and that one should not seek a template that is useful for all time and all purposes. It does matter, however, that such schemes illuminate in relation to what they are designed to illuminate, whether it be to give an overview of the curriculum for a traditional English grammar school education or to map the knowledge available for a range of vocational programmes. It should be noted that Hirst's Forms of Knowledge do not correspond exactly either to traditional grammar school subjects or even to newer ones. Thus the social sciences are put together as one form even though it is quite plausible to suggest that Economics and Psychology are methodologically distinct forms of enquiry, or, more radically, that different assumptions underlie different approaches to the respective subject matters of Economics and Psychology making them in effect more than one form of knowledge, albeit concerned with the same subject matter. To use a contemporary expression, the different subjects may each within themselves embrace different *paradigms*, each with its own central concepts, inferential warrants and modes of investigation and validation.

A central point about subjects (and by implication, the traditional subjects of the grammar school curriculum) is that they organize both already existing and new knowledge in a systematic way and imply procedures for the discovery and validation of knowledge. One could say that such a subject is a *systematic* way of organizing knowledge, bearing in mind that this is a potentially misleading way of expressing the matter. At a minimum a subject will have the features already mentioned. One writer has attempted to set out in more detail the kinds of inferences that are allowed in each subject, preferring the term 'forms of discussion' for this aspect of Hirstian Forms of Knowledge, which reflects the incomplete and dynamic nature of the forms (Mackenzie 1998).[10] Another approach would be to use Toulmin's (1958) account of argumentative structures and show how these vary in terms of backing statements and inferential warrants across different areas of knowledge.[11] However, it is not enough to characterize subjects in terms of inferential structures. There is a greater richness to the systematic nature of such enquiry than distinctness of inference suggests by itself.

There are usually *core assumptions* which, although rarely if ever articulated, nevertheless constitute working assumptions in a particular field of enquiry, for example, that measuring instruments retain a certain constancy in their results in various branches of the natural sciences or that there really are genuine traces of the past as in Archaeology, Geology and History. These are what Moyal-Sharrock has called 'local riverbed propositions', adapting Wittgenstein (1969).[12] There are very often also *key propositions* with a normative or quasi-normative status, such as formulae of Relativity Theory in Physics or Geometrical Axioms in Geometry, whose status is unlikely to be questioned except in the most unusual circumstances. There are also central organizing concepts particular to subjects, such as *agency* and *narrative* in History, or *energy* and *field* in Physics. The individual possession of concepts is itself a form of practical knowledge or know-how, as will be argued in Chapter 2.[13]

It can be seen therefore that the systematic organization of knowledge into subjects is something very different and much more subtle and complex than the definitions of knowledge to be found in much of the philosophical literature suggest, that usually attempt to account for what are the conditions for knowledge of single propositions. In German, there is a distinct noun, *Wissen* to denote systematic knowledge, as opposed to *Kenntnis* which refers to single propositions. Throughout much of this book, when the application of knowledge to practice is being discussed, it will, in the main, be the application of knowledge in the sense of *Wissen* rather than *Kenntnis* that will be discussed.

The Other Face of Expertise: Practical Knowledge

The main theme of this book is the concept of practical expertise. There is a tendency to think of practical expertise as something that contrasts with the subject expertise that we considered earlier, as if they two are largely independent of each other.[14] This is a significant mistake which obscures understanding both of subject and of practical expertise. Although the book will be much concerned with the detail of *knowledge how to do* various kinds of things, it is important to locate the discussion in relation to a conceptual framework for thinking about practical affairs that came to prominence with the publication in 1981 of Alastair MacIntyre's *After Virtue*,[15] which has since generated an extensive literature. In this book, MacIntyre argues that, central to our conceptions of worthwhile activity, and hence the concept of a virtue, itself central to our understanding of moral agency, is the concept of a *practice*. A practice is a recurrent social activity characterized by the following key features:

1. It has its own goals or *telos*, criteria for the achievement of which constitute the standards of excellence available in that practice. These constitute its internal goods, which are of two, related varieties. First the activities involved in achieving excellence are themselves of intrinsic value. Second, the fulfilment of criteria of excellence are also a central internal good.
2. Practices are historically constituted and involve taking account of and developing a tradition of activity, in relation to both kinds of internal good. Initiation into a practice is, to a large degree, initiation into established ways of working and established criteria of excellence. These may evolve, but do so usually in the context of respect

for and adaptation to traditional ways of working and criteria of excellence.

3. Each individual human life has a *narrative structure*, based on the life cycle of humans as part of nature, but located within practices. We understand the significance of our lives and their worthwhileness in relation to the practices in which they are located.

4. Not only do practices have internal goods, but they also have external goods, which have extrinsic value. The internal goods of a practice, when they are exchangeable, become external goods such as money or services and are the possession of some individual. External goods could be obtained in other ways than through the achievement of the internal goods of some particular practice.

Much has been written about MacIntyre's concept of a practice. I want, however, to concentrate on certain aspects of the notion of a practice which are particularly relevant to this discussion. Philosophers are prone to use technical terminology. There is nothing wrong with this and it is much to be commended provided such terminology assists rather than obscures understanding. The concept of a *practice* was introduced by MacIntyre in order to provide illumination of a range of phenomena clustered around the concept of moral agency. His discussion, however, suggests that the concept of a practice may not be as illuminating as has been widely thought. The main reason for this is that we already have a rich classificatory vocabulary, not only for human activity but for the social context in which it occurs. If we are to abandon such vocabulary in favour of a philosophically introduced concept of a practice with the characteristics describe above, it is reasonable to enquire whether or not it actually adds to our understanding of philosophical questions such as the nature of expertise. It is not clear that this is in fact the case.

What is a Practice?

More than one commentator has remarked on the fluidity of the MacIntyrean notion of a practice.[16] In itself this need not be a problem. There is no reason why MacIntyre should be rigidly bound to a particular definition of a practice. The notion was developed in order to elucidate philosophical questions, not to provide a sociological classificatory framework. However, if the notion of a practice both causes confusion and fails to enlighten then there are grounds for wondering whether or not it is worth adopting. One central problem with the notion of a practice is that of getting clear about what is and what is not one. Thus we learn that, for example, construction, fishing, architecture and farming are practices, suggesting that the notion is linked to other familiar concepts such as that of an economic sector, an occupation or a way of life. By contrast, bricklaying and planting turnips are not practices. This again suggests a contrast between, for example, occupation or professions on the one hand and trades or activities on the other hand. It can be argued, however, that *occupation* is a category superordinate to the more culturally specific *trade* so the exclusion of bricklaying is, on the face of it, puzzling.

However, matters become more complex in MacIntyre and Dunne (2002) where it is suggested by MacIntyre that teaching is not a practice but

a set of skills and habits put to the service of a variety of practices. (p. 5)

The practices in question are the subjects like History or Philosophy of the previous section of this chapter. In this set of distinctions we find more confusion. First, an occupation like teaching is reduced to a 'set of skills and habits', a description which is far too reductive of what it is to practice a complex occupation, even on MacIntyre's account of a practice, for example, architecture or farming. Second, although there may be merit in classifying subjects as practices they exhibit characteristics of internal goods: they have traditions; they are a site of the exercise of virtues and they help to structure the narrative of a human lives; they are not the same kinds of things as occupations. Occupations are primarily ways of organizing work for economic purposes, but they are also ways of organizing and acquiring knowledge.

One could argue that while practices are concerned with internal goods, institutions are concerned with external goods (status, prestige, money). But this distinction will not hold up, even for MacIntyre's preferred examples. Architecture, for example, is concerned not just with the production of excellent buildings, excellently conceived, but also with prestige, status and money as well as other external goods such as the enhancement of the environment or of the economic, legal or cultural life of a society. Indeed, architecture as a practice (in the sense of an ongoing human activity or *form of life*) would not be intelligible without reference to these external goods. One can distinguish between an institution (e g. the professional association of architects), the occupation (e.g. the historically evolved system of training, licensure, body of knowledge and skill associated with the design of buildings) in a particular country, and the practice (form of life) of architecture, that embraces the evolution of those activities characterized by the *telos* of architecture (the design of buildings), but it is worth doing so when there is a purpose for doing so, rather than constructing a classificatory scheme for its own sake.

Furthermore, one can detect within occupations, subjects, institutions and forms of life the characteristic of possession of internal goods that MacIntyre attributes to practices. MacIntyre has already acknowledged this to be the case for subjects, but the same can be said for professions, occupations and institutions. Thus, medicine has its own *telos* in terms of the achievement of health, bakery in terms of the production of breads and pastries, and a national army in terms of defence of the territory of the state.[17] There are 'internal goods' criteria in each, both in terms of the achievement of excellence in respect to the *telos* and in respect of ways of achieving that *telos*. One can conclude that the notion of a practice in MacIntyre's sense does not give any significant philosophical illumination to the matters that concern him in terms of moral agency, the narrative structure of human life and the production of internal and external goods, as these can be discussed at a detailed level in relation to established sociological categories of profession, occupation, way of life and institution (and, no doubt, others). Furthermore, it may well be that one needs a much finer-grained analysis than this in order, for example, to become clear about the development of virtue and of internal and external goods in relation to a culturally situated sociological category such as *Beruf* in Germany, which although loosely belonging to a sociologically superordinate category of *occupation* cannot nevertheless be understood independently of its cultural specificity.[18]

Knowledge and Practice

I will not, therefore, make use of MacIntyre's notion of a practice. The concerns, however, that MacIntyre wishes to explore through the notion of a practice are important, but they can be dealt with in greater detail and discrimination through established sociological categories. Those that I wish to explore in greater detail include both internal and external goods, although in the case of the latter, I will not be concerned with money, status and prestige, but with the 'outward' signs of excellence such as dealings with customers, patients, the public and society more generally.[19] But my concern is more specific than that as it is focussed on the personal attribute of expertise as a way of capturing the contribution of *individuals* to these goods. This expertise, as we have seen, can be related to the production, validation and safeguarding of systematic propositional knowledge in subjects. But it can also be related to the practice of professions, occupations and forms of life within various institutional contexts. This appears to shift the focus from propositional knowledge (knowing that) to knowing how and indeed it does. It is plausible to argue that there are some occupations, for example, what are sometimes known as *traditional crafts* such as pottery or wheel-making that do not rely on the drawing down of publicly available systematically organized knowledge for their practice.[20] They clearly depend on the exercise of *skill* and *professional judgement* and either rely on contingent knowledge (in the sense of *Kenntnis*) or on a personally generated store of systematic knowledge acquired during the growth of expertise (see Ryle 1946). These will form an important, but not exclusive part of my concern.

To account for expertise relying exclusively on the traditional craft model would be tempting. One would be spared the need for dealing with the apparent complexity and difficulty of showing how knowing that and knowing how interact with each other and, in particular, of showing how propositional knowledge or subject knowledge may inform skill or professional judgement. But this approach is, I believe, futile. We have already shown how expert subject knowledge is an amalgam of propositional and practical knowledge and have suggested that even traditional crafts cannot dispense with propositional knowledge. When we go on to look at trades, technical occupations, semi-professions and professions, such a limited approach will be even more implausible. Many occupations rely on systematically organized propositional knowledge for their practice. This is not just because they happen, as a matter of contingent fact, happened historically to have done so but because they could not be practised effectively, let alone with expertise, without doing so. This, of course, requires argument, not just concerning how it is that such knowledge is brought to bear on the practice of such occupations, but also concerning how expertise is facilitated through, but not exclusively through, the bringing to bear of such knowledge on practical judgement and activity.

In this respect, the *subjects* discussed in the previous section are highly significant, as some of them provide a principal source of the organized knowledge on which occupations draw. As already suggested, there are affinities between subjects and occupations. Both involve the mastery of practical abilities and judgement, both encompass the notion of expertise and both manifest themselves in diverse institutional forms. But it will be argued in Chapter 10 that the bearing of subjects on occupations has a wider significance than this in terms of individual and civic development within the context of occupational engagement. The question of the relationship between subjects and occupations is not then merely one of pragmatism (what knowledge is needed to carry out this occupation?) but also of how expertise is defined (what does one need to know in order to be an expert?), of how one grows personally as a result of subject expertise within the occupational context (what is it to be an educated member of an occupation) and of civic entitlement (how does being a member of this occupation contribute to one's being a citizen)?

Subjects and Occupations

The distinction between subjects and occupations is an important one. It is possible to be an expert in a subject (in the loose 'form of knowledge' sense in which the term has been used in this chapter) and it is possible to be an expert in the occupation sense (again this term is used in a loose sense). There are affinities, however. Mastery of a subject involves knowing how to acquire, use, manage and validate the propositions which are both the result of and the instruments of the established mode of enquiry which constitutes the subject. Mastery of an occupation involves practice of a traditionally established mode of economic activity with its own internal identity and standards of excellence.[21] It may or may not involve the use of organized knowledge, let alone the application of systematic methods of knowledge acquisition, but it frequently does do so and, for that reason there is bound to be a link between subject and occupational expertise. Of course, in the world of the universities and research institutes, practice of the subject as an occupation suggests a unity in practice of what are, conceptually two distinct types of expertise.[22]

An important question is that of the degree and type of subject knowledge that is required in order to engage in an occupation. Should it be the bare minimum necessary to perform certain tasks within the relevant occupation or should it approach that of the subject expert? There are different answers to this question but they all raise a common concern – is there such a thing as subject knowledge which is superfluous to the immediate practice of the occupation and how much of it should be imparted to the intending practitioner of the occupation? This concern relates to a number of issues that suggest that the attribution of expertise should be considered generously – it is not just to do with the possession either of large amounts of propositional knowledge nor with excellence in the carrying out of central occupational tasks.

For occupational expertise the important questions to be considered include the following:

1. The degree of autonomy of the practitioner in planning, controlling, co-ordinating and evaluating occupational work.
2. The permeability of occupational careers from direct practice into technology and research relevant to occupational practice.
3. The role of the occupation and its associated subject knowledge in relation to the civic and personal development of its practitioners.

Different responses to these concerns both reflect and define different conceptions of occupational expertise and divergent views on the role of occupational practice in broader conceptions of individual and social well-being in the societies in which they are practised.

Outline of the Argument of the Remainder of the Book

Chapter 2 explains and defends a particular view of the relationship between knowing how and knowing that which is broadly based on, although critical of some aspects of Ryle's distinction. Alternative accounts are considered and found wanting. Chapter 3 considers the concept of skill as the primary individual repository of knowing how to do something and illustrates some of its peculiarities and limitations, as well as its role in the broader picture of practical knowledge. Chapter 4 examines the relationship between moral and non-moral aspects of practical knowledge looking in particular at the relationship between *techne* and *phronesis* and considers different conceptions of competence as a category of practical knowledge conceptually related to various conceptions of occupation. Chapter 5 explains and defends an account of practical knowledge that locates understanding of it in the concept of *normative activities*. This account is defended in terms of actual and possible objections. A key feature of this defence is the claim that norms, to be adequately understood, need to be located within a broader cultural understanding. Chapter 6 takes up a feature of Ryle's account that Chapters 1 and 2 suggested was inadequate, its unwillingness to acknowledge the role of systematic knowledge in practical action. It is shown how Ryle's account can be modified to take account of this central element in professional judgement and action. Chapter 7 takes up the topic of tacit knowledge and describes the indispensable nature of that concept in our understanding of knowing how, while at the same time dispelling two distinct myths about tacit knowledge, associated with Oakeshott and Chomsky respectively. Chapter 8 critically examines the contention that there can be *theories* of expertise, paying particular attention to 'fluency' theories which suggest that expertise is a matter of, in some sense, the fluent performance of the relevant actions associated with an activity. Such theories are criticized for giving an inadequate account of the role of theory in much that can be termed 'expert practice'. Chapter 9 takes on the more constructive role of attempting to describe the senses in which one can be an expert and the various distinctions that lie on the novice – expert continuum. Important to this account is the distinction between 'vertical' aspects of expertise concerned with the application of propositional knowledge to practice, 'horizontal' aspects of expertise, associated with the evaluative aspects of the activity and 'scope' aspects of expertise, concerned with the breadth of operation of the occupational activity. Chapter 10 considers the implications of the positions developed, for the organization of both initial and continuing vocational education and critically analyses the European Qualification Framework (EQF). The construction of an adequately articulated relationship between initial and continuing vocational education is considered to be of particular importance.

Notes

[1] Ryle, G. (1946) 'Knowing how and knowing that', *Proceedings of the Aristotelian Society*, 56, pp. 212–25; (1949) *The Concept of Mind*, London, Hutchinson, pp. 25–60.

[2] White, A. R. (1982) *The Nature of Knowledge*, Totowa, Rowan and Littlefield, pp. 27–9.

[3] Ryle (1946), pp. 2–3.

[4] See the discussion in White (1982), ch. 2.

[5] Ibid. p. 27.

[6] This is not to say that there may be some simple actions of which it is true that all that one can say of them is that someone can or cannot perform them. But such isolated cases do not help to deal with the Degree Problem.

[7] Weil, S. (1949) *L'Enracinement*, Paris, Gallimard. Translated into English as *The Need for Roots* (2001) London, Routledge.

[8] Hirst, P. H. (1965) 'Liberal education and the nature of knowledge', in Archamabult, R. (ed.) *Philosophical Analysis and Education*, London, Routledge; Oakeshott, M. (1933) *Experience and Its Modes*, Cambridge, Cambridge University Press; Phenix, P. (1964) *Realms of Meaning*, New York, McGraw Hill.

[9] Cf. Brandom, R. B. (2000) *Articulating Reasons*, Cambridge, MA, Harvard University Press, esp. ch. 2.

[10] Mackenzie, J. (1998) 'Forms of knowledge and forms of discussion', *Educational Philosophy and Theory*, 30, 1, pp. 27–50.

[11] Toulmin, S. (1958), *The Uses of Argument*, Cambridge, Cambridge University Press; Newton, P., Driver, R., Osborne, J. (1999) 'The place of argumentation in the pedagogy of school science', *International Journal of Science Education*, *21*, 5, pp. 553–76.

[12] Moyal-Sharrock, D. (2003) 'Logic in action: Wittgenstein's *Logical Pragmatism* and the impotence of scepticism', *Philosophical Investigations*, 26, 2, pp. 125–48. Wittgenstein, L. (1969) *On Certainty*, Oxford, Blackwell.

[13] See also, Geach, P. (1958) *Mental Acts*, London, Routledge; Brandom (2000), chs 1, 2.

[14] A possible problem with Hirst's later work, see (1993) 'Education, knowledge and practices', in Barrow, R., White, P. (eds) *Beyond Liberal Education*, London, Routledge.

[15] MacIntyre, A. (1981) *After Virtue*, London, Duckworth.

[16] In what follows, I make extensive use of ideas set forth in Hager (2008) 'Refurbishing MacIntyre's account of a practice', unpublished ms.

[17] It has been argued that the *telos* can be contested in the case of professions but not of occupations, but there is no good reason to suppose this to be the case, as considerations of examples will show (see Carr 1999; Winch 2002). Although he does not use MacIntyre's terminology, Carr appears to think that an occupation like bakery can achieve excellence even where external goods factors like justice with regard to the public are violated, whereas this is not the case with professions. Once again, examples can show that this need not be the case. It is interesting, however, that such external goods as just dealings with customers have the characteristic of not merely being morally significant but of having intrinsic value.

[18] See Greinert, W-D. (2007) 'The German philosophy of vocational education', in Clarke, L., Winch, C. (eds), pp. 49–61, for the cultural specificity of *Beruf*; Winch (2006a, b) on the way in which the concept of *Beruf* is related to that of virtue).

[19] See, for example, Marquand, D. (2004) *The Decline of the Public*, London, Polity Press, on the importance of some of these in the British context, brought under the concept of the public realm.

[20] See, for example, Sturt, G. (1923) *The Wheelwright's Shop*, Cambridge, Cambridge University Press, on the wheelwright's trade, an example which will be drawn on elsewhere in this book.

[21] It is striking that an occupation in stronger conceptions, like the German *Beruf*, has many of the properties of MacIntyrean practices.

[22] *Occupation* is also an economic category as it is concerned with the production of goods and services and with the provision of a livelihood for its practitioners. However, it would be misleading to insist on too narrow a definition of 'economic' in characterizing occupations, for fear of missing some of their most important characteristics (including their economic characteristics).

Chapter 2

Current Philosophical Debates about Knowing How

Introduction: Ryle's Account of Knowing How and Knowing That

Contemporary philosophical discussion about the nature of practical knowledge or, more specifically, knowing how starts with Ryle's (1946) paper on 'Knowing How and Knowing That' and continues in a chapter of that title in his 'The Concept of Mind' (Ryle 1949). In both of these Ryle argues that *knowing how* is a distinct form of knowledge from *knowing that* and cannot be reduced to it. If we do not recognize this we cannot do justice to our understanding of knowing how and related concepts. He does not deny that knowing that can be implicated in knowing how, although he does not say too much about this. Ryle's principal concern in 1949 was to expose the shortcomings of Cartesian philosophy of mind. His strategy for doing so was based on a set of assumptions that Cartesians are committed to and which jointly mean that they cannot coherently present their preferred conception of *knowledge how* as a form of *knowledge that*. Whether it can be maintained that *knowing how* can be implicated in *knowing that* without Cartesian commitments is one of the themes of this chapter.

Much of the comment on Ryle's alleged distinction between knowing that and knowing how has been hostile, with many commentators denying that such a distinction exists in a meaningful epistemological sense (e.g. White 1982; Stanley and Williamson 2001). Sometimes, more sympathetic commentators like Carr (1980, 1981) have defended a distinction between propositional and practical knowledge without, however, endorsing the way in which Ryle makes this distinction.[1] In general, the defenders of some form of Ryle's distinction between knowing how and knowing that appear somewhat beleaguered. It is my belief that the full strength of Ryle's position has not been adequately brought out. Without endorsing it in its entirety therefore, the object of this chapter is to vindicate Ryle's distinction by drawing attention to the inadequacies of the attacks on it and also to the fact that, without it, we are unable to adequately understand a crucial feature of human activity, namely the concept of expertise. This is not to endorse Ryle's account of the knowing how/knowing that distinction wholeheartedly, as it is vitiated by one notable weakness.[2] But without some form of Ryle's distinction we will not make much progress in understanding expertise.

What then was Ryle saying? His account of the knowing how/knowing that distinction was based on a particular kind of argument. Assume that knowing how is a form of knowing that. Follow through the consequences of maintaining such a position. You will then see that it leads to unacceptable consequences. Therefore, the initial position that knowing how is a form of knowing that is untenable. But identifiable forms of both knowing that and knowing how are recognized in non-technical linguistic usage. Since the only plausible alternative view is that knowing how and knowing that are distinct (although perhaps related) we should accept that view.[3]

Ryle's argument against the claim that knowing how is a species of knowing that gets going by assuming the premises for the argument that knowing how is form of knowing that and then showing that they lead to unacceptable consequences. The premises are as follows:

1. If one acts in a certain way, one knows how to act in a certain way *w*.
2. If one employs knowledge that such-and-such is the case, one avows the proposition that such-and-such is the case.
3. Knowledge how to act in a certain way *w* is knowledge that, for some proposition, doing so-and-so is a way of doing *w*.[4]

Ryle argues that a certain theory of mind, Cartesianism, is committed to all three of these propositions. Cartesianism is the view that minds are ontologically distinct from bodies and that all intentional bodily activity is preceded by mental acts performed by the individual mind that is associated with a particular body. Mental activity is always conscious activity and the actor is immediately and incorrigibly aware that he is so acting.[5] Premise 1 is based on the assumption that the exercise of a skill involves knowing how to perform the activity on which the skill is exercised. Premise 2 is based on the idea that knowledge that involves the conscious entertaining of a proposition in one's mind, as it were, silently asserting it. Premise 3 asserts that, mentally speaking, which for a Cartesian is the only way in which agency can be spoken of, the *act* identified through someone's overt action or behaviour is, in fact, an example of knowing that there is a certain way to perform that act.

It follows from these assumptions that:

4. if one acts in a certain way *w*, one knows that doing so-and-so is a way of doing *w* (follows from 1, 3]).[6]

And thus,

5. if one knows that so-and-so is a way of doing *w*, then one avows it (2).[7]

It then follows that an act involves an avowal, since acting in a certain manner involves knowing that such-and-such is the way to act in a certain manner and knowing that involves avowal of the relevant proposition. But an avowal is itself an act of certain kind. Since this is so, one can ask of any particular avowal what one needs to know in order to carry out this avowal. And, repeating the pattern of reasoning outlined above, one can ask what proposition one needs to know in order to know how to carry out the avowal. Finally, since knowing that *second proposition* involves avowing it, one has to repeat the analysis for the avowing of the second proposition, and so on. The conclusion of Ryle's argument is that these three premises taken together offer an incoherent account of action because they are incapable of explaining how any action arises without implying that any action is preceded by infinitely many actions. Since these three premises are necessary commitments of the Cartesian position, the argument demonstrates that this position is untenable.

It has been objected that 1 and 2 in particular are false. There are certain things one can do without knowing how to do them, like breathing and digesting for example.[8] Premise 1 is only true when applied to intentional action. Likewise it is objected that possession of *knowledge that* does not necessarily involve silently asserting the proposition that expresses it. We can only accept 2 if it is interpreted *not* to mean conscious avowal. But since 1 is only true when action involves conscious intention, 1 and 2 cannot be true together. Ryle, however, is not committed to either 1 or 2 and indeed rejects them. The only questions that arise are, first whether he has correctly characterized the Cartesian position, second whether he has correctly pointed out that there is a regress, and third whether or not avowing that a certain proposition is the case necessarily involves knowing how to avow a further proposition. It is this last point that we shall return to.

Critiques of Ryle's Account of Knowing How

Ryle has been criticized by Stanley and Williamson for holding to claims that he in fact rejects so I will not detain myself over these criticisms.[9] It is worth, however, spending more time on the criticisms of Ryle's position urged by White (1982), because they well illustrate the misunderstandings that Ryle's arguments give rise to. Ryle as we have seen, is not committed to the view that all human activity involves knowledge of how to perform that activity. His claim relates to those activities, namely actions, of which it makes sense to say that they can be performed well or badly according to some criterion of what is a good or a bad performance related to the intention with which the action is carried out. Neither is he committed to the view that possession of know-how or a skill means that one can exercise that knowledge or skill in all relevant circumstances. Finally, neither is Ryle committed to the view that it is impossible to know and to be able to articulate the procedure for doing something without being able to do it.[10]

Ryle's central claim is that knowing how to do something involves being able to do that thing *under normal circumstances*. This disposes of the second objection. Ryle's view can perfectly well accommodate the suggestion that some activities, like explaining how something is to be done, can form part of one's repertoire without one having the requisite know-how or skill to actually carry out that activity. The ability to explain how something is done is not the same as the ability to do it, despite the fact that they frequently accompany each other. I want, however, to focus on two other criticisms of Ryle made by White that merit serious consideration. The first of these concerns the application of *intelligence concepts*, the second what was called in the previous chapter the *Degree Problem*. White objects that Ryle identifies knowing how with particular intelligence concepts, so that, for example, to describe someone as 'shrewd', 'prudent' or 'subtle' is to ascribe to them a particular ability, that of shrewdness, prudence or subtlety.[11] White objects, not unreasonably, that one cannot identify knowing how to do something with being good at it. It is obvious that one can know how to do something more or less well, in a way that one cannot know an individual proposition more or less well (see Chapter 1). To argue subtly is to argue in a certain way, not to argue *per se*. It is true that Ryle's formulation may look misleading to a certain extent, but is he committed to this view?

Ryle's central claim is that knowing how cannot be reduced to knowing that. We have seen how this claim was supported by an attempt to show how assumptions that lead to the contrary view end in absurdity. It is a further argument for his view that one can apply the range of concepts that he calls 'intelligence concepts' to propositions that express the fact that someone knows how to do something, whereas one cannot do this to propositions that express someone's factual knowledge. In other words, an account of knowing how is required that allows us to continue to use locutions central to our understanding of human action, namely a range of 'thick' or contentful evaluative concepts that characterize the manner in which something is done and how well it is done. For example, let us assume that *accuracy* is an intelligence concept applicable to the activity of measurement. Ryle is *not* suggesting, as White seems to imply, that to measure is to be accurate (whatever that might mean). Nor is he suggesting that to measure is to measure accurately. This would be a *reductio ad absurdum* of the position that Ryle seeks to defend. Take the following proposition:

1. John knows how to measure furniture components.

For Ryle, 1 is an attribution of know-how to John and the truth of the statement implies that, in normal circumstances, John can carry out certain kinds of actions. It does *not* imply anything about his expertise, simply that he satisfies basic criteria for being able to measure furniture components.

If we further assert,

2. John knows how to measure furniture components with great accuracy

we are employing an intelligence concept in order to provide an evaluation of *how well* John can measure. Ryle claims that one needs the knowing how / knowing that distinction in order to account for the distinctive character of knowing how that allows for the adverbial application of intelligence concepts. White may reply that some of Ryle's formulations suggest otherwise, but the view that he attributes to Ryle is evidently absurd and is not developed in any further way. A sympathetic interpretation of Ryle would, therefore, suggest that he intends intelligence concepts to be applicable to propositions used to claim that people know how to do certain things, in such a way as to qualify them evaluatively.

I conclude that the incoherence or falsity of Ryle's view has not been demonstrated.

Alternatives to Ryle's Account

The philosophical literature is now replete with alternative accounts of the nature of knowing how to that of Ryle. Broadly speaking, these fall into three categories:

Knowing how to do something is a form of propositional knowledge (Stanley and Williamson 2001)
Stanley and Williamson hold that someone who knows how to do something knows that there is a contextually relevant way that is the way to do it in a practical mode of presentation (2001, pp. 428–9). If persuasive, this analysis shows that the agent knows that a way is the way to do something in a third-person and *non-discursive* sense. The agent knows that w is a way to F and cannot necessarily articulate, but must be able to enact, his knowledge. In other words, he knows that, in a *weak* or ascriptive sense; his knowledge is shown through his behaviour and is attributed to him by others, rather than claimed by himself.[12] It could be true of someone that she knew how to light a fire, without it also being true that she could give an account of how to light a fire and be able justify her account. So we need to be clear that the *knowledge that* which Stanley and Williamson attribute to a practical knower is not comparable, although it is compatible, with the *knowledge that* of someone who successfully makes a 'knowledge that' claim. In some, but not all cases, the former knowledge is sufficient to signify professional competence. For assessment purposes, however, it may be inadequate, where, for example, the range of professional contexts is so numerous and complex that *in situ* professional performance is inadequate to infer occupational competence. In such cases, it may be necessary to ask the candidate to declare what she would do, or what her judgement would be in a hypothetical situation. An examination could be used to sample the range of circumstances in which the candidate could reasonably be expected to make professional judgements.[13] The point at issue, then, is whether *knowing how* practically is a form of *knowing that* in the weak sense. Stanley and Williamson's account can only be offered as a way of understanding *knowing how* as a *particular kind* of knowing that, and

not one that encompasses some of the principal examples, such as first-person declarative knowledge. Normally, to say that A knows that *p* is to imply that A can truthfully and with understanding utter 'I know that *p*'. To say that A knows how to F on Stanley and Williamson's account is *not* to imply that they can truthfully and with understanding utter 'I know that *w* is a way to F', since they may not know that *w* is a way to F in a discursive, as opposed to a practical, sense. They suggest that knowing that a way is a way to F in a practical mode of presentation involves the possession of certain dispositions (Rosefeldt 2004, pp. 374–5; Stanley and Williamson 2001, pp. 429–30).[14]

Furthermore,

> It is simply a feature of certain kinds of propositional knowledge that possession of it is related in complex ways to dispositional states. (Stanley and Williamson 2001, p. 430).

A natural question arises about the nature of these dispositional states. Weak propositional knowledge can be manifested dispositionally without a corresponding explanation. For example, we can say that someone successfully navigating their way through a city knows that A is nearer to B, displays this knowledge through the route that he takes without their being able to explain what it is that he is doing. Ryle's own account of *knowledge how* was in fact set out in terms of dispositions.[15] For him, these dispositions are such things as manual dexterity, hand-eye co-ordination, situational awareness, and so on. They are the kind of personal properties that we use to distinguish *knowledge that* from *knowledge how*. A person who knows how to do something acts appropriately in the relevant context, while someone who does not, does not. For Ryle, that *knowledge how* is to be explained in terms of complexes of dispositions which are activated in appropriate circumstances. Surprisingly, therefore, Stanley and Williamson's account looks similar to that of Ryle: both explain know-how in terms of individual dispositional qualities. Wallis (2008) has drawn further attention to the affinities between Rylean dispositional accounts of knowing how and Stanley and Williamson's analysis by pointing out that under Stanley and Williamson's account one could evidence know-how without evincing relevant beliefs (except, presumably, in the weak behavioural sense outlined above). Second, he points out that the context specificity of many action dispositions make them so complex that it is implausible to characterize them as indexical beliefs concerning the efficacy of ways of doing something, since it is impossible to exhaustively specify in advance the circumstances in which knowledge how to do something could be manifested.[16]

Another, closely related way of making this point about the dispositional nature of the Stanley and Williamson account is due to Koethe (2002). A way w of carrying out an action, if it is a correct way to carry out that action, is one that, if put into effect in normal circumstances means that an agent carrying it out *can* perform that action. Thus, if there is a correct way to F and someone can put that way into effect, then they *can* F in normal circumstances. This is tantamount to saying that they *know how to* effect that way and, in doing so, know how to F (Koethe 2002, p. 327). If this is so then the analysis needs to be repeated for the account of the way w of carrying out action F.[17] The Stanley and Williamson analysis is, then, prone to a regress argument, although not of the kind that Ryle described, since Stanley and Williamson are not committed to the agent's avowal of propositions in their account. What they are vulnerable to, however, is the charge that they have not eliminated an unanalysed concept of *knowing how to* in their account of *knowing how to* as a form of *knowledge that*.

Moreover, the Stanley and Williamson account has one significant disadvantage not present in Ryle's. It does not generally make sense to attribute skill or expertise to someone's knowing that p, or more generally, one cannot evaluate the quality of someone's knowledge of an individual proposition, whereas one can evaluate, in most circumstances, the character of an individual act.[18] It usually *does* make sense to ask how well someone knows how to do something. For many purposes, we need to make an appraisal of someone's knowledge how to, for example, in order to determine whether or not someone can or cannot perform a particular kind of task well and to assess their level of expertise. Generally speaking, we determine how well someone knows how to do something by an appraisal of their performance rather than an assessment of their propositional knowledge, using the rich array of 'intelligence concepts' that Ryle drew attention to. For this reason, the analysis offered by Stanley and Williamson is not helpful, since the practical mode of presentation is manifested through non-discursive *intentional action* generally rather than through *discourse*, and it is usually the ability to act rather than the ability to explain how to act that we are concerned with when making attributions of knowing how.[19] We judge knowledge how primarily through actions, not through explanations of how to act.[20] It could be said, then, that the Stanley and Williamson account is, in some respects, similar to that of Ryle without sharing in any of its significant strengths.

Knowing how to do something is a form of procedural knowledge
(White 1982; Carr 1980, 1981)

Carr's seminal articles defend the knowing how /knowing that distinction made by Ryle, but set out an alternative view of that relationship. Carr distinguishes between *knowing how* and *ability*, pointing out that the former may be present without the latter and *vice versa*. These points have now become a commonplace in the discussion.[21] Carr identifies *knowledge how to* as a mastery of practical modes of inference rather than as skill and characterizes it as follows:

A knows how to ø only if:

1. A may entertain øing as a purpose,
2. A is acquainted with a set of practical procedures necessary for successful øing,
3. A exhibits recognisable success at øing. (1981, p. 58)

A number of explanatory comments are necessary to make this clear:

1. øing is a place holder for actions. Thus practical knowledge is action-oriented.
2. Condition 1 asserts that action involving knowing how to do something is intentional. It does not necessarily imply that such entertaining has to be conscious.
3. The practical procedures involved in condition 2 can be spelled out as follows:

It is A's purpose to φ.
A understands that that ψ-ing is a satisfactory way to φ.
A ψs. (Carr 1981, p. 59)

4. Condition 3 implies that there is at least a loose conceptual connection between knowing how to ø and performing actions of type ø.

However, it is a characteristic of Carr's account that knowledge how is to be distinguished from *skill* or *ability* (1981, p. 60). This is implicit in the account offered above. One can have mastery of principles of practical inference without necessarily being able to put the conclusions of those inferences into effect. A skill is not the same kind of thing as the possession of knowledge of how to do something. Just as skill can be evaluated in terms of 'intelligence concepts', so knowing how to do something is a property that one either has or does not have, it is not susceptible either of presence in degree nor of being evaluated for its qualities.[22] A very similar position is arrived at by A. R. White, who writes that:

> It is simply a mistake to assert that knowledge how to do something is not to possess knowledge at all, but to be intelligent. Knowledge of both kinds of things is an ability, but knowledge of how to do something is not the ability to do the thing itself, but the ability either to show or to tell how to do it. The ability to do the thing itself is simply a consequence and, therefore, a proof of the ability to show how to do it. That a person tends or is able to do certain things well, correctly or efficiently, is not, as Ryle asserts, what we mean by describing him as knowing *how* to talk grammatically, to play chess or to fish. The former arises because of the latter. (White 1982, p. 29)

Unfortunately, this claim is incorrect as an account of how the concept of *knowing how* is employed in ordinary usage. Not only can we evaluate skills and abilities, but we also evaluate people's know-how using the same range of evaluative concepts that we bring to bear on skill, together with further ones for which the concept of skill is not applicable (see Chapters 3, 4). We have already seen how the concept of ability is distinguished from that of know-how. This does not mean that ability does not, in many cases, involve know-how. An artificial distinction has been made between *knowing how to* do something and *being able to* do something in order to articulate a particular philosophical position at the cost of revising our existing conceptual structure and thus losing us the ability to provide a philosophically satisfactory *description* of how concepts in this area work.

There is a further problem with White's account and, arguably also with that of Carr. White explicitly characterizes knowing how as an *ability* (see the quotation above). Specifically, it is an ability that causes the ability 'to do the thing itself'. In Carr's case, mastery of a practical mode of inference underlies action. Here too, it is quite plausible to suggest that such practical mastery is an ability underlying the ability to act. However, this means that the procedural knowledge account of knowing how to is incomplete. Knowing how is conceptualized as an ability that underlies an ability.[23] But reflection suggests that, in the absence of an explanation of what an ability is, we have not advanced very far in the understanding of knowing how. The original question was whether or not there was a form of knowledge (knowing how) that was distinct from propositional knowledge (knowing that) which explained what was involved in possessing an ability. Since the account of knowing how offered by White and Carr relies on the concept of an ability it can hardly be used to explain what abilities of a certain kind are. If they are not know-how type abilities we remain in the dark as to what they might be and how they are related to knowing how. If they are a form of knowing how themselves then the explanation of know-how is circular. Yet, according to these accounts, in order to understand knowing how we need to understand what an ability is. I conclude that the procedural knowledge account of knowing how is, in the forms in which it is currently offered, untenable. In fact, any account of the concept of knowing how which both sharply distinguishes it from the concept of ability and which also characterizes it as a kind of ability is, for reasons which should be obvious, bound to fail the test of explanatory illumination.

Knowing how to do something is a form of conceptual mastery
(Bengson and Moffett 2007)[24]
The account of knowing how to offered by Bengson and Moffett (2007) is different from the other two accounts considered above. Bengson and Moffett characterize their position as 'intellectualist' meaning that they locate *knowing how* as a feature of mind rather than action, in contrast to Ryle. Their position, however, is significantly different from the ones already considered. On the one hand Bengson and Moffett reject the claim that knowing how is a form of propositional knowledge and on the other hand they do not think that it involves mastery of practical inference. They do, however, characterize it as *conceptual mastery* (ibid. p. 33). To know how to do something is to have reasonable mastery of the concepts implicated in the relevant action, which in turn entails an understanding of what is involved in performing that action. Understanding what is involved in performing the action is normally a necessary condition for the performance of that action. Although it is true of some types of knowing how that reasonable mastery of the relevant concept entails possession of the corresponding ability, this is not generally true. Thus, having a reasonable mastery of the concept of multiplication entails that one can do some multiplying.[25] Having a reasonable mastery of the concept of *aviation* does not however entail that one has the ability to fly an aeroplane.

Bengson and Moffett reject the claim that 'knowing how to F' is ambiguous between 'being able to show or give an account of how to F' and 'being able to F'. There is but one sense of the verb *knows how to F* and that is to be explained in terms of reasonable mastery of the concept F, even if in some cases, having such reasonable mastery entails being able to F. Why is this? Bengson and Moffett want *knowing how to F* to be part, in most circumstances, of the explanation of why F is performed, even though there are peculiar circumstances in which F might be carried out without the agent knowing how to do so. But they also recognize that there are numerous circumstances in which one can know how to F and yet not be able to do so. The thrust of their account is to show that knowing how to do something does not entail being able to do it. However, since knowing how to do it does involve understanding how to do it, it is therefore a necessary condition for being able to do it in the right kind of way, that is, with understanding. One can have conceptual grasp without being able to carry out the action associated with the concept, even though conceptual grasp is a form of know-how.

> Abilities, it seems, are at most reliable dispositions to intentional behaviour, whereas know-how involves some degree of understanding. (ibid. p. 46)[26]

It seems then that knowing how to do something, when thought of as conceptual mastery of the relevant action cannot, at the same time, be thought of as the ability to do the action itself. How could this be so? Bengson and Moffett consider a complex example which involves a manoeuvre in ice-skating called a *salchow* (pronounced 'sal-kow'). This is

> a figure skating jump with a takeoff from the back inside edge and landing on the back outside edge of the opposite foot after one or more rotations in the air. The quintuple salchow would then require five complete rotations in the air. To our knowledge, no skater has ever landed a quintuple salchow. (ibid. p. 32, fn.2)

Furthermore, assuming that all world-class figure skaters know how to do a quintuple salchow but few, if any, have the ability to do so owing to the 'athletic difficulty of the jump' we can say that knowing how to do a quintuple salchow is distinct from being able to do one (ibid. p. 34). It won't do simply to say that all world-class figure skaters can give an account of how to do a quintuple salchow, since this would not distinguish them from non-skaters. We should assume that all world-class skaters will be able to do (for example) a quadruple salchow, entailing that not only do they have the athletic ability to do so, but the knowledge (tacit or explicit or both) of what the manoeuvre involves in practice. Their knowing how to do a quintuple salchow is thus implicated in their ability to perform a like activity and a practical conceptual mastery (understanding) of how to do that activity.

How convincing is this example? We can say the following of world-class figure skaters who know how to do a quintuple salchow but are unable to do one:

1. They can perform a related activity which involves essentially employing the same concepts as the one in question.
2. They know how to do this related activity.
3. They lack the athletic ability to perform the action in question.

From this, it is alleged to follow that they know how do a quintuple salchow even though they are unable to do one and this knowing how to cannot be simply explained as being able to give an account of how to do one.

Consider, for instance, the Olympic figure skater Irina Slutskaya. We are quite confident that Irina knows how to perform a quintuple salchow. We are equally confident that she is unable to perform it. Since there is no epistemic tension in this pair of beliefs, there is good reason to think that knowing how to do a quintuple salchow does not entail the ability to do one. (ibid. p. 34)

The example, however, does not show what it purports to show. No-one would deny Bengson and Moffett's claim, but the interpretation that they put on it is disputable. It is clear that Irina's *understanding* of how to do a quintuple salchow is greater than that of a non-skater. But this is true of the weaker sense of *knowing how* more generally, since the kind of account that can be given of what is involved in *any* activity can demonstrate greater or lesser understanding. In this case, world-class figure skaters can give an enactive account: 'it's like *this* only with five rotations' without being able to do it. It cannot be maintained, however that Irina knows how to do a quintuple salchow in the relevant sense of being able to do it, in the sense, for example, that she would still know how to do it had she possessed the athletic ability to do so but had temporarily hurt her ankle and was thus unable to do so. Bengson and Moffett's treatment of their example presupposes what it seeks to prove, namely that there is a sense of knowing how to do something which does not involve being able to do it, in the sense in which we would normally understand knowing how to φ without ability to φ. More generally, as White correctly pointed out, the use of examples is crucial to this discussion. Although intriguing as a special case on the end of a continuum of situations where conceptual mastery can be practically demonstrated, it cannot bear the weight of the distinction that it seeks to make between *knowing how to* and *ability.*

To take another example, let us consider a plumber who knew how to plumb a house but lacked the ability to insert pipes into a particularly tight space in a particular house. For him to tell a customer that he knew how to plumb that particular house would be misleading, since the customer would correctly infer that he *could* do it. In this type of situation, there would be no *implicature* involved in the plumber saying that he knew how to plumb the house *implicating* that he was not able to do. In this context an equivalence between *knowing how to* and *being able to* would be assumed. He would not receive a sympathetic hearing were he to inform his customer, 'I know how to fit these pipes but I am unable to do so.'

Thus, the way of avoiding Bengson and Moffett's conclusion, which, in common with Stanley and Williamson and Carr, makes a clear distinction between *ability to F* and *knowing how to F,* is to claim that 'knowing how' is ambiguous between 'being able to give an account of how to F' (weak sense) and 'being, in normal circumstances, able to F' (strong sense) (see Carr 1981). It would then be possible to show understanding of how to F (knowing how in the weak sense) without being able to do it, while knowing how to do it in the strong sense would entail being able to do it, provided the agent was not sick, lacked the requisite materials, and so on. Pointing to this ambiguity clears the way for a Rylean account of knowing how, although does not entail it. Carr, for example, maintains that the strong sense is tantamount to a claim of ability, while the weak sense provides the philosophically interesting sense of 'knows how'. On Carr's account, the philosophically interesting case of knowing how is possession of mastery of principles of practical discourse, which *prescribe* rather than *describe* procedures. Theoretical knowledge, which entails describing principles underlying procedures, is thus irrelevant to the possession of knowledge how to in the weak sense.[27]

For the claim that there are weak and strong senses of *knowing how,* to hold however, it is necessary to show that attributions of *knowing how* are ambiguous. This is precisely what Bengson and Moffett seek to deny. To reinforce the point made by the example above, they suggest four arguments based on four linguistic features of English that suggest that 'knows how' is unambiguous and that there is no weaker or stronger sense of the verb, just one unitary sense.

First they suggest that one cannot construct zeugmas using *knows how to*, as in

1. She came home in a bath chair and a flood of tears.

Second, they argue that there is no grammatically anomalous reading of

2. I don't know how to do a quintuple salchow but Irina does.

Third, they argue that there is no non-contradictory reading of

3. Irina knows how to do a quintuple salchow, but she doesn't know how to do one.

Finally, they claim that if 'knows how' were ambiguous, there would be four distinct readings of

4. Irina knows how to do a quintuple salchow and she knows how to add.

Namely: weak sense + weak sense
Weak sense + strong sense
Strong sense + weak sense
Strong sense + strong sense.

But, 'theoretical prejudices aside' this sentence does not have four separate readings (Bengson and Moffett 2007, pp. 38–40).

The following are weak arguments:

To take the first case, it is easy to construct a zeugma using 'knows how' as in, for example,

5. Irina knows how to fly to the Moon and do elementary addition.

The absurdity of the above sentence depends on the amalgamation of two senses of the verb in one instantiation of it, thus illustrating the ambiguity of 'knows how'.

The second case, of 2, can be grammatically anomalous, when, for example, it means that I cannot give an account of how to do a quintuple salchow but Irina can actually do one. To say that it cannot be grammatically ambiguous is to beg the question at issue. Likewise, for example, 3.

In this case, Irina can give an account of how to do a quintuple salchow but cannot perform one. It is left as an exercise to the reader to construct four senses for 4. It is worth noting, however, to deny that this is possible is to be motivated by 'theoretical prejudices' in favour of the position set out by Bengson and Moffett. But whether or not these reservations are 'prejudices' or well-founded beliefs in a philosophically important distinction is precisely what is at issue and cannot simply be a question begged in favour of Bengson and Moffett's view.

There is a further important linguistic consideration concerning these examples, which was drawn attention to by Rumfitt (2003).[28] This is the point that the ambiguity is signalled explicitly in some languages such as French and German, even though it is not in English. For example, German uses the verb *können* for the strong sense of being able to perform and *wissen wie* for the weak sense of being able to give an account of how to perform. French signals the difference with *savoir faire* and *savoir comment faire* respectively (Rumfitt 2003). A meaningful conceptual distinction is made linguistically explicit. One cannot erect a philosophical thesis on the peculiarities of one language, namely English.

Thus,

6. Irina knows how to do a quintuple salchow and elementary addition

is, according to Bengson and Moffett, non-zeugmatic. But

7. *Irina sait comment faire un quintuple salchow, et elle sait faire des additions*

doesn't even have the appearance of being a zeugma precisely because the two senses of 'knows how to' are clearly signalled by different verbs with different usages. Thus, the grammatical deletion of one of the verb phrases would not be allowable in French or German because two senses are expressed in two different verbs. The third case is obviously non-contradictory when translated as

8. *Irina sait comment faire un quintuple salchow, mais elle ne sait pas le faire.*

In fact 8 has a perfectly intelligible sense. Irina can give an account of how to do a quintuple salchow, but cannot actually perform one. The German and French renderings of the four possible senses of 4 are left to the interested reader, but the point should, by now, be obvious that there is a systematic ambiguity in 'knows how to' in English which is largely avoided in

French and German. It is a methodological mistake to attribute grammatical similarities in one language to the absence of a putative philosophical distinction without examining a broader range of linguistic examples.

However, Bengson and Moffett's account of *knowing how* as reasonable conceptual mastery of how to do something is highly plausible. It is undoubtedly true that mastery of a concept F does not entail, except in particular cases, that one can actually *do* F. Concept mastery is itself an ability even if someone's reasonable mastery of a concept F is not sufficient for them to actually do F.[29] It is a strength of Bengson and Moffett's account that it allows one to conceptualize mastery as degrees of expertise, hence neutralizing the Degree Problem. It is a weakness, however, that, like White and Carr's account, *knowing how to* F is explained as a form of ability, namely that of *having reasonable conceptual mastery of what is involved in doing F.* An explanation of what it is to know how to do something is explained in terms of a relevant ability which is an intentional ability (one that requires intention to realize it, at least in some circumstances) rather than a physical one, like digestion. As such it involves *knowing how* itself and cannot serve as a general explanation of what it is to know how to do something.

Conclusion

Any account of knowing how to do something has to address the Degree Problem. Although not perhaps designed to do this, Ryle's distinction between *knowing how* and *knowing that* is able to do so by showing how intelligence concepts apply to knowing how but not to knowing that. Alternative accounts to that of Ryle were considered.

Stanley and Williamson's suggestion that *knowing how* is a species of *knowing that* manifested in dispositions to act in certain ways that manifest that knowledge practically was considered. By characterizing knowing how as a form of knowing that the Degree Problem is not addressed and a dispositional account of this kind suggests either that they adopt a view similar to Ryle's without explaining how intelligence concepts can be deployed, or that they conceal within their account, an assumption that know-how is necessary to explain the relevant dispositions (see the criticisms of Koethe and Wallis). Carr's account of know-how in terms of mastery of certain forms of practical inference also fails to solve the Degree Problem, although Carr does not think that this is a problem for accounts of know-how, which he is inclined to explain in terms of the ability to give an account through displays of inferential ability in practical (prescriptive) discourse. Both Carr and White, whose account is similar, explain knowledge how to F in terms of ability to give an account of how to F in a prescriptive sense, thus leaving a *lacuna* in the explanation of how such an ability could be described without the concept of know-how. Bengson and Moffett fail to establish that there is only one relevant sense of know-how and, although they seem equipped to deal with the Degree Problem, their characterization of know-how as a kind of ability leaves them open to the same charge as Carr and White.

Our conclusion, therefore, is that Ryle's claim that there is a distinction between *knowing how* and *knowing that* holds. It has the particular virtue of completely avoiding the Degree Problem and of indicating how evaluative concepts are allied with descriptions of knowing how to do something. It is also necessary to consider the fact that an agent's knowing how to do something, on Ryle's account, typically results in *action* of the relevant kind. Although they are not prominent features of Ryle's account, both *intentionality* and *normativity* are essential features of human action and therefore any satisfactory account of knowing how to do something and hence of expertise, has to take account of these two features. Ryle's account is largely consistent with these two conditions although he does not make much of them. Chapters 3 and 4 will, however, give intentionality its due place in an account of knowing how to, while Chapter 5 will describe the normative basis and context for human knowing how and hence human action. It will be shown how it is against a normative background that we can best understand knowing how.

There is, however, a serious difficulty with Ryle's account, namely in accounting for judgement in action. Consideration of this issue must await treatment in Chapter 6.

Notes

[1] White (1982); Stanley, J., Williamson, T. (2001) 'Knowing how', *Journal of Philosophy*, ref. Carr, D. 'The logic of knowing how and knowing that', 'Knowledge in practice'; more sympathetic commentary can be found in, for example, Koethe, J. (2002) 'Stanley and Williamson on knowing how', *Journal of Philosophy*, 99, 6, June, pp. 325–8; Rosefeldt, T. (2004) 'Is knowing-how simply a case of knowing-that?' *Philosophical Investigations*, 27, 4, pp. 370–9 and Wallis, C. (2008) 'Consciousness, context, and know-how', *Synthèse*, 160, pp. 123–53.

[2] See Winch, C. (2009) 'Ryle, knowing how and the possibility of vocational education', *Journal of Applied Philosophy*, 26, 1, pp. 88–101 for further discussion.

[3] One might perhaps maintain that knowing that is a form of knowing how. Ryle does not attempt this and it seems an unpromising approach to take, much more

so than the weaker claim that one cannot understand knowing that without realizing that knowing how is implicated in it.

[4] This way of setting out Ryle's case can be found in Stanley, J., Williamson, T. (2001) 'Knowing how', *Journal of Philosophy*, 98, 8, August, pp. 411–44, p. 413. The intellectualist assumptions set out by Ryle can be found, for example, at Ryle (1946), p. 212, where 2 and 3 are set out explicitly and 1 can be reasonably inferred from the general intellectualist position. 2 can also be clearly seen at Ryle (1949), p. 29.

[5] Cartesianism is arguably an oversimplified and inaccurate summary of Descartes' own views. For alternative readings, see Cottingham, J. (1986) *Descartes*, Oxford, Blackwell; Baker, G. P., Morris, K. (1996) *Descartes' Dualism*, London, Routledge.

[6] In more technical language, if p then q, and if q then r, then if p then r.

[7] A simple case of a substitution instance of the principle set out in 2.

[8] Ref. Stanley and Williamson 2002; White 1982.

[9] See Winch 2009.

[10] See Rumfitt (2003) for more on this point.

[11] See, for example, Ryle (1949), pp. 27–8.

[12] He may of course be able to *articulate* his knowledge how, but this is not a necessary feature of *possession* of knowledge how.

[13] See, for example, Prais, S. J. (1991) 'Vocational qualifications in Britain and Europe: theory and practice', *National Institute Economic Review*, 136, May, pp. 86–9.

[14] 'Then (29) {Hannahi knows [how PROi to ride a bicycle].} is true relative to a context c if and only if there is some contextually relevant way w such that Hannah stands in the knowledge that relation to the Russellian proposition that w is a way for Hannah to ride a bicycle, and Hannah entertains this proposition under a practical mode of presentation' (Stanley and Williamson 2001, p. 430).

[15] Following other commentators, I use the phrase 'knowledge how to' to distinguish the subject of discussion from other forms of 'knowing how' such as the propositional 'knows how the 2nd World War occurred', but only where it is appropriate to do so.

[16] Wallis (2008), p. 139.

[17] Koethe (2002). More formally:

1. A knows that w is a way to F (assumption)

entails that

2. A knows how to w (suppose the contrary, then A would not know how to F, since knowing how to w is a necessary condition for knowing how to F)

which, in turn implies that

3. A knows that w' (in a practical mode of presentation) is a way to w (since any knowing how to entails knowledge that some way is a way to act).

4. But, since for any form of know how to, there is an analysis in terms of knowledge that a certain way is the way in which the relevant action is carried out, this analysis is repeated *ad infinitum* and so one never reaches a point at which one has explained any action.

[18] White is wrong in his claim that one cannot make like for like comparisons of the differences between *knowing how* and *knowing that* in such a way as to bring out these differences – see the discussion of subject expertise in the previous chapter.

[19] A football coach will be able to do the latter without necessarily being able to do the former, but his ability *qua* football coach is not that of a footballer. Thanks to Geoff Hinchliffe and John Gingell for this example.

[20] This is not, however, to say that such considerations are never relevant, for example, when we wish to determine someone's ability to apply theoretical knowledge to a practical problem in a hypothetical situation.

[21] See, for example, Snowdon, P. (2003) 'Knowing how and knowing that: a distinction reconsidered', address delivered to the Aristotelian Society, 13 October, pp. 1–29.

[22] Carr, D. (1981) 'Knowledge in practice', *American Philosophical Quarterly*, 18, 1, pp. 53–61, p. 60.

[23] It is not an ability like breathing or digesting which might be said to be necessary conditions for action, but the kind of ability that requires knowing how to do the particular thing in question, namely to make a practical inference or to give an account, a point which makes the circularity of the account even more obvious.

[24] Bengson, J., Moffett, M. A. (2007) 'Know-how and concept possession', *Philosophical Studies*, 136, pp. 31–57.

[25] A point also made by Carr.

[26] This condition is to take account of fluke performances which are successful despite misunderstanding of the procedures necessary for successful performances (Bengson and Moffett 2007, p. 46).

[27] Carr (1981), p. 61.

[28] Rumfitt, I. (2003) 'Savoir faire', *Journal of Philosophy*, 100, 3, pp. 158–66.

[29] See also Rowbottom, D. P. (2007) 'Demystifying threshold concepts', *Journal of Philosophy of Education*, 41, 2, pp. 263–70.

Chapter 3

Skills and Their Discontents

Introduction

The use of the English word 'skill' is a central feature of debates about practical knowledge and vocational education. This chapter addresses the relationship between this culturally bound concept and the broader concepts of practical knowledge and knowing how. What is the problem with the concept of skill? It will be maintained that the exercise of skill in its core use presupposes action and hence the exercise of skill involves intentionality within a normative context. These points will be further developed in this and the following two chapters.

There are, however, five further issues to consider as follows:

1. Ryle's account of knowing how and how it is related to the concept of skill.
2. Skill and its relationship to the concepts of task, job and occupation, together with alternative concepts of practical knowledge that relate to occupational capacity, such as the German *Fähigkeit*.
3. Skill and conceptual inflation: the introduction of generic, social, soft skills – and the potential problems that can occur when the concept of skill is moved far beyond a range of central cases.
4. The moral dimension of skilled action and the distinction and relation between skill and virtue.
5. The conflation of skill with behaviourally based notions of competence and the resulting development of Competence Based Education and Training (CBET).

The conclusion of the previous chapter was a cautious endorsement of Ryle's general position on distinguishing *knowing how to* from *knowing that*. Particularly important is the claim that knowing how to do something is, with *caveats*, the ability to do that thing. We have looked at some criticism of this idea from Carr, Stanley and Williamson, and Bengson and Moffett and have seen that their arguments are by no means convincing. It is the task of the current chapter to consider what the implications of Ryle's position are and what difficulties it poses in giving an adequate account of practical knowledge in terms of skill.

Knowledge how to do something is, then, in normal circumstances, the ability that an individual has to do that thing. It is possible to call that ability a disposition, as Ryle did. However, there is a danger that, in leaving abilities characterized as nothing more than dispositions, we run the risk of assimilating them to other aspects of our activity that do not involve knowing how to, particularly those that involve neither *intentionality* nor *normativity*. Examples have already been discussed in a previous chapter. Digestion, for example, can perhaps only with strain be described as something that one does, but it certainly does not require individual know-how.[1] Breathing, on the other hand, is an ability and can be described as something that one does, even though we would not normally describe it as something that requires know-how although there are circumstances when one would, for example, when one is required to control one's breathing during contractions.

Skill

It seems natural, in English, to use the term 'skill' to describe such abilities. But we need to exercise caution about this. There are many things that we do which, in some sense, require know-how, even if it would be an exaggeration to say that they require skill. Even an activity like walking is bound by social convention and there are 'correct' and 'incorrect' ways of walking according to the kind of situation that one is in. Indeed there are rules which set out when it is and when it is not correct to walk.[2] Walking is unlike breathing in the sense that it is normally voluntary and, in most cases it involves purpose. It is like breathing in being a normal physical activity of a human being. It is *unlike* breathing in, as just noticed, being subject to some kind of normative constraint (see Chapter 5). While we do not normally say that someone knows how to breathe, we do say that they know how to walk if, for example, they are a toddler or if they are recovering powers of locomotion after an accident or if, for example, it is a particular kind of walk that is in question. But we do not normally say that walking is an activity in which one exercises skill. It is, therefore, misleading to identify knowing how to F with a skill, although knowing how to F often does involve skill.

Skill is the ability that is usually subject to normative appraisal. Normally, one can exercise a skill more or less well. One can, of course, walk more or less well, depending on one's physical state but this is not a matter of skill, but of physical capacity. It is also not normally true to say that, for animal abilities like walking, an animal that can walk knows how to walk.[3] However, there is nothing strained in the assertion that a certain tiger is, for example, a skilled hunter and thus knows how to hunt skilfully. It is, therefore possible to talk, in a limited sense, of a tiger's possessing the skill of hunting. We can attribute intention to the animal and, in a third-person sense, we can attribute norms to the activity, although that does not and should not commit us to saying that a tiger follows rules in its hunting. While there is limited scope in the case of some abilities like walking or eating to normatively appraise the way in which the activity is carried out, this is not the case with skilled activities, where normative appraisal of the way in which something is done is central to our talk about skill.

Animal know-how and skill need not cause problems to those who maintain that knowing how to do something is either a form of propositional knowledge or a kind of intellectual ability. Thus, one may well make third-person attributions of knowledge to animals engaged in activity that evidences belief. Carr's account of know-how as practical mastery explicitly detaches know-how from the exercise of skill.[4] Bengson and Moffett accept that animals can display conceptual mastery in those activities that they carry out to which know-how can be attributed. In Chapter 5, I will try and show how in a limited sense this may be true.

This chapter will concentrate on the concept of skill for the following reason. Our overall concern is to provide a descriptively adequate account of that part of our language concerned with expertise. So far it has been argued that know-how is expressed in activities apt for at least some degree of normative appraisal. The concept of a *skill* seems to be the ability concept which opens up the vista of normative appraisal in terms of the *degree* to which an activity can be performed well or badly. A skill is thus an ability which is subject to normative appraisal in terms of the degree to which it can be well or badly accomplished. Just as an ability is the property of an individual, so a skill is also a property of an individual and the individual can normally be appraised in terms of their possession or exercise of a skill. Skill should be distinguished from *technique* which is not, in anything like the same sense, a property of individuals. A technique is a particular *way* of carrying out a procedure and can itself be subject to normative appraisal. Thus one can say that the proper technique for calming a class down is to do so-and-so, like waiting for the noise to subside before talking. One cannot say that the skill for calming a class down is such-and-such. It is, of course, also true that one can say, for example, that Andrew's driving technique is good. This suggests that the technique is *his*. But it is reasonable to suggest that all this means is that the way that Andrew drives is good, or that his skill consists, at least partly, in the exercise of that particular technique. Without getting into metaphysical distinctions between skill and technique, there is an important and worthwhile distinction which it is worth keeping, between ways in which things are done, of which techniques are a species, and skills, which are in some sense what individuals acquire, possess, exercise, lose, and so on.[5]

The English Concept of a Skill: A Paradigm Case? Conceptual Links: Tasks, Dexterity, Sensorimotor Co-ordination

In Chapter 2, the danger of conceptual analysis that does not pay sufficient attention to linguistic variation was indicated. A similar problem arises with the central concept of the current chapter, namely *skill*. 'Skill' is an English word that is not easily translated into some other languages, yet it is taken to be an explanatory concept of great significance and has show signs of being imported into other languages, such as German.[6] We will examine the scope and limits of the concept of *skill*. Distinctions between related concepts are drawn in different ways: some, particularly in technical subjects, have tight, easily identifiable boundaries. Others are *ramified*, there is neither a central core of usage nor clear boundaries. Wittgenstein's examples of *game* and *thinking* fall into this category. Generally speaking, those concepts central to many areas of human concern and activity which are also of great antiquity, fall into this category.

> Our language can be seen as an ancient city: a maze of little streets and squares, of old and new houses, and houses with additions from various periods; and this surrounded by a multitude of new boroughs with straight regular streets and uniform houses.[7]

This quotation from Wittgenstein is particularly apposite to our current concerns. In English, 'skill' represents one of the old houses, but with additions (and demolitions) from the contemporary period. Like family resemblance concepts, its use ramifies but at the same time it has a central core of usage of some antiquity such that it is plausible to talk, in this instance, of 'paradigm cases'.[8] A paradigm case is an example of a 'central core' of usage, the oldest and still most commonly used part of the conceptual 'house', a point of reference when examining conceptual change and a starting-point for hermeneutical consideration of the development of a concept over time. Crucially, paradigm cases can be used to form judgements about whether or not the terminology employed in a conceptual expansion, employing as it does the words used in paradigm cases, still retains enough links to the original case to warrant continuing to be judged to be conceptually connected to such cases. One can even ask whether such conceptual expansion continues to leave anything coherent in the new usage or whether it merely results in confusion.

Skills as Individual Dispositions

A skill is an ability, usually learned, to act in certain ways in relation to tasks (activities generally restricted both in scope of outcome and in duration of exercise). Paradigmatically, skills are activities that involve dexterity and sensorimotor co-ordination, such as archery, swimming and climbing. It is also acceptable in English to talk of someone having the skill of carpentry or of cooking. However, in these cases it is also quite in order to respond to someone who says that John has the skill of cooking to ask what specific skills he has? Can he, for example, make pastry or steam fish? It is evident that the possession of skill by an individual is subject to normative appraisal and we use the term 'skilful' as approbation for the effective use of a skill. However, one can possess a skill without being particularly skilful with respect to that skill, a point that will be returned to in Chapter 9.[9] The adjective 'skilful' and the adverb 'skilfully' qualify verbs signifying actions involving know-how and are placeholders for Rylean 'intelligence concepts'. To say that someone is a skilled worker or that they acted skilfully is to invite a fuller specification of what they did in terms of the evaluative concepts associated with that type of action. *Pace* White's interpretation of Ryle, to act skilfully is not to perform a type of act, but to act in a certain (praiseworthy) way.

It has already been noted that skill involves the use of method or technique, which is usually learned. However, it is plausible to suggest that skill involves more than this. Technique is often difficult to acquire. This means that in the acquisition of technique certain qualities are acquired, such as persistence and attention to detail, which are needed when the technique is exercised, as well as more mundane *habits* such as cleaning one's tools before one planes a plank of wood. It may also involve the development of *physical strength* and, as Ryle reminds us, this can take many different forms in relation to different kinds of activities.[10] In addition, certain refined perceptual discriminations are necessary for the practice of certain skills, for example, the ability to spot an offside violation for a football referee, or to detect animal movement against a vegetative background for a hunter.[11] Skill also involves knowledge in the propositional sense. A hunter not only entertains beliefs about the habits of his prey, he must know what these are as well, if he is to catch them. A significant point here is that the knowledge in question may be manifested enactively rather than verbally, but is nevertheless knowledge displayed in the exercise of the skill.[12] Finally, but by no means least importantly, the exercise of skill frequently if not invariably involves judgement. It is not just a question of judging *when* to use a technique, although this can be complicated enough, but also of the employment of the technique, for example, judging that the target is at a sufficient distance for the weapon still to be effective. We can see, therefore, that the exercise of skill involves technique, perceptual ability, certain moral qualities, habits and propositional knowledge.

Evidently, to possess a skill is to possess something complex, with different integrated and interrelated aspects. The point is a very important one in relation to those charged with the development of skill and is all too often lost in discussions of the subject. The development of skill cannot involve mere acquaintance with a technique, as the technique needs to be practised successfully.[13] Neither can it be nothing more than the development of habit as it requires judgement as well as technique. On the other hand, the development of judgement is not sufficient either, since judgement may require underlying perceptual ability and steady habits. Evidently the learning of propositional knowledge will not do either, since there is no guarantee that possession of relevant knowledge will result in adequate development of technique, habit or perception. It follows that skill development may well be a highly complex affair. Such, it is plausible to maintain, is the paradigmatic employment of the skill concept, embedded in everyday and traditional usage.

Tasks

It has been argued that skills are exercised in relation to tasks which broadly speaking are specific actions or action sequences.[14] The description of a task entails a description of what the corresponding skill involves in terms of actions. Description of the task may only hint at the complexity of what is involved in exercise of the corresponding skill. This is why it is mistaken to think of the curriculum for the development of skills purely in terms of task description. Likewise, it is mistaken to think of the pedagogy of skill development as always consisting of no more than increasing practice of the target task. Given the complexity of skill, it cannot be assumed that working 'on task' is always and only the best way to acquire the relevant skill.

The concept of a task belongs to a larger family of activity concepts concerned with actions and sequences of actions, such as *job* or *occupation*. Unlike these, it is relatively narrow in range, applying paradigmatically to the construction of an artefact, the delivery of a service or a performance of some kind. The pursuit of a hobby, for example, may involve carrying out a range of tasks. This is also true of a paid job, recruitment for which may involve a 'job specification' in which a range of tasks to be performed is outlined. We may, though, be suspicious of the idea that a job is merely an aggregation of related tasks. This point applies with even more force to the concept of an *occupation*, which is more akin to a broadly conceived type of human activity, usually related to economic purposes or the fulfilment of human need, such as carpentry, medicine or banking.

Conceptual Deflation

Skills are focused on tasks, which are typically a fairly narrow type of activity. However, it is possible, as already suggested, to underestimate what is involved in exercise of a skill and hence of what it needed to acquire one. To think of skills purely in terms of technique or of habit or overt task performance is to engage in a process of *conceptual deflation* in which key attributes of the concept of skill are stripped away to reveal a limited version of the original concept. This, arguably is what has tended to happen in the case of certain kinds of training in the United Kingdom, where the concept of an action has been thinned out into a conception of behaviour. Actions can be described 'thickly' in terms of the perceptual, judgemental, epistemic and moral aspects that a full understanding of them needs to display. This, essentially is what Ryle offers in his numerous examples in *The Concept of Mind*, although it is arguable that he underplays the role of explicit judgement in action, a point that will be returned to in Chapters 6 and 8. 'Thin' action description, on the other hand, at its extreme, confines itself to the description of bodily movement in the performance of the action in such a way as to evacuate all sense of intention or purpose from the description.[15] Action description can obviously vary in terms of degree of thickness. A seminal figure in this approach is Gilbert Jessup, one of the architects of National Vocational Qualifications (NVQs), who writes

> Skills can only be demonstrated through their application in performance (doing something) while knowledge can be elicited through the more abstract means of conversation, questioning or talking.[16]

Much of course hangs on what is meant by 'doing something', but the very fact that 'doing something' encompasses a range of behaviour, including the non-intentional, should make us suspicious. Although it is true that observation of a performance can tell us much about the underlying abilities that are being exercised, it is also the case that, even when using 'task' in the type rather than token sense, such as in 'can report a problem to a supervisor' much is left underspecified. It is not sufficient that a token occurrence of reporting a problem to a supervisor would be adequate to ascribe the ability type to an operative. Even if the application of 'intelligence concepts' are left out of the picture and when a certificate is awarded for 'A does F adequately' where A is the agent and F is the token task under assessment, it is doubtful whether a token instance of doing F could lead safely to the inference that 'A can do F', where F is the type of task under consideration. This could only be done when token instances of F are virtually qualitatively identical, which is only likely to be the case with the simplest of tasks.

These examples make clearer Noë's point that one can do F without knowing how to do so. It might not just be a matter of 'beginner's luck', but of not knowing adequately how to perform *that type of task*, even though the odd token task might be managed. And even the adequate performance of the type of task which the skill requires is scarcely sufficient to assess the *degree* to which a skill is possessed. The point about 'intelligence' concepts is that they provide detailed ways of appraising the grasp of the skill and the manner in which it is exercised. We can say, therefore, of a skill like that of diagnosing a car engine fault that a mechanic acts 'knowledgeably' (e.g. he deploys his theoretical knowledge of the internal combustion engine in his work), 'responsibly' (e.g. he takes the customer and colleagues into consideration in providing a good service or following safety procedures), 'judiciously' (he makes a judgement only after careful consideration of the alternatives in difficult situations), and so on. The deployment of intelligence concepts in making judgements about a person's skilfulness indicates the complexity of a concept which has been thinned out in some currently influential conceptions of training.

Are Skills Dispositions?

While there is nothing wrong in describing a skill as an agent's disposition to do certain things in appropriate circumstances, such an account does little to explain what it is to have a skill. Why should we want to know what it is to have a skill? There is no general answer to this question but specific answers related to purposes that we might have, such as the development, learning and assessment of skills. When we want to identify skills, to say that we want to identify dispositions of a certain kind is not to say very much.

Ryle's original account of dispositions, which he contrasts with episodes or 'occurrences'[17] was developed as a general explanatory category for many mental concepts, including that of *knowing how*. The account was developed on the basis of an analogy with physical dispositional concepts, such as brittleness. Thus

1. If glass is brittle it breaks when struck.

Explains what brittleness is.

There is, however, a problem with this account which has been drawn attention to by Smith and Jones (1997).[18] If 'brittleness' means 'breaks when struck' substitution yields

2. If glass breaks when struck, it breaks when struck

which is vacuous. So dispositional accounts of physical properties cannot do what Ryle hopes that they will do without some further explanation. Smith and Jones' suggestion is that to characterize a physical property such as brittleness as a disposition only has explanatory value if it can itself be explained in terms of states of the material in question which are not themselves dispositional.[19] For the example above, this would have to be in terms of the physical structure of materials like glass, which are not dispositional. It is not clear that this is a devastating objection to the attempt to use dispositions as explanatory concepts. It does rather depend on what kind of explanation one is looking for. In some cases, to say that a material is brittle might be sufficient to explain to someone considering using it for load-bearing purposes to desist. Someone else might want to know about the degree of load-bearing capacity of glass (for a coffee table, for instance) and would, therefore, want to know more about the properties of the glass in question. These properties may themselves be explained dispositionally, for example,

  3. If glass is brittle to degree D, it breaks when 13k of load is placed on it

or categorically,

  4. Because the glass is only 2mm thick it breaks when a 13k load is placed on it.

The kind of explanation offered will depend on the audience and the purpose for which it is being offered. 3, for example, might be offered to a more specialist audience than 4. In this case, the intention is to explain the physical categorical state that makes the disposition possible. The context will determine whether or not the explanation is deemed to be adequate (given that it is an accurate explanation).

How does this affect descriptions of skill? Let us take an example of a skill description expressed in apparently dispositional terms.

  5. If A can measure accurately, then she can predict whether her furniture will fit in the new house

suggests a dispositional account of skills. But it is also evident that many different consequents will make the hypothetical statement true, since the skill of measuring can be exercised in many different circumstances. The antecedent of the hypothetical may also serve as a starting-point for further enquiry, which might yield descriptions of A's dexterity in tight corners, co-ordination, calculation and carefulness. These may themselves be dispositional or they may be categorical. For example, I may cite an instance of A's subtracting the height of the shelf from that of the wash basin in determining what kind of tap might fit in the bathroom. Dispositional statements characterizing skills can, therefore, have more than minimal explanatory value. On the other hand, to rest satisfied with the description of skills as dispositions is inadequate for many purposes.

This is because we are very often concerned not merely with *whether* someone possesses a skill or the *range of circumstances* in which that skill can be exercised, but *the way in which* it is exercised and *how well* it is exercised. In order to answer these types of question, it is necessary to look at different aspects of the exercise of a skill. Sometimes these will have a dispositional quality, such as the care with which a skill is exercised, when this can be determined by overt action in a recurrent situation. However, there will often be specific acts connected with the exercise of the skill whose occurrence we may wish to check. In another case, where, for example, an accident has occurred, it may not be sufficient to determine whether or not someone has not violated certain procedures but whether, given the unusual concatenation of circumstances, they had made a judgement taking account of all available evidence. In such a case, culpability may not necessarily be assigned to an agent even though an accident had occurred, because that agent had followed procedures but, given her level of current *expertise*, was not capable of making a sound judgement in the unusual circumstances that obtained on that occasion.

Ryle does not, of course, think that dispositional statements are adequate on their own to determine whether and to what extent someone possesses a skill or an ability. 'Heed' or attention concepts are deployed episodically as well as dispositionally. We want to know, for example, whether or not someone was taking care on a particular occasion, not whether or not certain persons are careful, or are people who exercise their skill carefully.

His acting in that frame of mind was a clockable occurrence[20]

writes Ryle of the application of a heed concept like that of taking care. While this is true, there is still a sense in which it is not enough. It may well be adequate for certain purposes to determine that a lorry driver was paying attention to the road over a crucial 5-minute period, for example, and that would clearly be a 'clockable occurrence', it may also not be enough of an account of what we wish to know about the circumstances. It might be crucial to know, in an inquest, for example, whether or not the driver judged that the vehicle would clear the bridge that it was approaching. It's not merely that such a judgement is 'clockable', but that it may be a mental rather than a physical occurrence.[21] The exercise of skill has to take into account the exercise of judgement, and, while judgement may be overt it need not be. It may not be precisely clockable, but definitely occurs within determinate periods of time. Any account of skill that does not give an adequate account of how judgement in this sense is possible and relates to action is going to be inadequate, not merely for philosophical, but for many practical purposes as well. This topic will be returned to in Chapter 6.

Moderate Conceptual Inflation of the Skill Concept: To Take in Non-physical Abilities, Transferable Skills

The previous section but one discussed the phenomenon of *conceptual deflation*, whereby the action concepts relating to skill were partly reduced to behavioural characteristics. Curiously, a parallel process of *conceptual inflation* has also been taking place in recent years in the areas of vocational and professional education.

The first of these processes will be called 'moderate conceptual inflation' and is, I will argue, essentially benign. The second, 'immoderate conceptual inflation', is confused and the consequences are misleading and lead to incoherence. Moderate conceptual inflation of the concept of skill involves the recognition that, beyond the paradigm cases discussed earlier, which involve physical activity, there exist also cases of *mental skills*, such as the ability to do mental arithmetic and *transferable skills*, such as numeracy and literacy.[22] Let us take *mental skills* first. If one can perform actions whose descriptions are not exhausted by an account of the observable physical manifestation of that action and such actions can be described as the exercise of skill, then it is difficult to see why one could not possess 'mental skills' as well as 'physical skills'. Such skills possess the right kind of complexity that was previously attributed to 'paradigm case' skills. Indeed, for reasons that we have already begun to examine, it is rarely correct to suppose that one can adequately describe 'physical skills' solely in terms of bodily activity. The difference between mental and physical skills is one of degree: the degree to which descriptive adequacy is to be achieved, either by an account of physical action or of a process of reasoning or of arriving at a judgement.[23]

Transferable skills are those which have applications in a number of different contexts. Therefore, their acquisition may be particularly valuable. The skills involved in fly-fishing are certainly relevant to successful fly-fishing, but of limited relevance elsewhere, except perhaps, to the academic study of the feeding habits of trout. On the other hand, the ability to read and write (literacy) and the ability to handle non-algebraic calculation at a simple level (numeracy) *do* have obvious value in a variety of contexts outside the classroom where they were originally acquired. That is why they enjoy a central place in the primary school curriculum. Such skills are applicable to tasks or to a range of tasks which can be specified quite clearly. Thus the ability to write can be applied to tasks such as writing letters or invitations, or perhaps, to stories.[24] To say that a skill is transferable is not to imply that is necessarily unproblematically transferable. In order to be able to add and subtract, for example, when measuring for the furnishings in a house, it is necessary to realize that it *can* be done and it is also necessary to be able to do it in circumstances that may be different from those that obtain in a classroom. Nevertheless, without having acquired the skill in the first place (not necessarily in a classroom), it will not be possible to practice it in such situations. It is also true that it may be difficult to learn to practice such skills in unfamiliar circumstances, where their utility is not immediately obvious or where operational conditions make it difficult to do so. In other words the skill may need to be developed further in order to ensure that it is transferable. These cautions, should not, however, prevent us from accepting at least some transferable skills into the conceptual family of skills. A crucial point is that the degree to which a skill is transferable cannot be settled *a priori* but needs empirical confirmation.

Immoderate Conceptual Inflation (1): General Skills and Whether There Could be Such Things

The same, however, cannot be said of some appropriations of skill terminology. It is claimed that some skills are *general* in nature (Siegel 2010). So-called thinking and problem-solving skills are often said to fall into this category. It is not just that they are claimed to be *transferable*, but that, once acquired, they can be applied to many subject matters without much difficulty and hence are, in a sense, *generally transferable*. In other words, their nature is such that not only do they underlie many different kinds of tasks, but that they are directly relevant to the successful carrying out of such tasks with the additional acquisition of some minimal degree of non-systematic knowledge or *Kenntnis*.[25] This cannot even be claimed of skills that are no more than transferable. Acknowledgement of the existence of such general skills would need to meet certain conditions such as the following:

They are immediately or very rapidly applicable to a wide variety of different kinds of tasks (otherwise why characterize them as *general skills?*).
They can be applied to a range of particular tasks without significant new knowledge or additional skills (otherwise they are incomplete).

For thinking and problem-solving skills to satisfy the claims that are often made for them, it would be necessary to show that they can be deployed whenever thinking or problem-solving are involved in an activity. But since thinking is required whenever an activity requires thought, and problem-solving ability is required whenever there are problems to be solved, the range of tasks to which these skills can allegedly be applied is potentially vast, depending on what one takes thinking skills to be. However, since what we normally recognize as paradigm cases of skills can be applied to a varying number of tasks, we cannot dismiss out of hand the idea that there may be skills of broad applicability. To some extent, this is an evidential issue: one can test the range of application of an acquired skill that is thought to be general and assess how wide the range of its applicability actually is. But that would not, of itself determine that it was *general* rather than *transferable*. For the former to be true it would need to be shown that, for example, *thinking about F* or *solving a problem of kind F* are essentially exercises of the same kind of skill over a wide range of arguments for F. This can be done by showing, for example, that all problems of a certain type are essentially the same or similar, or that thinking about a range of different subject matters is the same kind of activity whenever it occurs. But this is a conceptual, rather than an empirical task and the proponents of such skills need to be able to show that their proposed inflation of the concept of a skill will, in fact, be successful.[26] It would, however, be a sign of conceptual confusion were the alleged general skill not be useable without a significant amount of systematic specialist knowledge, as this would suggest that the expertise involved in, say, solving a problem in pharmacology, was not possible without extensive knowledge of pharmacology.[27]

It should not be assumed, however, that anything that is offered under the name of 'thinking' or 'problem-solving' skills is necessarily useless. It may well be the case, for example, that learning principles of inductive and deductive reasoning will enhance learning in a variety of different specialist subject matters. This just seems to be an empirical possibility.

A related case is that of the use of the skill concept in relation to occupational practice. It does make sense to talk of 'the skill of a carpenter', for example, but such a remark can quite legitimately be followed by 'and what skills does he have?' In other words, the occupational use of the term is shorthand for the collection of skills that the carpenter has, not some general skill of being a carpenter. One of the difficulties here is that it is quite right to suppose that being a proficient carpenter is to have more than a collection of skills, but to have them in an integrated way so as to make up an occupational capacity. But the concept of a skill is not really equipped to deal with this need, which we will consider in more detail in Chapter 4.

Immoderate Conceptual Inflation (2): Social Skills

There is another form of appropriation of skills terminology that needs to be addressed with some scepticism. This is the use of the term 'skill' in conjunction with personal attributes implicated in dealings with other people. In this connection, terms such as 'social', 'soft' or 'personal' skills are often used to describe the range of attributes that people deploy in their dealings with others. Why should this be a problem? There is one major reason. It is that the concept of 'skill' is in large measure inappropriate in its application to dealing with others. A full explanation of why this is so will have to wait until Chapter 4, but can be outlined here.

A skill, as already remarked, applies paradigmatically to a task. Tasks, are usually goal-oriented, they are carried out with a purpose in mind. A skill relevant to a task is, therefore, deployed successfully to the extent that it accomplishes that task. We also noted that, in paradigmatic usage, skills can be thought of in relation to the creation of artefacts or to the accomplishment of some physical goals such as hitting a target or catching a fish. There is an important sense in which the worth of the pot, the target or the fish is as an instrumental value, something that we appropriate for our purposes and which has worth largely as the servant of our purposes. This is not to say, of course, that a pot may not have intrinsic value, nor that the making of the pot may have intrinsic value. However, the object of the exercise of the skill is not conceived of as having moral worth in the way that a human being has, something which acts as an absolute boundary on the ways in which we can deal with them.[28] It cannot ever, therefore, be adequate to subsume our dealings with other human beings into the categories in which we deal with inanimate objects or with animals. Any use of such terms as 'social skills' which fails to recognize this is inadequate and confused.

We should, nevertheless, be careful. It is not the case that there is no legitimate application of the concept of skill to our dealings with others. There are times when we wish to accomplish particular tasks in relation to other people, such as to follow rules of politeness, to set them at their ease or to elicit clear information from them. In these instances of etiquette, politeness or clarity of communication, it does not seem absurd to talk of 'social skills'. It is worth noting that they have a considerable use in professional and vocational as well as in normal social situations and may be considered a vital part of *occupational capacity* (see Chapter 4). It is, of course, the case that some people consider that their dealings with other, or with certain categories of people, are solely of the skill variety. Such people see the others as entities to be *manipulated*, that is, to be got to act in ways desired by the manipulator, without realizing that this is happening to them. Were they to do so, of course, they would probably not be inclined to act in the ways that they are being directed towards.

The problem with conceptualizing all our dealings with other as skills is that it distorts our proper moral orientation towards other people, setting it more in the direction of the way in which we operate with materials and animals rather than the way in which we *should* deal with people. Such dealings should respect their agency and their integrity should not see them as obstacles to be overcome.[29] Those who talk about social skills rarely if ever, make this distinction. It is worrying to see the inability to make this distinction carried into vocational contexts when, for example, a bank employee is trained to 'recognize purchasing behaviour' on the part of a client, and to act on it, rather than to present and explain financial services that are in the client's interests.[30]

Concluding Remarks on Skill

The concept of skill is of limited but essential use. It has a complexity that is often insufficiently recognized. In particular, Ryle's analysis of know-how and the related concept of skill has the enormous strength of making sense of the fact that we have a rich evaluative vocabulary to apply to the skill concept, that Ryle terms 'intelligence concepts'. Ryle's largely successful attempt to relate *knowing how* to ability and to skill in particular does, however, have serious shortcomings which will be addressed in subsequent chapters. Attempts to inflate the concept of skill into something that either leads to unintelligibility or to unacceptability should be resisted. However, *skill* is quite inadequate as a concept to provide us with a framework for thinking about practical knowledge or even *knowing how* in the broad sense that we need in order to understand professional and vocational practices. Skill, as we have seen is not a general term for practice broadly conceived.

Although the term 'skill' does incorporate a moral dimension, it is not a suitable term for the majority of our dealings with other people, even though a person's character is very often implicated in the way in which he exercises a skill (see Chapter 4). Neither is it a term that really captures the integrated nature of many of our activities, nor the way in which an experienced professional is able to have an overview of and relate and integrate the range of occupational tasks in which he is engaged. Finally, neither is Ryle's treatment of the role of knowledge in particular and of judgement in general in his account of the exercise of know-how adequate. This is a matter that will be dealt with in more detail in Chapter 6.

Notes

[1] Noë is doubtful about even this claim. See Noë, A. (2005) 'Against intellectualism', *Analysis*, 65, 4, pp. 278–90, p. 279.

[2] See Hutchinson, P., Read, R., Sharrock, W. (2008) *There is No Such Thing as Social Science*, London, Routledge.

[3] See Bengson and Moffett (2007), p. 54, fn. 41.

[4] See Carr (1981).

[5] 'Skills have methods where habits and inclinations have sources' (Ryle 1949, p. 134). We shall see that skills do have methods, but they also require habits and inclinations, as Ryle acknowledges later.

[6] See, for example, Kraus, K. (2008) 'Does employability put the German vocational order at risk?' in Gonon, P., Kraus, K., Oelkers, J., Stolz, S. (eds) *Work, Education and Employability*, Bern, Peter Lang.

[7] Wittgenstein (1953) *Philosophical Investigations*, Oxford, Blackwell, §18.

[8] For a defence of the use of paradigm cases in conceptual inquiry, see Hanfling (2000) *Ordinary Language and Philosophy*, ch. 5, pp. 74–93.

[9] One should treat the expressions 'unskilled labour' or 'unskilled work' with some care as they can be subject to misinterpretation. Activities that rely on habit and nothing else can be regarded as unskilled in the terms of this section, but very often 'unskilled work' is work that has many if not all of the attributes mentioned here, but is not recognized for remuneration purposes as 'skilled'. Sometimes, the exercise of physical strength is taken to be a mark of skill in the economic sense.

[10] Ryle, G. (1974) 'Intelligence and the logic of the nature-nurture issue: reply to J. P. White', *Proceedings of the Philosophy of Education Society of Great Britain*, 8, 1, pp. 52–60.

[11] These two examples indicate in the first instance a concept-dependent perception, and, in the other, one that may, but need not be so.

[12] See the remarks of Ryle (1949), pp. 134–5, including the curious remark about the contrast between knowledge and belief.

[13] 'There is scarce any common mechanic trade, on the contrary, of which all the operations may not be as compleatly and distinctly explained in a pamphlet of a very few pages, as it is possible for words illustrated by figures to explain them.' Smith, A. [1776] (1981) *An Inquiry into the Causes of the Wealth of Nations*, Indianapolis, Liberty Fund, Bk 1, section 1, p. 4. See also the discussion of tacit knowledge in Chapter 7.

14 One can also of course talk about the task of running the country, but here it is perfectly legitimate to ask what tasks this involves, since to talk of the task of running the country with no further specification on request is to describe something vacuous.

15 See Taylor, C. (1964) *The Explanation of Behaviour*, London, Routledge, for a description of the behaviourist account of action as 'neutral behaviour'.

16 Jessup, G. (1991) 'Implications for individuals: the autonomous learner', in Jessup, G. (ed.) *Outcomes: NVQs and the Emerging Model of Education and Training*, Brighton, Falmer Press, p. 121.

17 Ryle (1949), ch. 5.

18 Smith, P., Jones, O. R. (1997) *Philosophy of Mind*, Cambridge, Cambridge University Press, ch. 10. Their argument against a Rylean account of psychological concepts rests on the non-equivalence of dispositional propositions and those unpacked dispositionally along Rylean lines, which are 'multi-track'. Thus 'John is grumpy' would be analysed as 'If John is disturbed while reading the paper he will storm out of the room, if John is interrupted, he will shout, if John is frustrated, he will stamp his feet' and these two statements are plainly not equivalent, so the analysis of psychological concepts along dispositional lines will fail (pp. 146–7).

19 This is not to identify the disposition with a categorical state, but to maintain that the existence of the categorical state explains why the glass, for example, is brittle. See Hacker, P. M. S. (2008) *Human Beings: The Categorical Concepts*, Oxford, Blackwell, ch. 4, pp. 118–21.

20 Ryle (1949), p. 140.

21 Whether or not it is a brain activity or is accompanied by one is not the point here. It is not a physical action.

22 Bengson and Moffett use this as an example where possession of, say, the concept of multiplication entails multiplicative ability (2007, p. 40). In the German statutory specifications of know-how associated with particular occupations, a distinction is made between *Fertigkeiten* which broadly have a physical specific manifestation, like planing wood, for example, and *Fähigkeiten* which have a less physical presence and manifest themselves in different activities. Examples would include planning, calculating, communicating problems, and so on. Such *Fähigkeiten* in the plural should be contrasted with the singular notion of an occupational *Fähigkeit* which is a broader concept internally related to that of an occupation (see Chapter 4). Hanf, G. (2009) 'National report on German vocational education', unpublished report to Nuffield Foundation, p. 21.

23 There are different methods of calculating mentally, as can be ascertained by asking people who calculate. Different methods may affect the relative skilfulness of different calculators.

24 An important point here is that a skill like writing may take a while before the individual who possesses it acquires a reasonably full range of its application. Writing is done in different genres, the acquisition of which may take time and practice. It is no contradiction to say, 'A can write but she can't write fairy stories', for example.

25 See the discussion on systematic and non-systematic knowledge in Chapter 1.

[26] An example of a specific, but transferable skill would be the ability to use a certain tool for repairing a motor vehicle, which had a potentially wide application to a variety of models of car.

[27] In fact, moderate defenders of the concept of thinking skills such as Siegel (2010) neither insist on the term 'skill' to capture the kind of practical ability that they have in mind, nor do they allow the intelligibility of anything that purports to be a thinking skill, for example, *comparing*, as opposed to quite specific general abilities connected with reasoning.

[28] See, for example, Weil, S. (2001) *Oppression and Liberty*, London, Routledge, p. 68. The point is, not that such boundaries are never violated, but that we cannot help recognize them as boundaries.

[29] Again, one has to recognize a certain range of exceptions as in a criminal investigation, when a suspect is trying to conceal information. It is important to stress, though, that these are exceptions.

[30] Straka, G. A. (2002) 'Empirical comparisons between the English national vocational qualifications and the educational and training goals of the German dual system – an analysis for the banking sector', in Achtenhagen, F., Thång, P.-O. (eds) *Transferability, Flexibility and Mobility as Targets of Vocational Education and Training*. Proceedings of the final conference of the COST action A11, Gothenburg, 13–16 June 2002. Göttingen: Seminar für Wirtschaftspädagogik der Georg-August-Universität, pp. 227–40.

Chapter 4

Beyond Skill – the Complexities of Competence

Introduction

In the previous chapter the concept of *skill* was described and its complexities as well as its limitations laid bare. However, *skill* is an utterly inadequate concept to describe all the complexities of practical knowledge, including what we have termed 'knowing how to'. In this chapter, a more adequate account of action, particularly in work contexts, will be set out. It will incorporate *skill* but much else besides and will provide a framework for talking about the different dimensions of expertise. In doing so, examples will be taken from the European context in order to show how the conceptual patterning of practical knowledge is significantly different from (and possibly more illuminating than) that available in English.[1] This follows up a point already made in Chapter 2, namely that we should not rely on usage in one language, namely English, in order to make conceptual points applicable across a range of languages.

There is a related point of philosophical methodology to be made here related to overreliance on one language. We need to distinguish between linguistic and conceptual variation. There is no doubt that the same or very similar concepts can be expressed in different ways linguistically.[2] However, Hanfling suggests that the common form of human life itself suggests a conceptual unity within linguistic diversity.

It is no accident that concepts are shared, to a large extent, by different societies; they are part of the human condition, reflecting the needs and interests of humans living in a social world.[3]

However, the 'human condition', although it has certain universal features, consists of humans living in different societies whose ways of life may differ significantly. This is not to suggest that the concepts that express these differences are going to remain impervious to attempts to understand them, but that it is easy to overlook these differences unless one takes care. This is partly because we tend to make the lazy assumption that other societies must organize their lives in the way in which we organize ours and partly because we are misled by homologies, subtle mistranslations and linguistic 'false friends' into thinking that all their distinctions are ours as well and hence that our usage alone can confidently be relied on to achieve philosophical clarity. It is also the case that apparent similarity of usage in one language can lead us to adopt a stance of maintaining *prima facie* conceptual identity in our analysis of a central concept such as that of knowledge, where the root verb 'to know' expresses what German would express by *wissen*, *können* and *kennen*, leaving us prone to the temptation of conceptual assimilation (Rumfitt 2003).

In this chapter, we shall see how the term 'competence' and its cognates in other European languages can lead to such confusions, as can the concepts of 'skill' and 'knowledge'. But we will start the discussion of the contemporary concept of competence by looking at a distinction made by Aristotle between two kinds of practical knowledge, *techne* and *phronesis*.

Techne and Phronesis – a Misused Distinction?

Aristotle's ethics offers two aspects of practical knowledge which are currently very influential, but which are also susceptible to oversimplification and misunderstanding. Briefly put, *techne* is 'a state of capacity to make, involving a true course of reasoning'.[4] The reasoning involved concerns the means to achieve a given end. Aristotle's account therefore says something significant about the *intentionality* involved in the exercise of know-how, although it limits the invocation of intentionality to the choice of means to ends. It is natural to think that this course of reasoning eventually becomes simplified and codified into the description of a *technique* or way of doing things, which has conditional normative force, the antecedent setting out a personal objective, the consequent the injunction:

If you want to achieve F (goal), do G (rule).

This natural tendency is, perhaps, one of the reasons why philosophers have tended to look down on practical knowledge expressible in terms of a technique (sometimes known as technical knowledge). But we should bear in mind the point made in Chapter 3, that a skill is a personal attribute and a technique a way of doing things that can be described or enacted within the exercise of skill.[5] *Conceptual conflation* will lead us to think of skill and technique as virtually identical and a skill as a description of a way of doing something, or even a stilted recipe for carrying out a procedure. It should be noted that the description of a technique might be quite 'thin' and procedural while a demonstration of that technique may be complex and nuanced, embodied in the personal skill of the practitioner of that technique – taking account of the particular needs of the situation (in its broadest sense), materials, time limitations, and so on. We need, then, to distinguish between a technique, as a codification of a way of doing something, and the practice of a technique. Failure to do so can lead to philosophical confusion. Arguably Adam Smith falls into this confusion in passages like the following:

> But when both (watches and watchmaking machinery – CW) have been fairly invented, and are well understood, to explain to any young man, in the completest manner, how to apply the instruments, and how to construct the machines, cannot well require the lessons of more than a few weeks; perhaps those of a few days might be sufficient.[6]

Admittedly Smith goes on to say that dexterity of hand may require a long time to acquire fully, but the above quotation shows how easy it is to conflate skill and technique.

Techne, then, in the sense that Aristotle uses it in many of his remarks, is akin to the use of the English term 'technique'; it is a way of doing things. The *exercise* of technique, on the other hand, with all the nuances of situational awareness and use of experience that this term entails suggests that it has aspects that make it more akin to *phronesis*.[7] The Aristotelian term also brings out a key feature of the concept of knowing how to do something, its *intentionality*. Thus, *techne* when considered as a form of action is goal-directed and intentional, even in those circumstances where the goal is not explicitly formulated by the agent prior to its exercise. It is a way of achieving a particular kind of goal.

Phronesis, on the other hand, is the exercise of practical wisdom. *Phronesis* involves doing the right thing in the right way at the right time in the moral sense of 'right', which in Aristotelian terms is directed towards *eudaemonia* or a state of morally significant well-being (which includes being well-regarded).[8] It is thus the desired manner in which an individual should exercise moral virtues such as justice, courage and honesty.[9] *Phronesis* cannot be prescribed; it is best thought of as a way of acting, not a set of prescriptions. As such it requires experience of diverse situations in which the exercise of the virtues is called for. Each particular situation requires an appropriate response in which the moral integrity of the individuals concerned needs to be considered. Honesty, for example, is a virtue, but acting honestly although causing unnecessary pain and offence to someone in being honest is not necessarily an exercise of *phronesis*. The development of practical wisdom, then, is a complex achievement which requires experience, but on a basis of conditioning, training (in the Rylean sense), explanation, vicarious experience[10] and first-hand experience of a wide variety of different situations.

Virtue is an attribute of how something is done – the virtuous person exhibits *phronesis* in his exercise of the virtue. Typically the virtues such as courage, honesty, kindness and patience are exercised in our dealings with other people and they involve treating people as one would oneself – as of supreme value, rather than as a means to an end. Virtue is generally exercised in social situations – one is inclined to think of it as practical wisdom in dealing rightly with people (i.e. according to what is morally right).

What, then, is the difference between an action involving skill and a virtuous action? This is not a particularly easy question to answer. A skill is an individual attribute and is exercised in action, usually by the employment of one or more techniques. It is possible, for example, to perform an action like *measuring a bathroom* employing skill. One can further say that the ability to measure involves the exercise of skill.[11] To elaborate further, to describe an action as one that requires a skill (an exercise of a way of doing things – a technique), is to offer that action under a certain description: 'A performed F by doing G.' And one can, of course, apply 'intelligence concepts' to such descriptions. 'A measured the bathroom by using the tape measure carefully and accurately', for example.

The contrast with accounts of the virtues is subtle but significant. To describe a virtuous action is to offer an *aspect* of the way in which the action was done, it is not to describe the action under a description of what was done, but rather one feature of the manner in which it was done. To say that *A defended his moral position courageously* is not to characterize a type of action that must involve courage, but is to say that this was the way in which the action was performed. It might not have been, A might have defended his moral position half-heartedly or in a cowardly way, but one could still say that he defended his position. By contrast, to measure a room is to exercise skill with a measuring instrument; not to use a measuring instrument to measure a room is the same as failing to measure a room. The exercise of a skill is a specific action. Although there are actions in which archery or pottery consist, which involve the exercise of the relevant skills, there are no actions in which courage or patience consists which are the exercise of patience or courage. Rather these are aspects of the ways in which these actions are carried out and may, unfortunately often are, carried out without the exercise of these virtues. Indeed, it is possible to exercise a skill such as measuring, exercising *phronesis*. Thus, it is possible to measure the room, not just carefully and accurately (i.e. skilfully), but with patience and consideration. Indeed, these might even be aspects of the *skilfulness* in which one measures the room, rather than merely aspects of the exercise of the skill. In other words, they are a kind of moral intelligence concept.[12] The analogy is thus more between skilfulness and virtue than between skill and virtue. To say that an action is skilful is not just to say that it is the exercise of a skill, but that it is a praiseworthy exercise of that skill, it is an aspect of the way in which the skill is exercised.

The differences between skills and virtues are subtle, but nevertheless significant. One can be an expert in a skill, that is, someone who not only possesses the skill, but also practices it with a degree of excellence, which is related to the purposes for which the skill was acquired. An expert can instruct, demonstrate, train an individual in how to get better at the skill, to be skilful. The expert may, but need not be in all cases, skilful themselves, although they do need to be knowledgeable about what exercise of the skill involves.

Why can't there be experts in virtue? There can obviously be people who exercise a virtue in varying degrees. The virtues are exemplified in action. It does make sense to say that someone may possess a virtue, just as one may possess a skill. Nor is it that one must want to be virtuous in order to be virtuous. Generally, one must want to acquire a skill in order to do so. It is rather that although a skill is something that one possesses, the exercise of the virtue of an individual (the way he or she acts) is that person's way – it is part of what he or she is *in terms of character*, and is thus partly constitutive of the kind of person that person is. To the extent that the exercise of skill is an action, it embodies, or fails to embody, virtues. To cease to practice certain virtues is to cease *constitutively* to have quite the same character that one once had, and this applies as much to one's actions that involve the exercise of skill as it does to actions that do not involve skill.[13]

But this has a further consequence. It is not just that the virtues that one possesses and exercises are partly constitutive of the character that one has, it is that the way in which they are exercised is individual to the person who exercises them. The way in which A exercises a skill may be subtly different from the way in which B does so, but they both recognizably perform the same types of action, say in measuring or archery, by using a ruler or drawing a bow, that is, they employ the same or a similar technique. The exercise of say, the virtues of justice by A or B may be quite different in the case of two individuals, because of the kinds of individuals that they are and result in quite different actions. The possession of a virtue is the possession of *that individual qua that individual.* The most striking example of the importance of this point is offered by Peter Winch.[14] In Melville's story, 'Billy Budd' the eponymous sailor strikes an officer in time of war, a capital offence. The captain, Vere, condemns Billy to death, knowing full well the pure nature of Billy's character and the provocation that he was subject to by the officer, Claggart.

> Faced with the demands of two incompatible 'oughts', Vere reflects what he ought to do; and the outcome of his reflection is that he ought to ensure that the law takes its course.[15]

In this example, the demands of the virtue of justice pull in two directions. Vere, with his military background and sense of the importance of the integrity of naval discipline to which he himself is morally committed, makes the decision that he does while fully cognizant of Billy's moral innocence.

> But somebody else in such a situation (i.e. Vere's C. W.), considering those very same arguments, might conclude that the moral possibilities were different for him without necessarily making any further judgment about what the corresponding possibilities were for Vere or for anybody else and without being committed to any such further judgment.[16]

We may, therefore, say a number of things concerning the relationship between skill and virtue. First, skills can be exercised virtuously or with a lack of virtue, as well as with or without skilfulness. Second, the demands of the virtues are somewhat different from those of skills. Skills are usually directed towards the achievement of aims that the agent has, irrespective of the moral value of those aims. One can employ skills towards the achievement of wicked aims, for example. The practice of virtue, on the other hand, is principally directed towards the good, and this usually means to the good of other people, not necessarily to the well-being of oneself. An action that requires skill is an identifiable type of action. The exercise of virtues is not the performance of an identifiable type of action, but an aspect of the way in which an action aimed at the good is done.[17] Skills are a property of the individual, the virtues or, rather, the way in which they are or are not practiced, are an important aspect of a person's character, part of what makes him or her what they are. We cannot assume, therefore, that the type of action that two people carry out, in the same type of circumstances, embodying the same virtue, is necessarily the same. This answers our question about expertise in virtue. Our exercise of the virtues is part of the development of our character, something that is partly achieved, through our endeavours and our learning from others, something partly that also emerges through our experiences and our discovery of who we really are; it is not the application of any technique.[18]

There is, however, an important complicating factor in this story. If a skill can be exercised with virtue, when, for example, one flies a plane courageously, then isn't the way in which the skill is exercised partially constitutive of character? The answer must be 'yes'. The skill itself may not be part of one's character, but one's actions when they embody skill may exemplify virtue. However, if it is possible to exercise a skill, say, diligently and if doing so is an aspect of character, then it cannot be the case that the virtues, or at least some of them, are unambiguously directed towards the good. For skills can be misdirected by someone who has adopted bad principles or values, even though those skills are exercised diligently, prudently, and so on. This suggests a disjuncture between the 'petty' or 'bourgeois' virtues that are subordinated to the exercise of technique and the 'civic' or 'major' virtues that are aimed at some good. This is not an altogether sharp distinction, because it is the case that even a virtue like courage can be exemplified in bad actions. However, it is the case that the petty virtues are generally subordinated to the good of oneself (they are self-regarding rather than other-regarding) and, for that reason, not as valued as the other-regarding virtues. This is why thinkers such as Kerschensteiner, who recognize the role of virtue in the exercise of technique, are, at the same time, at pains to stress the limitations of virtue inculcation when applied solely to the exercise of technique, arguing that it can be distortive of one's perception of the importance and significance of what one is doing. Any inculcation of 'bourgeois' virtues must, therefore, be balanced by the development of the 'civic' virtues that necessitate the consideration of a social rather than merely an individual good.[19] It can be seen, therefore, that the exercise of a skill can be done in a certain way that embodies one or more virtues (or vices). It is thus not the possession of a skill as such that is partly constitutive of character, but the way in which that skill is exercised. In this respect the exercise of skills are in the same position in relation to the virtues as any other kind of action.

One final point of distinction between skill and virtues needs to be made. It has been argued that the primary home of the concept of skill lies with that of *task*, a relatively restricted form of intentional human activity. Virtues can be manifested in the ways in which tasks are carried out, but their scope is much wider and includes actions more broadly and also, importantly, activity types of broad scope, such as occupational activity. The virtues of a soldier or carpenter, for example, do not merely consist in the way in which they practice tasks belonging to those occupations but also to their practice of the occupation as such. A carpenter *qua* carpenter can exercise the virtues of his occupation, which include the way in which he deals with employees, customers and apprentices as well as with the reputation of his occupation and the way in which it relates to the broader concerns of the society in which it is practiced. One can, then, be a *technically virtuous* carpenter independently of being an *occupationally virtuous* one. That is, one can practice the skills of carpentry according to the virtues that promote excellence in those tasks, and one can pursue the occupation of a carpenter in a way that enhances the reputation both of oneself as a human being and of the occupation itself. Unfortunately the two types of virtue are not always found together in the same person.[20]

Techne – Phronesis in Modern Guise – Three Influential Reductive Accounts of Practical Knowledge

The discussion so far leads us to the view that there are two aspects of practical ability, each subtly interwoven with the other, because they deal with different dimensions of human action. Technique is a way of doing something in the sense of a procedure, while virtue is an aspect, relevant to the morally good, of the way in which an individual acts. They are, in the sense, complementary, not in conflict with each other. This is not, however, the way in which they are often seen by modern and contemporary commentators and, in this section, reductive accounts of the differences will be explored and largely rejected. Such commentary tends to regard the practice of technique, particularly in an economic context, as essentially demeaning, while action in the sense of civic or political engagement or in the sense of the pursuit of disinterested friendship is of ultimate value in human life.

Aristotle's philosophical legacy comes in a sociological one, which continues to be influential in our understanding of his philosophical theses about practical knowledge. But they need to be unpicked in order to gain a better understanding of contemporary forms of vocational education, at least in countries other than England. The conventional account of the acquisition of the virtues is that they are formed through experiences: training, habituation, exemplification and emulation, vicarious experience, independent experience and judgement and reflection on that experience.[21] One needs to have the right kind of experiences. Beyond the early stages of training and habituation, these must provide scope for, and indeed *demand* the exercise of moral judgement. Such experiences can be specified in a loose way and their characteristics indicate a spectrum of situations of varying degrees of moral seriousness. Such a specification relates to what I call *operational conditions*, which have certain characteristics to various degrees. The presence or absence of these features gives us some indication of the moral significance of such situations and the scope they offer for moral formation. Such experiences, involving operational conditions, have the following features to a greater or lesser degree: they involve (a) personal responsibility for oneself and others; (b) lack of complete control over the environment in which action takes place; (c) the moral seriousness of the consequences of action in terms of one's welfare and that of others; (d) the immediacy of the need for decision and action. Examples of areas of life in which operational conditions obtain, which are typical but by no means exhaustive include war, work[22] and civic affairs.[23] Work and business activities thus have no ultimate value, although they may embody activities that have some intrinsic value.

This poses a problem for the general idea of employing operational conditions as indicators for the scope for moral action. Although there may still be situations in which virtue may be developed (and Aristotle, for example, thinks that some experience of them may be necessary for this to happen), it is also clear that he regards such conditions and the formation that takes place in them as preliminaries to a life in which valued activities are enjoyed for their own sake.[24] War and work may, therefore, be components, even necessary components, of *preparation* for a worthwhile life, but are not themselves spheres of life to which ultimate value attaches. Civic action, leisure and contemplation are such components, however, and the first two, particularly where leisure involves the cultivation of friendship, are proper areas for morally significant action. Thus, an educated man may work in order to gain leisure in which noble activities are enjoyed for their own sake. His work *qua employment* can have no ultimate value, however, for it is menial and not a component of a worthwhile life. If it has to be engaged in, it must be as a means to the end of engagement in worthwhile activities. The *actions* that he undertakes as part of that work, however, may have intrinsic value.[25]

This is abundantly clear in Aristotle's treatment of musical education in Bk 8 of the *Politics*, where he maintains that a musical education for leisure, in which music is appreciated rather than seriously played, needs to be preceded by the learning of an instrument. Leisure which involves the appreciation of music requires a first-hand appreciation of the difficulties and the art of playing. Such accomplishment should not, however, attain the degree of expertise of a professional musician as that would put the man of leisure in the invidious position of practicing music for employment rather than leisure.[26] Vocational education, although it is properly concerned with the achievement of excellence in the chosen occupation, is not a preparation for the life of a citizen. The excellence in an activity demanded by a vocation is not appropriate for an educated man.[27] Education does not, therefore, require excellence in arts and crafts but a semi-vicarious appreciation of what is involved in attaining excellence. In this sense, too close an appreciation of the operational conditions of the working life of a professional musician is not desirable, because experience of those operational conditions is demeaning, in a way that experience of the operational conditions of battle or the *agora* are not. We could further say, using the idiom of value, that the music produced and the skills and virtues used to produce it may be of intrinsic value, but the way of life in which it is produced and those skills and virtues exercised are not, and cannot be, a worthwhile mode of existence.

This thesis expresses a particular conception of the free man, someone who does not have to work for a living, at least not as a major component of his life. It is a gentlemanly ideal of the cultivated, leisured and civically engaged person for whom a thoroughgoing liberal education is thought most appropriate because it is the right kind of preparation for the kind of life considered to be worthwhile. It is an ideal that has carried over into most conceptions of liberal education that still retain influence, both those that owe their inspiration to Plato and Aristotle, such as the earlier work of R. S. Peters and those that stem from Rousseau (although in this case there are important qualifications to be made, since Émile needs to learn various vocational skills). However, the citizen of a modern liberal democracy is thought to be, not merely independent like the Aristotelian gentleman, but *autonomous*, someone who is able to chart his own course in life, albeit autonomous under conditions which necessitate, for most people, the experience of paid employment. For such a person, it can be argued, the achievement of excellence in a *techne* may not just be an economic necessity, but a constituent of an activity that has ultimate value for the citizen.

But these liberal educational positions are based on an assumption that a citizen's life is to be one of independent leisured pursuits in which the necessities of earning one's living play, at worst, a relatively minor role. For people who are to enjoy such a destiny there is a lot of sense in the kind of education that Aristotle prescribes. Most of us, however, differ from the Aristotelian gentleman in two important respects: first we are expected to be *autonomous* rather than just independent; second, earning a living plays a dominant role in our lives in terms of the time and, in many cases, of the emotional and cognitive commitment required. The significance of autonomy is that, in choosing a particular course of life, we are of necessity constrained to also choose an occupational path that we think suits us. This kind of choice is often problematic and prone to false starts, since it is only through sustained occupational engagement that we can safely say that our choices are, or are not validated through a process of self-discovery within employment.[28] For most people constrained to earn a living, such exploration must lead to a permanent engagement with work for which, perhaps, one's earlier engagement is a culmination of previous education.

The sociologically based disparagement of the exercise of *techne* in favour of action in leisure and civic or political contexts has had a profound influence, despite the subtlety of Aristotle's account of *techne*. Aristotle does not deny, indeed affirms, that the pursuit of excellence in the purpose of the exercise of the *techne* is a matter or ardour and care, but is demeaning not because of that, but because excellence is pursued for economic rather than entertainment or aesthetic reasons. Neither does Aristotle deny that a *techne* may be practiced in a social context. Nonetheless, a tradition of thinking about the *techne/phronesis* distinction has arisen which largely ignores these points.

Against Reductive Accounts of Agency in Economic Contexts

Arendt's account of three aspects of human activity, as it is set out in *The Human Condition*, is a good example of the reworking of the Aristotelian sociological theme in an epistemological guise.[29] According to Arendt, one may regard human activity under three distinct, although related, aspects: man as *animal laborans*, as *homo faber* and as participant in the *vita activa*.

As *animal laborans*, man is primarily a biological entity whose existence lies in the production and reproduction of his existence. This is a very wide category, which includes the physical functions necessary to individual sustenance and reproduction of the race. Labour in childbirth, for example, is a function of *animal laborans*. But it also includes all kinds of tasks which are necessary to sustain life, such as hunting, gathering, building shelter. Arendt conceives of *animal laborans*, however, as a solitary, at least as far as these activities are concerned. The term used by Arendt to characterize this type of human activity is 'Arbeit', perhaps best translated in this context as 'labour'.

Contrasted with this aspect of existence is man as planner and creator, as *homo faber*, who conceives of and puts into effect designs which employ raw materials which nature provides. Unlike the effects of labour, the outcome of *homo faber*'s efforts, a more or less permanent product, is not a biological necessity but part of an attempt to create a permanent artificial physical environment for humans to live in. *Homo faber*, however, like man as *animal laborans*, is essentially a solitary. The work of design and production can be conceived of as arising from the plan of an individual and the putting into effect of that plan by an individual, although often with the assistance of others. But the others are the handmaidens of *homo faber* in this sense, not participants in a common enterprise. Arendt uses the term *Werk* or 'making' in this context.

The *vita activa*, on the other hand, is the characteristic of life in the *polis*. Man's social life is essentially political: it involves the discussion, determination and direction of the collective life of the *polis*. It is concerned as much with ends as with means and is not concerned primarily either with the conditions of existence or with the construction of artefacts. It is clear that Arendt sees the *vita activa* as most expressive of the distinctive aspect of human life, namely its social character and this social character is, in turn, most fully manifested in the direction of man's political and ethical affairs in the broadest sense. Arendt, it is important to note, is not denying that the same person may not exemplify all three aspects of human activity and in this sense is not insisting on the kind of sociological separatism to be found in Aristotle or Plato. She does, however, share with them the view that it is in the courtroom, the meeting place and the parliament or council chamber that man realizes himself to the highest degree. In this sense the Aristotelian hierarchy of political and leisure activity over economic and productive activity is maintained.

There is something profoundly unsatisfactory about Arendt's account of human activity in general and her account of labour and work in particular. Taking the first two of her distinctions, *Arbeit* in her sense covers both voluntary and involuntary (excretion and digestion) and also some forms of intentional action, such as hunting. It is also apparent, as she herself notes, that the *Arbeit/Werk* distinction is not always clear, since some of the outcomes of both may be similar in their permanence or lack of it. But there are two problems with her concept of *Arbeit*, the first one being that it does not discriminate between *being able to do something* and *knowing how to do so* (see Chapter 2). Neither, within the category of intentional action, does it discriminate between conceptually dependent action (where some form of conceptual mastery is necessary for practical mastery) and non-conceptually dependent action (where it is not). It is thus unable to distinguish between animal and human labour. This point is further strengthened by the characterization of *Arbeit* as something largely non-social, the solitary activity of the body. This may be true of digestion but is certainly not true of a wide range of activities that fall within *Arbeit*, such as hunting and even eating (where this is done as a social practice).

Werk, on the other hand, is clearly intentional. Man forms a plan for an artefact and puts that plan into effect. Although she does not put it this way, *Werk* does require conceptual mastery and thus *animals* cannot carry out *Werk*. However, Arendt, in common with Marx, does not place much, if any, emphasis on the social character of *Werk*. This category has much in common with Marx's concept of *unalienated labour* and Kerschensteiner's *produktive Arbeit* which both involve planning and putting into effect.[30] Neither Marx nor Arendt deny the social nature of this kind of human activity that involves intention and the production of something more or less permanent.[31] It is rather that it does not enter their account in any significant way. Indeed, in Marx's writings, it is through the *division of labour,* that we encounter the social organization of human economic activity. While it is true that one can work in this sense in a solitary way, it is to be doubted whether such work could ever have originated outside a social context.[32] But, more than that, it is a misdescription of both *Arbeit* and *Werk* in Arendt's senses to consider them under the aspect of solitary activity. Not only is this because they nearly always occur within a social context, but also because they usually are themselves in one way or another, social activities. We cannot adequately characterize them as the kinds of activities that they are without recognizing this feature. One of the main features of the difference between these two categories of labour and the *vita activa* is therefore, undermined. One writer who recognized this fully and also understood the importance of the social aspect of work to human spiritual needs was Simone Weil, who writes

> a team of workers on a production-line under the eye of a foreman is a sorry spectacle, whereas it is a fine sight to see a handful of workmen in the building trade, checked by some difficulty, ponder the problem each for himself, make various suggestions for dealing with it, and then apply unanimously the method conceived by one of them, who may or may not have any official authority over the remainder. At such moments the image of a free community appears almost in its purity.[33]

Arendt may of course, acknowledge this aspect of *Werk* but nevertheless claim first of all that it is a contingent feature of it that it is, in this instance, social rather than solitary. Dealing with this objection will have to wait for a fuller treatment until the next chapter (Chapter 5). However, a further consideration that she would undoubtedly urge is that in Weil's example the workers are deliberating on *means* rather than *ends* and this makes all the difference to the significance of the example. The participant in the *vita activa* has the opportunity, with his fellow citizens, to determine what is worth pursuing, as well as how to pursue it. He is not just independent, but *autonomous*, to put the matter in a modern idiom. This means more than what it might have meant in the Aristotelian context, that the political ends of the state may be determined, but rather that what is worthwhile as a human life also has a certain openness about it.

This is undoubtedly an important point but it should not make us lose sight of the importance of independence in the workplace. Control over one's work is an important source of human satisfaction and, where work is dependent on the co-operation of others, that control has to be co-operatively exercised. The exercise of independence, the taking of responsibility, the planning, control and assessment of what one is doing are all important aspects of work that contribute to human satisfaction and a sense of the worthwhileness of what is being done. This, as we shall see, is something that is widely recognized in modern work practices in Europe.[34]

However, Arendt's larger point can be answered as well. The determination of the ends of work is not something that need be left to professional politicians or an élite. It is important to consider, as did, for example, Kerschensteiner, workers as citizens rather than subjects (*Bürger* rather than *Untertanen* in his terminology) able, through the political structures of their state, to play a role in the determination of such ends. But this ability need not be confined to the sphere of national politics. Civil society has a role to play as well, through trade union activity and the practice of *social partnership* and also, through its presence in countries such as Germany, of some form of industrial democracy or *Mitbestimmung* in which, not only do employees have a say in the control of their workplace, but a significant determination of the strategic course of their enterprise as well.[35] These considerations together suggest that it is not helpful to make a sharp conceptual separation between different types of human agency in work and in other contexts, even though, in particular contexts, there may be a significant practical separation.

Conceptions of Competence

It is now time to consider a broader category of action than that indicated by the concept of skill. It is known, to the English ear somewhat misleadingly, by the term 'competence' in English, by *compétence* in French and *Kompetenz* in German. In order to understand this broader action category it is necessary to move the focus of attention away from *tasks* and towards *occupations*. An occupation is a broad category of economic activity related to the production of some recognizable type of product or service. There is an important sense, therefore, in which occupations have goals or end, or as MacIntyre might put it, 'internal goods' with standards of excellence internal to the occupation itself. As a broad category it encompasses professions, crafts and trades. In German, the term *Beruf* signifies 'occupation' but in a broader sense which is more equivalent to the English term 'vocation', which signifies an ethical calling but also as a term that signifies the social identity of the person practicing the *Beruf.*

> 'Most Germans are not looking for just a job, they want a *Beruf*,[36] a lifelong one, and one about which they can be passionate. And any government that does not meet that aspiration must fail, sooner or later. If you have a *Beruf* in Germany, you are someone. If you just have a job, you aren't.' So wrote Ullrich Fichtner in the weekly current affairs magazine, *Der Spiegel*, on 30 May 2005.[37]

Looking at practical knowledge under the aspect of occupation rather than that of task, brings with it a number of points that tend to be overlooked in task-focused English discussions. The 'English' conception of competence is that of skill exercised to an acceptable standard. In modern accreditation systems, especially those based on a 'learning outcomes' approach such as National Vocational Qualifications (NVQs), competence is thought of task-based, performance of the task being conceived of in behavioural terms.[38] In setting out the 'continental' concept of competence I will concentrate on what is perhaps the richest manifestation of this, the German one, referring to French and Dutch cases where appropriate.

As already noted, the *Beruf* concept is much more nuanced than that of the generic 'occupation'. It has an existence, both in the everyday linguistic sense, but also an official usage to indicate the kind of vocational education one has undergone, as well as the kind of occupation one is pursuing as paid employment. In the official usage, to have successfully completed vocational education, particularly in the Dual System, a modern form of apprenticeship with a significant formal educational element, is to have mastered a *berufliche Handlungsfähigkeit* or occupational action capacity.[39] In order to understand this concept it is first necessary to distinguish between two forms of know-how recognized in the German language.

First, there are *Fertigkeiten*, which are roughly equivalent to skills, or even to knacks, which are task-related. A *Fertigkeit* is, then, closely related to skill. Second, there are *Fähigkeiten*, which are abilities which do not necessarily have a typical physical manifestation, such as communicating, planning, evaluating; in other words, transferable in the sense outlined in Chapter 3. Finally the term is used in the singular, in the vocational context, to denote the overall, integrated capacity of, for example, being a carpenter, priest or doctor. The *Fähigkeit* in this sense is more than a bundle of *Fertigkeiten* and *Fähigkeiten* for a number of reasons. The first of these concerns the independence that a worker is expected to exercise over his work. This involves, to varying degrees, the planning, control, co-ordination, assessment and finishing of a wide range of occupational tasks. A typical *Beruf* is not narrowly conceived but encompasses a range of related activities which may well be much greater in *scope* than those expected in analogous occupations in other countries like England. Bricklaying would be a good example of this. Second, the worker is expected to be able to co-ordinate operations with other members of a work team as well as with other workers in related occupations in the same sector. Third, the work itself is thought to necessitate, not just the application of contingent knowledge (*Kenntnis*) to practice, but also systematic (and theoretical) knowledge relevant to the occupation. This includes knowledge in sufficient depth to be able to anticipate and understand new developments in the occupational field. Fourth, *Kompetenz* includes complex moral and civic dispositions and attitudes which are more or less immediately bound up with the labour process. These include the ability to apply standards and take responsibility for one's work, to develop personal characteristics of commitment to moral values and to take responsibility for the consequences of the practice of one's occupation in the wider social and political context. *Berufliche Handlungsfähigkeit* does, then, include important elements of *Bildung* or education that encompass character development as well as knowledge and skill acquisition. It is also intended to be the foundation for continuing personal development, not just as a worker and a citizen, but as an individual with unique characteristics, what is known from the work of Wilhelm von Humboldt as *allgemeine Menschenbildung* or general human education.[40]

It can be seen that this concept of competence takes us a long way from the accounts of practical knowledge offered in Philosophy, with the notable exception of the work of Georg Kerschensteiner. It is of much broader scope than the practice of a *techne* and incorporates the idea of pursuit of excellence as internal to the practice of the occupation. *Pace* Aristotle, there is no dishonour in pursuing excellence in a work environment, indeed to do so is an aspect of self-realization. Furthermore, the work environment is a locus of social and moral activity (*pace* Arendt) and the responsibilities of the worker do not end in the workplace but extend into the direction of the enterprise, the occupation and the place of the occupation within society.

The complexity of competence in this sense preserves one important feature of know-how applied to skill, namely the applicability of 'intelligence concepts'. However, we can now understand the growth of expertise as something that involves more than task-related intelligence concepts. The range of evaluative concepts applicable to an occupational *Fähigkeit* will be far broader and will include the evaluation of moral, social and civic characteristics of the person possessing the *Fähigkeit*.

Conclusion

The discussion in this and the previous chapter has been long and complex. However, some clear conclusions stand out:

1. Know-how can be understood in both dispositional and categoric terms depending on the context of discussion.
2. The concept of skill primarily concerns the individual possession of task-related abilities.
3. Skills and other forms of practical ability are subject to evaluation in terms of the ability of their possessors to meet standards or ideals of excellence. They can also be evaluated in moral terms.

4. The concept of skill cannot do justice to all categories of practical ability, for which a wider set of concepts is required, such as that of *Handlungsfähigkeit*.

5. Skills and other forms of practical ability should be distinguished from the virtues, which concern morally relevant features of how actions are performed, even though, as actions, the exercise of skill or competence may reveal the virtues possessed by the agent through the way in which the ability is exercised and the circumstances in which it is exercised.

Notes

[1] This section draws heavily on the Nuffield Foundation Crossnational Project on the Transferability of Qualifications and to the contributions of Linda Clarke, Michaela Brockmann, Georg Hanf, Anneke Westerhuis and Philippe Méhaut.

[2] I am assuming here that concepts can *broadly* be delineated by the use of the words that express them. See Wittgenstein (1953, §43).

[3] Hanfling (2000), p. 72.

[4] Aristotle (1925) *Nichomachean Ethics*, Ross translation, London, Dent, Bk 6, section 4, p. 141.

[5] It is this latter use of 'technique' that seems to be most responsible for the skill-technique conflation.

[6] Smith [1776] (1981), Bk 1, ch. 10, p. 71.

[7] For detailed scholarly support for this view from a variety of Aristotelian texts, see Dunne, J. (1993) *Back to the Rough Ground*, Chicago, Notre Dame Press, esp. ch. 10.

[8] Aristotle (1925) is the main source for his views on *phronesis*.

[9] Although Aristotle is concerned with the virtues valued in his time, his account is meant to apply and can apply to different ideas about virtue – Homeric, Christian, and so on.

[10] On the importance of this, see Simpson, E. (1989) *Good Lives and Moral Education*, New York, Peter Lang.

[11] I ignore here unusual cases of 'beginner's luck' or flukes, which do not undermine the normal case.

[12] What Kerschensteiner (1964) refers to as the 'bourgeois virtues' (*bürgerliche Tugenden*). It is arguable that 'carefully' falls into this category as well.

[13] Not, of course, in the sense of ceasing to be the same person, but in no longer being the kind of person that one once was.

[14] Winch, P. (1965) 'The universalizability of moral judgements', available in Winch, P. (1972) *Ethics and Action*, London, Routledge. Winch does not frame his discussion in terms of the exercise of the virtues, but the point that he is making illustrates an important aspect of virtue.

15　Winch (1965), p. 162.

16　Ibid. p. 169. Raz, J. (2003) *Engaging Reason*, ch. 40 argues that the growth of the exercise of judgement in such situations is an aspect of the development of one's character.

17　Or in the case of a vice, aimed at the bad; but then it is not an exercise of virtue.

18　This is one of the central themes of the Germanic *Bildungsroman* genre of novels of coming of age and self-discovery, usually within an occupational context. See Goethe, J. W., *Wilhelm Meister's Lehrjahre* and Keller, G., *Der Grüne Heinrich*, for example.

19　See, for example, Kerschensteiner, G. [1901] (1964) 'Staatsbürgerliche Erziehung der deutschen Jugend', in *Ausgewählte Pädagogische Texte*, Band 1, Paderborn, Ferdinand Schöningh.

20　Carr (1999); Winch (2002). The distinction between technical and occupational virtues made here is similar to, although not identical with that made by Kerschensteiner between *bourgeois* and *civic* virtues.

21　Aristotle (1925); Simpson, E. (1989) *Good Lives and Moral Education*, New York, Peter Lang, for a good account.

22　Aristotle (1988) *The Politics*, Bks 7, 8. Stephen Everson edition, Cambridge University Press.

23　Arendt, H. (1958) *The Human Condition*, Chicago, University of Chicago Press, ch. 5.

24　Aristotle (1988), Bk 8, section 13, in Everson edition, pp. 189–92.

25　For the distinction between intrinsic and ultimate value, see Raz (1986). I will use this distinction in discussing the Aristotelian idea of a worthwhile life, while recognizing that Aristotle himself did not employ this terminology.

26　Aristotle (1988), Bk 8, section 5, pp. 189–90.

27　See also Plato (1975) *Laws*, Bk 1, where training for excellence in trade is explicitly discounted as a form of education, London, Penguin, p. 73.

28　See, for example, Keller, G. [1854–5] (1951) *Der grüne Heinrich*, Zurich, Atlantis Verlag; Goethe, J. [1796] (1980) *Wilhelm Meister's Lehrjahre*, Frankfurt am Main, Fischer Verlag. J. R. R. Tolkien's *The Hobbit* also follows the *Bildungsroman* pattern (London, Allen and Unwin, 1937).

29　See Arendt, H. (1958) *The Human Condition*, Chicago, University of Chicago Press. For related treatments, see also Lave, J., Wenger, E. (1991) *Situated Learning: Legitimate Peripheral Participation*, Cambridge, Cambridge University Press; Oakeshott, M. (1962a) 'Rationalism in politics', in *Rationalism in Politics and Other Essays*, London, Methuen, pp. 1–36.

30　Refer Marx, K. (1970a) (1887) *Capital*, London, Lawrence and Wishart, volume 1, p. 178; Kerschensteiner, G. (1906) 'Produktiver Arbeit und ihr Erziehungswert', in *Ausgewählte Pädagogische Texte*, Band 2 (1968).

31　See in particular Marx, K. (1964) (1858) *Precapitalist Economic Formations*, London, Lawrence and Wishart, pp. 87–8.

32　See Chapter 5 on concept-dependent activity.

33　Weil, S. (2001) *Oppression and Liberty*, London, Routledge, p. 95.

34　There is good empirical evidence to support this thesis. See, for example, Wilkinson, R. (2005) *The Impact of Inequality: How to Make Sick Societies Healthier*, London, Routledge.

[35] For a good account of *Mitbestimmung*, see Streeck, W. (1992) *Social Institutions and Economic Performance*, New York, Sage, ch. 5.

[36] Translator's note: the German term *Beruf* is one that does not have a single equivalent in English and can be rendered as 'occupation', 'profession' or 'career'. However, training and status are always involved. In this chapter, it will not be translated but left in German.

[37] Greinert, W-D. (2007) 'The German philosophy of vocational education', in Clarke, L., Winch, C. (eds) *Vocational Education: International Perspectives, Developments and Systems*, London, Routledge, pp. 49–61, p. 49.

[38] On learning outcomes, see Brockmann, M., Clarke, L., Winch, C. (2007) 'Can performance-related learning outcomes have standards?' *Journal of European Industrial Training*, 32, 2/3, pp. 99–113. On English CBET, see Hyland, T. (1993) 'Competence, knowledge and education', *Journal of Philosophy of Education*, 27, 1, pp. 57–68.

[39] For further explanation, see Hanf, G. (2007) 'Quick scan of the German VET system' on http://www.kcl.ac.uk/content/1/c6/01/57/15/GermanyQuickScan-Nov07.pdf

[40] For a detailed account see Benner, D. (2003) *Wilhelm von Humboldt's Bildungstheorie*, Munich, Juventa; Brockmann, M., Clarke, L., Méhaut, P., Winch, C. (2008) 'Competence-based Vocational Education and Training (VET): the cases of England and France in a European perspective', *Vocations and Learning*, 1, pp. 227–44. The French concept suggests a more narrowly focused occupational field but emphasizes the ability to make judgements and take action in complex situations, while the Dutch concept emphasizes underlying attitudes that enable one to deal with critical situations in operational conditions.

Chapter 5

To Follow a Rule . . . The Normative Basis of Practical Knowledge

Introduction

It may be useful to sum up the argument so far:

The claim that knowing how is a distinct epistemic category, which serves certain distinct purposes was defended. One of these purposes was to give an account, in practically relevant situations, of the nature of expertise (Chapter 1). In Chapter 2, a particular version of the distinction between *knowing how* and *knowing that*, based on an account of know-how manifested primarily in action was defended. In Chapter 3, this claim was filled out in relation to the concept of skill, some of whose hidden complexities were discussed. At the same time, inadequacies in the account offered by Ryle were alluded to. Chapter 4 put the concept of skill within a broader category of action concepts which refer to the moral dimension of action, to such social categories as that of an occupation and to the integration of virtue, independence and responsibility, declarative knowledge and skill in an action-concept adequate to describe contemporary vocational and professional action.

The task of this chapter is, first, to address the way in which we can best understand know-how and related concepts for this purpose. The argument is that know-how is based on capacities for normative response that are part of human species-nature, and that know-how both in its broad and narrow senses, is best to be understood as norm-related action. This claim is amplified in order to show how it can take account of expertise, one of the central concerns of this book, and also to show how such an understanding of know-how can be defended against some obvious objections.

To Follow a Rule: The Role of Normative Activities in the Understanding of Practical Knowledge

A good place to start is with Ryle's account of knowing how and the consideration of possible inadequacies with it. We saw in Chapter 3 that Ryle offers an account of knowing how that is based on intelligent action. Intelligent action involves both the individual possession of dispositions and of 'clockable occurrences' of the exercise of specific abilities. Nevertheless, it is fair to say that the account is mainly dispositional; without some actual occurrences, it would be hard to see what work the concept of an action disposition would be doing. However, as Smith and Jones pointed out, simply to offer a dispositional account in which a description of disposition occurrences is substituted for a label for the disposition is to offer an account that is largely vacuous.[1] What is needed, they argue, is an account of the states that underlies the disposition which in turn provides much of the explanation for why a disposition resulted in occurrences in particular situations.

Smith and Jones suggested that a proper understanding of the categorical states underlying human action should be understood *nomologically*, as the law-like properties of the human physical constitution. Here it is understood that a large part of the explanation of the necessary conditions for the application of know-how concepts is to be understood in terms of such states but that it cannot be the whole story. We need, as well, to understand both the *normative* basis and the normative nature of knowing how to do something. In order to get to grips with these issues it is first useful to make a distinction made by Anthony Kenny, between a *capacity* and an *ability*.[2] A capacity is the ability to acquire an ability. In what follows I will use the term in the sense of those states of human beings that provide the necessary conditions for the genesis of abilities, including those that involve know-how. It is by now a commonplace that many such capacities are underpinned by our neurological constitution, which, although it does not provide a complete explanation of how abilities arise, does provide us with an increasingly good understanding of the *necessary conditions* for their genesis.[3]

However, such accounts of capacity cannot be exhaustive as they cannot provide adequate explanations of our normative capacity, that is, our capacity to recognize and follow norms as opposed to physical laws. We need, in addition, to postulate a normative capacity whose realization does not involve just our physical constitution, but also the social milieu of our existence. It is important to realize that there is an important sense in which such normative capacity could be understood nomologically as Wittgenstein acknowledged.[4] However, in order to understand normative activities in terms of *norms* rather than *laws*, it is necessary to understand them in normative rather than nomological terms and, in order to do this, it is necessary to move beyond accounts of human physical constitution to an understanding of what is involved in social interaction. This in turn involves understanding what it is to participate in the typical *normative activities* of habituation, training, instruction, correction, explanation, interpretation and justification.[5] Participation in these activities is both a condition of our becoming full participants in these practices but is also constitutive of our being so. We are bound by such norms as conditions of our being participants in such practices and, indeed in being subject to the evaluative concepts internal to these practices but we are not compelled by them in the sense that we are said to be subject to laws of nature. These activities are, by their nature, social, involving more than one person.[6] Normative activities do not exist in isolation, but are organized around an institution or activity from which they derive their sense, such as hunting, building, farming or conducting political life. Grasping how they fit together in an institutional context is part of understanding the norms that they express. Indeed, one should say that to claim that someone understands an activity is to assert that he has at least an adequate grasp of these normative activities and how they hang together in an institutional unity through his participation in them. If we did not have the *capacity* for participation in normative activities of this kind, we would not acquire normatively understood abilities which involve know-how.

We are now in a better position to see at least part of what is missing from Ryle's account. He does have the beginnings of a framework for talking about the acquisition and practice of know-how, in his account of training and in reference to intelligence concepts. Here Ryle's thinking appears to indicate that criteria internal to the skill that an individual is learning are brought to bear both in the process of training and also on its evaluation, but nothing is said about this. In order to account for these phenomena we need the language of norms to describe what it is to train someone what to do as opposed to *conditioning* them to do so.[7] This is connected with the concept of *understanding* which Ryle does discuss, but without the normative background that makes such explanations intelligible. When we ask for an explanation of *what* it is that someone understands, or *why* we think that they understand it, or *how well* they understand it, we offer an account in terms of the norms that constitute that activity and the extent to which mastery of the activity is displayed through facility with the normative structure that constitutes it. What underlies our accounts of the possession of the skills and competences that an individual possesses is, then, something that has explanatory value. We can explain what it is that the skill or competence consists in through reference to its constituent normative structure, and this is what constitutes the activity which practicing the skill or competence involves. We can explain expertise in terms of *mastery* which usually involves at least implicit reference to the *purposes* for which the activity is carried out as well as the *constraints* which achieving those purposes are subject to. Such purposes may themselves, although this is rarer than many suppose, be understood completely through a description of the activity itself. It is more likely however, that they can be best understood through a grasp of how that particular activity fits broader patterns of human life and institutions, so that such connections shed light, not just on these broader patterns, but on the activity itself.

It is important to realize that, in many if not most cases, the normative structure of an activity is not disclosed explicitly or discursively through the promulgation of *rules* but implicitly and sometimes non-discursively through observation of the patterning of the activity itself and of the normative activities that underpin it. Although Wittgenstein's account of normativity is frequently couched in the language of rules (Regeln) it is not an account of normativity in terms of explicit rules, but in terms of the primitive practices that underlie the promulgation and enforcing of formal and explicit rules which are themselves a part of the broader family of normative activities and institutions.

MacIntyre and Practices Again

Is there something substantive that can be said about the social context of normativity? Probably the most significant recent work in this area has been that of Alastair MacIntyre who, as we saw in Chapter 1, introduced the notion of a *practice* in order to provide a conceptual framework for understanding the full range of human activity.[8] It is also necessary however to juxtapose MacIntyre's treatment of these issues with that of Rush Rhees and his criticisms of Wittgenstein's notion of a *language game*.[9] MacIntyre's claim is that a practice is

> any coherent or complex form of socially established cooperative human activity through which goods internal to that form of activity are realised in the course of trying to achieve those standards of excellence which are appropriate to, and partly definitive of, that form of activity, with the result that human powers to achieve excellence, and humans conceptions of the ends and goods involved, are systematically extended.[10]

MacIntyre's account of a practice, following the Aristotelian tradition, marks an advance on the reductive account of activity offered previously by Arendt. MacIntyre, whose main aim in this book, was to provide an historical interpretation of the evolution of moral concepts, is quite clear that economically productive activity should be considered as a central part of human life, not just the leisure, contemplative, military and civic spheres of life that figure more prominently in Aristotle's work. Also of significance is MacIntyre's willingness to embrace the teleological nature of much of what people do. Occupations, in particular, can meaningfully be said to have a *telos*, farming, one of MacIntyre's examples of a practice, the production of food, soldiering, the defence of the *polis*, and so on. The idea of excellence is related to the *telos* of the practice, to the goods for which it exists to produce.[11] Very significant aspects of the normative structure of a practice can, then, be elucidated in terms of this *telos*.

Nevertheless, as we have already noted, there are some serious problems with this way of providing a sociological framework for the discussion of normativity. A suitable starting-place would be the *rigidity* of MacIntyre's structure. It is possible to make all kinds of distinctions between different aspects of the social world. There is no one way of doing so, but different ways, each dependent on the kind of objective that we have in mind in making such distinctions. It is sometimes hard to see what purpose MacIntyre has, as the ground seems to shift between different characterizations with no apparent reason why one rather than another has been chosen.

It is not at all clear that it is helpful to describe all institutions and practices in terms of an overriding *telos*. Do we want, for example, to be given a purpose for religious practices or for family life? No doubt there are many purposes which are accomplished by these institutions, but it would be misleading to say that their *raison d'être* exists for these purposes.[12] Even those that do have, arguably, a purpose such as marriage (here contrasted with family life), do not have standards of excellence to which the husband and wife need to aspire.

Even if our ways of life, practices, institutions do not always have purposes, they do, however, have a *point* in the sense that, if they are to be valued by their participants, they are partly constitutive of a worthwhile human life. Sometimes this point may be conferred by the activity of producing the appropriate internal goods and by the goods produced themselves. Sometimes, however, this point is to be found in its place in the wider scheme of human life. A principal criticism by Rhees of Wittgenstein's recommendation that we see the 'Builder's Game' at the beginning of *Philosophical Investigations* as a complete language is that seen as a self-existent form of life it lacks sense, not because the purpose of what the builders are doing is not clear, but because it is not clear how what they are doing has significance as part of a human life. As Rhees puts it

> And the activity of the builders does not give you an idea of a people with a definite sort of life. Do they have songs and dances and festivals, and do they have legends and stories? Are they horrified by certain sorts of crimes, and do they expose people to public ridicule? The description of them on the building site, if you add 'this may be all', makes them look like marionettes. On the other hand, if they do have a life, then to say that their speaking is part of that life would be different from saying that their speaking is part of this activity of building.[13]

There is no point to speaking *as such* as part of life, although there is usually a point to speaking in the context of different activities. Nevertheless, life can make sense because the whole and the connections between the parts of the whole make sense, taken together.[14] This is not a matter of producing goods, but of having a sense that a way of life is one worth living and worth preserving. This making sense also grounds much of the normative structure of particular ways of life as the articulation of different aspects of human life lend point to each other. Thus, the point of education is illuminated by the areas of life for which it is a preparation, economic activity by the goods that it confers on people, and so on.

One gets a clearer sense of this by considering what MacIntyre has to say about *external* goods. These are not internal to the practice in the way that *internal* goods are, but can only be produced through engagement in the practice with which they are associated. Examples of external goods that are given by MacIntyre include prestige, status and money.[15] Internal goods are *public* in the sense that their achievement is a good for the whole community who participate in the practice while external goods are *private* possessions and are *positional*, their acquisition is typically to the detriment of someone else.[16]

Seen from the perspective of the interconnectedness of different aspects of human life and their making sense as a whole, as a culture and way of life, the distinction between internal and external goods looks strained and arbitrary. There seems to be a conflation between the realizability and enjoyment of goods within a practice and their intrinsic or even ultimate value. We cannot exclude the possibility that goods that are used outside the practice or that could have been produced within other practices might themselves have intrinsic value, for example, an orchestral performance.[17]

Some of the goods produced within a practice may have the characteristics of 'external goods', for example, a favour done to a fellow workman may be regarded as a bargaining chip or an entitlement to an economic exchange, even if it possesses intrinsic value as well. Furthermore, the same good may be regarded as internal or external depending on the perspective that is adopted. For example, one might argue, to use one of MacIntyre's examples, that the practice of fishing generates internal goods like those engendered by appreciating and experiencing the practice, together with the development of character and an understanding of what it is to live as a fisherman.[18]

But it is reasonable to include the fish caught as themselves one of the internal goods of the practice. Indeed, were one to exclude them, it would be difficult to see what the point of the practice of fishing would be. But it is also obvious that, unless the fish are exclusively consumed by the fishermen and their families they are tradeable and hence *external goods*. One might say that they are tradeable as food and hence, since food could be obtained through other practices, they are external goods. However, since they are tradeable as fish and since fish, rather than food generally may be the commodity sought (or even these particular fish from this particular fishing ground), this distinction is arbitrary.[19] Rhees' more general point is that the meaning that human life has is not simply to be found in an activity or practice itself, but in the role which that practice plays in life as a whole, which includes in nearly all societies, interconnected activities and institutions, understood through the possession of a common language. One will need to understand the normative structures underlying activities and institutions through close study of those activities and institutions themselves, but this is usually not adequate. It is only, for example, because we understand the broader role that catching fish or building cathedrals play in human life that we can grasp why some of the norms that apply to the activity or institution do so. For example, although the maintenance of sustainable fishing practices may be seen as an internal good of fishing, the importance of maintaining stocks of fish for the way of life of a larger community will also need to be appreciated in order to understand the norms underlying sustainable fishing.[20]

Problems with the Notion of a Practice as a Philosophically Illuminating Category

I suggest that the problems that arise with MacIntyre's category of practices as a philosophically illuminating innovation do not arise from the identification of different kinds of good, but through the use of a vague category which is assumed to be invariant no matter what purposes it is to be used for. As already noted in Chapter 1, it is not as if there is not a well-developed vocabulary for discussing different aspects of human activity. We generally find no difficulty in talking about ways of life, societies, institutions, occupations, jobs, tasks, economic sectors, and so on. In talking about each of these different kinds of phenomena, the roles of internal and external goods may play a part, often a different one in different discourses. Indeed, as already suggested, it may be that the same fish, cathedral or performance will assume the aspect of an internal or an external good, depending on which category we are considering it under, in what context and for what purpose. It is not clear, therefore, that there is a philosophical 'added value' in the concept of a practice and there may even be the potential for confusion.[21]

However, as stated, there is much of value in MacIntyre's discussion of human activity which helps us to better understand its normative structure and the normative activities that underpin it.

First, MacIntyre makes clear the social nature of normatively guided activity. Second, it is illuminating to know that activities can produce different kinds of goods, with both intrinsic and instrumental value. Third, MacIntyre shows how there needs to be an evaluative component within our understanding of normatively guided practices. Finally, and by no means least, the scope of practices as sites of meaningful human activity, which include economic and productive activity, mark a significant advance on previous discussions of most modern philosophical discussions of these topics, with the notable exception of that of Simone Weil.

Objections to a Normative Account of Activity and Agency

Understanding know-how as normatively guided activity raises some clear objections which must now be considered.

Much Activity is Not Rule-Governed

It has been objected that some activities and, by implication, some forms of know-how cannot be characterized as rule-following without a risk of grossly misunderstanding the nature of such activities. MacIntyre himself claims, for example, that such activities as smoking or walking cannot, without distortion be described as being governed by rules.[22] It is

mistaken, therefore, to consider that rule-governedness is the primary
category under which we should consider human action. It is certainly
true that many activities are not describable by formal rules. As we have
seen also, there is a range of abilities which are not really describable as
subject to agency. Digestion, for example, is more plausibly described as
a bodily process than it is as an ability.[23] Activities governed by one's auto-
nomic nervous system would not normally be considered to be even voluntary. Breathing is one such, although certain aspects of breathing, such
as controlling one's breathing rate or holding one's breath are partially
voluntary activities. What, though, about walking around a waiting room,
smoking a cigarette or twiddling one's thumbs? These are voluntary activities, although scarcely intentional ones. Then again, what about walking
to work or waiting for the bus? These seem to be intentional but to say that
they are rule-governed is highly implausible. But they are also plausible
examples of know-how. So, if they cannot be said to be rule-governed,
how can it plausibly be said that knowing how to do something is to have
a grasp of a rule?

Once one has made the distinction between rules and normative activities this question is not difficult to answer. A rule, as a stateable normative
practice, is an important type of norm but not the only one. Norms can
reveal themselves through the normative activities that delineate them,
without necessarily being stated explicitly. There are no *rules* for walking
as such, although there are often rules, for example, for marching or for
crossing expensive and fragile parquet floors. However, it does not follow
that walking is not subject to norms, nor that it does not make sense to say
how one should walk in certain circumstances. For this to be clear, one
should consider the kinds of transgressive behaviour that some kinds of
walking in some contexts could constitute. A defendant swaggering into
a courtroom, for example, may be thought to be violating implicit norms
of respect for the court.[24] Shuffling along while holding up a queue might
well also be considered bad form. In both these cases, and in many others, people can be criticized and corrected and, maybe, instructed, in
how not to violate norms of etiquette, politeness, respect or consider-
ateness that relate to the way in which one performs certain activities.
To take another example, smokers who exhale into other people's faces
are likely to be disapproved of for similar reasons. Even an apparently
non-voluntary activity like breathing can, in certain circumstances, be
thought of as norm-governed. One example would be the techniques of
breathing control practiced by singers, who need guidance and practice
to achieve them. One would intentionally work towards such a result,

even though breathing is not normally a voluntary activity. Once mastered, it would be one's intention to practice breath control while singing, even though one does not intentionally control one's breath while singing. However, it would be true to say of someone who has mastered such a technique that they have, at least partly, brought their breathing under voluntary control. It is also true to say that such a person *knows how to* practice breath control.

To sum up, the term 'rule' is a useful shorthand term for the ensemble of normative activities that constitute the established practice of a norm. Very often, norms are delineated negatively, they are constituted by what is considered to be acceptable or commendable as judged by the practices of teaching, correcting, praising, and so on that constitute them. It is not uncommon that one enters into the practice of such norms by gradual and increasing participation, being guided by the normative activities that constitute the practice. The promulgation of rules in the explicit sense is, often, a pedagogically efficient way of transmitting such rules, for example, to someone outside a practice who wants to know how it works, or just as likely, as a summary guide to someone who wishes to commence participation in the practice. It is also possible, as an external observer, to try to build up a systematic description of a norm-governed institution in terms of the rules through which it is conducted, even though such rules are neither explicitly taught nor recognized within the practice by the participants.[25] Much of what we do, then, although not explicitly rule-governed is most certainly norm-governed and is underpinned not merely by the mastery of technique, but also by a larger cultural awareness of the culture in which the technique has a life. Such normative awareness, for example, has a role to play in our choices of when to use a technique, or the manner in which we use it, as well as in our inclination to classify an activity as one sort rather than another.

The treatment of this objection also gives an important clue as to the treatment of another one, that it is not possible to state some rules or even how some normative activities work, because no description would adequately capture their nuances. It is best to concede that this is the case but to argue that it is not an objection to the claim that know-how involves participation in and grasp of normative activities. A fuller treatment of this issue must wait until Chapter 7, but it should be clear from the discussion that it is not a condition of participation in normative activities that one should be able to state precisely what one is doing when one is participating in them. It is often enough that one meets the criteria implicit in their practice to the satisfaction of other participants.

One Can Master Some Forms of Ability without Reference to Rules, Even Though These Activities Can be Described in Terms of Rules

One objection to attempts to characterize know-how as ability as we saw in Chapter 2 is that it is possible to be able to do something without knowing how to do it. We are not here dealing with the cases covered in the previous subsection such as breathing and digesting, but a much broader range of abilities that would normally be said to be voluntary or even intentional in character. The objection goes like the following:

1. The criterion for A being able to F is A doing F in appropriate circumstances.
2. Criteria for the successful doing of F can be set out or taught according to implicit norms.
3. It is possible for A to do F without learning the rules or fully (or even at all) participating in the appropriate normative activities.
4. Therefore, one does not need to know how to F in order to be able to do F.[26]
5. On the claim that know-how involves grasp of norms it is not therefore true that possession of abilities involving know-how entails that one has a grasp of the relevant norms.

For example, A might hit the bull's eye in archery, catch a fish on the seashore or deliver a speech to a large crowd without ever having learned rules for doing so or participating in those normative activities that constitute teaching or training in the activity.

The objection, then, is not that the activity cannot be described in terms of norms, but rather than one does not need to follow norms in order to possess the ability to perform that activity. There are two versions of this case. One is that *on occasion* someone can do F without knowing how to. The other, stronger, claim is that it is *generally* possible to F without knowing how to do so. The first case is innocuous. Cases of fluke and beginner's luck are well-known in a wide variety of activities and do not constitute a serious counter-example.[27] The more general objection brings in some more difficult considerations. If it is actually the case that someone is able to do F without knowing how to do so (as conceded), why then should it not be possible for anyone to do F consistently without knowing how to do so?[28] The appeal here is to a modal law to the effect that if Fa then possibly for all x, Fx; a theorem that would be accepted in modal systems relying on possible world semantics.[29]

Animal Know-How and Concept Possession. Most would maintain that animals possess practical knowledge or know-how. Much of what they do is intentional and they can learn from their elders and from their own mistakes to become better at achieving their purposes. Some maintain that animals have some form of concept possession. It is more difficult to maintain, however, that animal behaviour is norm-governed in the sense that this has been explained in this chapter. Adumbrations of normative behaviour can be found among social animals, but no-one would claim that they carry out anything like the range of normative activities that humans do, let alone do so in the cultural surroundings that give point to human life.[30] Furthermore, it makes perfect sense to attribute know-how to some animals on the basis of their actions in the light of their known intentions. If know-how were normatively governed, animals would not possess it, but they do. Therefore know-how cannot be norm-governed.

In order to address this point it is best to consider the types of abilities that underlie normative activity. These abilities are, ultimately, *capacities* or potentials to acquire abilities. Crucial among these in the human case are the capacities to form and master concepts. Can one do so without also having the capacity to engage in normative activities? Put in this way, the question suggests that we need to understand whether concept formation, possession and mastery are themselves norm-governed abilities. The view taken here, although not argued for at length, is that conceptual ability is dependent on possession of a language in which those concepts are expressed.[31] Indeed, the possession of language and of concepts depend on each other and they arise from a common capacity to engage in normatively regulated communicative practices. Some of the kinds of discriminatory abilities in relation to the environment required by animals do not necessarily require language or even communicative ability. However, in humans conceptual ability involves being able to distinguish between correct and incorrect, truth and falsity, fulfilment and non-fulfilment, compliance and non-compliance, sincerity and insincerity. These abilities all depend on our ability to use language.

However, it is also patently the case that discriminatory abilities are presupposed by conceptual ability in this full sense and that not only do animals possess many such abilities but humans do as well. This makes it clear that many animals share with humans *proto-conceptual* abilities concerned with discrimination within the environment. But to call these abilities conceptual is to stretch the use of the term 'conceptual' in a way that brings little benefit and much potential confusion. It might be replied to this that there are *ability-based concepts* whose possession relies solely on possession of the relevant ability, precisely because possession of the concept is non-discursive.[32] Into this category would fall, for example, all kinds of physical skills whose mastery could not be adequately be explained, if explained at all, via speech or writing. Animal abilities would seem to be of this kind, but among humans one could identify ways of planing wood or bowling a ball that are of this kind.[33] It is also clear that these are skills, not abilities like breathing or processes like digesting. They involve learning, and intelligence concepts can be applied to them. In the human case they clearly are normatively governed. Why then should such skills not be said to be dependent on conceptual mastery?

Animal skills are *perception dependent*; they would not exist and cannot be understood except in terms of the animal's ability, through its senses, to discriminate between features of its environment. But they are not *concept dependent* in the sense that their acquisition and exercise could not be comprehensible except in terms of the possession of relevant concepts.[34] Of the first kind of skills, we can make third-person attributions of know-how and of belief to humans just as we can of animals without implying that first-person accounts are going to be forthcoming from the humans. Many skills and competences would, however, not be comprehensible as skills or competences without at the same time attributing to their possessor some mastery of the relevant concepts. Thus, although the skill of planing a wagon wheel rim in a certain way, or spin bowling in a certain fashion may not be fully explicable, they are, nevertheless part of larger practices from which they gain their sense, the trade of wheel-making in the one case and the game of cricket in the other. Mastery of these skills, even though their transmission to others must remain at least partly non-discursive, is not independent of the concepts used to make sense of cricket and wheel-making. Although concept possession is itself a type of ability, concept possession or even reasonable conceptual mastery is very often not sufficient for know-how, which often requires in addition, physical skill and judgement.[35]

There is, therefore, nothing puzzling about our practice of attributing know-how or even skills to some animals. We observe these animals identify their intentions and come to understand the ways that they use to achieve those intentions. We also note that, in many cases, animals can teach their offspring these ways and that they can sometimes learn them from their own experience. We can also apply intelligence concepts to a limited degree to the ways in which they exercise skill. None of this implies either that animals possess concepts nor that they engage in normative activities. What it does imply is that they share capacities with humans for sensory discrimination and learning which are developed into abilities that bear some relationship with human concept dependent and hence normatively governed abilities, skills and forms of know-how. It does not threaten an account of human know-how in terms of concept possession and of norms rather than laws of nature.

The Circularity Objection. It might be objected to the account of rule-following offered above, that the characteristics of normative activities are themselves normatively grounded, so that the explanation offered of them is circular. That is to say teaching, correcting, training, and so on are all themselves normative activities *par excellence.* Likewise, concept possession, a presumed precondition of know-how, itself involves norm-governed abilities and hence know-how. How could normative activities ever have got started? Two issues are at stake here. The first is the claim that the *explanation* of what know-how is, is itself viciously circular. The second is that the *ontogenesis* of know-how is left obscure by the explanatory circularity of the account offered of know-how. Taking the first point first, the answer to this conundrum is that the normative activities that underlie norm-governed activities are particular practices within particular cultures of teaching, explaining, correcting, interpreting, and so on. In order to understand them and the place that they have in a culture one needs to see how they fit into the wider pattern of related activities and of the culture. There is a sense in which a certain degree of cultural understanding is required in order to make sense of particular practices so that light, in a sense, 'dawns over the whole'. But there is nothing mysterious about this. If one wants to understand certain patterns of activity one has to see how they hang together with many of the other customs, habits and institutions that make a culture. There is no foundational explanation of know-how, because there is not a foundational practice of normative activities on which it rests. There are particular ways of doing things which, once one understands them and the place that they have in a culture, are sufficient to explain, for most purposes what knowing how to do a particular kind of activity consists in. As for the ontogenetic question, concept possession and hence know-how rest on normative activities which, although qualitatively different from non-normative activities yet have affinities with them, and can be seen as part of the story of an evolutionary path from adumbrated normative behaviour to be found in some animal species. There is thus no vicious circularity involved in the account of know-how as being grounded in norms and hence normative activities.

Rules of Grammar and Rules of Cooking

We now turn to particular features of the normative nature of know-how. As already remarked, the use of language and the possession of concepts that it entails are fundamental to our understanding of practical knowledge. The normative nature of what Wittgenstein calls 'grammar', the ensemble of norms that apply to the use of language are, in a sense, arbitrary. They are not defined by the ends for which language is used, for language as such has no ends. They are also *constitutive* of the language; if one does not follow them one does not speak the language badly but not at all. There is a close analogy with games. If I do not follow the rules of chess I do not play chess badly, but do not play it at all. But there is no explanation in terms of the ends of chess as to why the rules are as they are. Wittgenstein contrasts this kind of rule with the example of cookery rules. If you do not follow these rules you will cook badly even though you are still cooking. Cooking is defined by the end of cookery, while language is not defined by any end because it has none.[36]

It follows from this distinction that evaluative or intelligence concepts are applicable to the non-arbitrary kind of rule, one associated with an activity or practice that has an end, such as cookery. So the kind of normative activities with which our concepts of know-how are associated are those associated with ends, such as the ends of occupations. This does not make them any the less normatively governed but does suggest that such activities and institutions need to be understood in terms of their ends, whether they be explicit or implicit, before their normative structure can be fully understood. It follows, therefore, that in understanding such evaluative concepts as skilfulness or expertise, we will need to do so in relation to the ends for which know-how is practiced.

Nevertheless, it is important to remove one misunderstanding before we adopt this approach. Just as there is a sense in which non-teleological human practices like the use of language do not have an end, there is also a sense in which particular uses of language do. Using one's language to tell a story, win an argument, explain a plan or to issue instructions demands the use of the language's resources in a way that is directed to one's purpose. There are norms governing such uses of language and sometimes they are even taught, as in classes on rhetoric. So there is a sense in which the rules of grammar, understood as all the rules that apply to language, are not entirely arbitrary, since some of them will be directed towards the achievement of an individual's ends. Conversely, there is a constitutive element to ends-governed activities like cooking. Some activities simply do not count as cooking because they do not follow the constitutive rules that make cooking what it is and not something else. Nor is it especially easy to describe particular practices of cooking solely in terms of some end such as preparing food for consumption. As is well-known, the diverse customs of cooking around the world have norms which relate, not merely to making food edible, safe or tasty, but to religious and aesthetic considerations as well. These norms are constraints but they are not always to be explained in terms of ends, but have an arbitrary quality about them as well. It is characteristic of these features of teleological activities that their significance can often only be understood in aspects of the culture that lie outside the custom, activity or institution itself. This reinforces the point made earlier about internal goods. If the among the internal goods of cooking are to be found dishes of food, then their excellence often consists, at least partly, in their wider cultural significance, not merely in their conforming to norms within the practice of cooking.

Nor is it true that 'rules of cooking' simply owe their validity to laws of nature.[37] Such activities are indeed constrained by laws of nature, just as the conventions of language are dependent on the laws of physics and the human physical constitution. Some investigations into language, undertaken for some purposes, might wish to take these features of language into account. It is true of course, that the physical, chemical and biological properties of foods have to be taken account of in cooking and that part of the explanation of why foods are prepared in particular ways is going to be connected with such considerations, but these do not exhaust the explanation of why the rules are as they are. That is also determined by a variety of norms relating to the preferred ways in which a society organizes its affairs.

To summarize, for someone to know how to do something is for that person to engage in intentional activities whose nature is constitutively circumscribed by the kind of activity involved, chess, for example, being constituted by the rules for the playing of chess. However, abilities that involve knowing how to do something are capable of *evaluation* in terms of the ways in which they achieve their goals *and* in terms of the ways in which they are carried out. The conceptual field that marks the evaluation of abilities of this kind is, to a large extent, specific to that kind of activity and consequently the *telos* of the activity and the preferred ways of carrying out that activity. We should not consider the *telos* to be one, simple, thing either. Cooking, for example, is directed at nourishment but must also satisfy aesthetic, hygienic, ethical, religious and social criteria if it is to be accepted as an appropriate or praiseworthy example of cooking in a particular social environment. The complex nature of such a *telos* can only be understood when the particular activity is related to its broader social context. Thus the evaluative concepts which are deployed to assess how well something is done, although particular to the activity, are also connected to broader social considerations and it is the case that they cannot be deployed with full effect by someone who is not able to understand this broader social context. These evaluative concepts, like those that constitute the activity, are normatively applied; they manifest themselves in normative activities just like any other human activity involving knowing how to do something, and these evaluative concepts, both formal and informal, implicit and explicit, provide the framework in which excellence in the activity is assessed. They do not, however, in the main determine whether an exercise of know-how is such-and-such an action, but how well that action has been carried out.

It is, of course, a *formal* possibility that all instances of successfully F-ing are done without knowing how to F in the sense that formal modal logic allows it. One can, however, question the intuition that lies behind this principle, particularly in the kinds of cases that we are discussing. The fact is that we do not entertain the possibility that abilities that require knowing how to do something can *as a generality* be achieved without our knowing how to do so, even though we are perfectly prepared to concede that there may be individual cases. The fact that we engage in such normative activities as teaching and training suggest that we consider that there are *correct* rather than *incorrect* ways of doing such things and that general success requires mastery of a technique that we consider to be correct. It is, of course, no objection to say that someone has mastered F without knowing how to F in the secondary sense of being able to give an account of how to F. We have already seen that such is often the case. It is, however, a problem for those, like Bengson and Moffett who deny that there are two senses of knowing how but claim that agency involves know-how. We can put the point in another way. It is sometimes possible to successfully perform a norm-governed activity F in accordance with the rules or norms for doing F. What is not possible is the chance performance of norm-governed activities on a regular basis. Why is this so? It is due to a fact of human natural history, that in order to perform many complex activities successfully and on repeated occasions, normally developed by inculcation through participation in normative activities, humans need to participate in those normative activities.[38]

Notes

[1] Smith and Jones (1997).

[2] Kenny, A. (1968) *Descartes*, New York, Random House, ch. 5.

[3] For a description of the explanatory role of neurological concepts in the explanation of human abilities and the scope and limits of the explanatory value of such concepts, see Bennett, M., Hacker, P. M. S. (2003) *The Philosophical Foundations of Neuroscience*, Oxford, Blackwell.

[4] See, for example, Wittgenstein, L. (1974) *Philosophical Grammar*, Oxford, Blackwell, p. 188. For similar and related remarks, see *Blue and Brown Books* (1958), Oxford, Blackwell, pp. 12, 97; *Philosophical Investigations* (1953), para 495. See also, for a fuller discussion, Winch, C. (1998) *The Philosophy of Human Learning*, London, Routledge, ch. 4. It is important to realize that it could be a project to effect a nomologically reductive account of normative practices. Wittgenstein is not excluding the possibility of such a project for certain purposes (whatever he thinks might be the prospects of its success). The kind of primitive normative practices described in Bennett's apian fable might be susceptible to this kind of account. Bennett, J. (1964) *Rationality*, London, Routledge.

[5] Cf. Baker, G. P., Hacker, P. M. S. (1985) *Rules, Grammar and Necessity*, Oxford, Blackwell, pp. 45–7 for further discussion.

[6] Much of the debate about the private language argument and private rule-following has centred around whether or not *ab initio* self-correction is a coherent possibility. Here it will be assumed that it is not. See, for example, Verheggen, C. (1995) 'Wittgenstein and "solitary" languages', *Philosophical Investigations*, 18, 4, pp. 329–47.

[7] Ryle (1949) distinguishes between training and drilling and appears to suggest that activities that involve drilling do not involve understanding, while those that involve training do (ch. 5). However, it is possible to drill someone, to habituate them to do something which involves learning to follow rules in a rigid way, but in such a way that their performance can be evaluated. The term 'conditioning' better captures the purely mechanical inculcation of non-normative abilities and habits.

[8] MacIntyre, A. (1981) *After Virtue*, London, Duckworth.

[9] Rhees, R. (1970) *Discussions of Wittgenstein*, London, Routledge ('Wittgenstein's Builders', pp. 71–84); (1998) *Wittgenstein and the Possibility of Discourse*, Cambridge, Cambridge University Press.

[10] MacIntyre (1981), p. 175.

[11] 'Goods' can, in this context, also be safely taken to include services such as child-rearing or accommodation, and need not necessarily be considered to be provided in a commercial context.

[12] Unless, for example, one wishes to *ascribe* a function to an institution that has not *assigned* itself one. See Searle, J. R. (1995) *The Construction of Social Reality*, London, Penguin, ch. 3.

[13] Rhees (1970), p. 83.

[14] For more on this, see Winch 2006b.

[15] I am indebted here to the discussion in Hager, P. (2008) 'Refurbishing MacIntyre's account of practice'.

[16] MacIntyre (1981), p. 178.

[17] Hager's (2008) example.

[18] MacIntyre (1994) 'A partial response to my critics', in Horton, J., Mendus, S. (eds) *After MacIntyre: Critical Perspectives on the Work of Alasdair MacIntyre*, Cambridge, Polity Press, in association with Basil Blackwell Publishers, Oxford, pp. 283–304. See also Higgins, C. (2003) 'MacIntyre's moral theory and the possibility of an aretaic ethics of teaching', *Journal of Philosophy of Education*, 37, 2, pp. 279–92.

[19] Hager (2008) uses the example of St Paul's Cathedral, which may be considered both as an internal good of the construction industry or as an external good for the benefit of churchgoers, tourists, aestheticians, and so on, p. 8.

[20] Ibid. p. 6.

[21] Consider the MacIntyre's own discussion about whether or not bricklaying is not a practice, whereas architecture is (both are occupations), or whether History is a practice and teaching is not (one is a subject, the other an occupation). Cf. MacIntyre, A., Dunne, J. (2002) 'Alasdair MacIntyre on education: in conversation with Joseph Dunne, *Journal of Philosophy of Education*, 36, 1, pp. 1–19.

[22] MacIntyre, A., Bell, D. R. (1967) 'Symposium: the idea of a social science', *Proceedings of the Aristotelian Society, Supplementary Volumes*, 41, pp. 95–132.

[23] Noë (2005).

[24] An example to be found in Wolfe, T.'s (1987) novel, *The Bonfire of the Vanities*, New York, Picador.

[25] See, for example, Frake, C. O. (1964) 'How to ask for a cup of tea Subanun', in Giglioli, P-P. (1972) *Language and Social Context*, London, Penguin, pp. 87–94. More generally of course our mother tongue is norm-governed in this sense, although we do not learn it by learning to follow explicit rules, except, for example, when we are learning to read and write.

[26] Of course, one can know how to F without being able to do it, for reasons already explored in Chapter 2.

[27] Noë (2005).

[28] Ibid. See, for example, Wittgenstein, L. (1953), para. 520.

[29] If Fa in the actual world it is *a fortiori* occurrent in a possible world. For a proposition to be possible in all possible worlds, an instance must be true in at least one possible world, for example, the actual world.

[30] See Baker, G. P., Hacker, P. M. S. (1984) *Language, Sense and Nonsense*, Oxford, Blackwell, ch. 7; Bennett, J. (1964) on how social animals might develop a normative structure.

[31] For a more detailed account, see Winch (1998), ch. 9.

[32] See, for example, Bengson and Moffett (2007).

[33] Sturt, G. (1923) *The Wheelwright's Shop*, Cambridge, Cambridge University Press.

[34] Cf. McNaughton, D. (1988) *Moral Vision* Oxford, Blackwell, for this distinction.

[35] Cf. Rowbottom, D. P. (2007) 'Demystifying threshold concepts', *Journal of Philosophy of Education*, 41, 2, pp. 263–70, pp. 265–6.

[36] Wittgenstein, L. (1974) 'X', in *Philosophical Grammar*, Oxford, Blackwell, p. 184.

[37] Glüer, K. (2001) 'Dreams and nightmares: conventions, norms and meaning in Davidson's philosophy of language', pp. 1–22, p. 20, http://people.su.se/~kgl/Nightmares.pdf, consulted 28 May 2008.

[38] This is not to deny, of course, that there are different rates of learning and that some people may master some activities with minimal participation. But these considerations do not alter the general point.

Chapter 6

Theory, Underpinning Knowledge and Practice

Theory, Underpinning Knowledge and Practice

Chapter 2 defended the distinction between propositional and practical knowledge, using some of Ryle's arguments as a principal support. Ryle, however, says relatively little about the *relationships* between knowing how and knowing that and it is arguable at least that he finds some aspects of that relationship problematic. However, the other commentators that we considered do not shed enough light on it either and so the question merits further investigation, as it is not possible to arrive at an adequate understanding of skill, competence and expertise without some understanding of this relationship. Stanley and Williamson, we may recall, see *knowing how* to do something as a form of propositional knowledge, but in a practical mode. They say nothing about how propositional knowledge in a non-practical mode may have a bearing on knowing how to do something. White argues that 'knowledge of how to do something is not the ability to do the thing itself, but the ability either to show or to tell how to do it.'[1] This account leaves the relationship between *this* ability and the ability described or shown problematic. Furthermore, it leaves it unclear how *knowledge that p* could have a bearing on someone's *knowledge that such-and-such is a way to do something.* Carr' account of practical knowledge in terms of mastery of practical modes of inference appears to leave a role for the assertion of facts as premises having a bearing on practical conclusions. Carr himself appears to rule out an extensive role for theoretical knowledge in practice, arguing that a plumber, for example, does not need knowledge of the theory of hydraulics in order to successfully carry out his work.[2] Whether Carr can consistently hold such a view will be considered in this chapter. Finally Bengson and Moffett take knowledge how to do something as reasonable conceptual mastery of the task to be performed, including the mastery of ability concepts that have to be manifested in action. They likewise leave it unclear how propositional knowledge could have a bearing on such mastery.

Third-Person Attributions of Propositional Knowledge on the Basis of Action

There is one important sense in which the attribution of non-discursive propositional knowledge to a third party is philosophically unproblematic. When someone rides a bicycle it is possible to say of that person that they know that one has to apply pressure to the pedals in order to ride it successfully. Likewise, in cases of propositional knowledge that are potentially discursive, one may say that someone knows that in the United Kingdom one drives on the left through observation of their cycling behaviour. It is a common point of agreement for Stanley and Williamson, White, Carr, Ryle, and Bengson and Moffett that attributions of propositional knowledge on the basis of action may be made in this way.[3] These, however, are not particularly interesting cases for our investigation. The question is, 'How do we understand the role of judgement that results in the deployment of propositional knowledge in action?' Why is this important? Simply because much action is of this kind, particularly in the professional and vocational fields which are our main foci. An account of practical knowledge that cannot give an intelligible explanation of how this is possible is inadequate as an account of practical knowledge. It is not being claimed that any of the accounts so far considered is incapable of doing this, rather that it has not yet been done. The particular challenge will be to show that the favoured account of *knowing how*, which claims that it is best understood as ability to act in the relevant way, is capable of incorporating, without strain, this aspect of knowledge issuing in judgement and/or action.

Ryle on the Role of Knowledge in Action[4]

Ryle's defence of the knowing how/knowing that distinction is part of a larger project of critiquing the dualism often associated with Descartes.[5] For our purposes Ryle is critical of the Cartesian theory of knowledge, which holds that knowledge involves judgement. Ryle thus reconstructs the Cartesian position, showing that it is internally incoherent and leads to a vicious regress, which should lead to rejection, not only of the Cartesian account of the possession of knowledge, but also of the Cartesian account of judgement. While successful, Ryle's attack seems to have had the unfortunate side-effect of leaving him bereft of a satisfactory theory of

judgement and so unwilling and seemingly unable to incorporate a satisfactory account of judgement into his account of knowing how.[6]

Spelled out in detail, this is the argument that Ryle appears to construct
as a form of *reductio ad absurdum* of the Cartesian position, by showing it to
involve a vicious regress.

1. If A knows how to F, then A knows that øF (øF is the procedure for
   F-ing) – *Premise.*
2. If A knows that øF then this involves A's judgement that øF (to know that
   something is the case is to consciously judge that it is the case) – *Premise.*
3. If A judges that øF then A avows that øF (judgement that øF involves
   the non-verbal assertion that øF) – *Premise.*
4. If A avows that øF then A knows how to avow that øF. *Premise: avowing is
   an action that involves knowing how to avow – Premise.*
5. A knows how to G (G = A knows how to avow that øF is a way to F).
   *Premise, needed because avowal is an action which requires knowing how to
   perform it in order to perform it.*
6. If A knows how to G, then A knows that øG (øG is the procedure for
   G-ing). *Substitute G for F and øG for øF in 1 above.*
7. A knows that øG. *Modus ponens 5, 6 above.*
8. If A knows that øG, then A judges that øG (*substitute ' øG' 'øF' in 2 above*).
9. A judges that øG (*from 7, 8 by modus ponens*).
10. A avows that øG (*substitution of 'øG' for 'øF' in 3 and modus ponens 9*).
11. A knows how to avow that øG (*substitute 'øG' for 'øF' in 4 and modus ponens
    4, 10*).
12. If A knows how to avow that øH (øH is the way to avow that øG) (*substitu-
    tion H for G in 11, based on 5*).

The regress starts, since knowing how to avow that such-and-such is the
procedure for avowing a proposition will itself involve a further knowledge, judgement and avowal, for which the argument must once again be
repeated. One can never, therefore, get to the point where one can assert
that someone knows how to do something or indeed that someone knows
that something is the case.

Ryle's conclusion apparently looks too strong, as if one accepts the
premises it is difficult to avoid the conclusion of the impossibility of knowing that something is the case. However, we must remember that Ryle need
not be committed to any of the claims. It is obvious, for example, that he
would deny 1, 2 and 3. Rejection of any one of the premises stops the regress
in its tracks, but still allows Ryle's anti-Cartesian argument to be developed,

since 1 to 3 are Cartesian commitments. Even if he is, in some sense, committed to 4 then the regress cannot work without the support of the other premises. In any event, it is simply not the case that some forms of knowing how to do something always require knowledge of a procedure in the sense that such a procedure must be internally avowed prior to the action taking place. Ryle is certainly not committed to this interpretation of 4. There is no reason either for Ryle to suppose that avowals involve conscious propositional knowledge of a procedure for how to avow, in the sense of the formation of a judgement to the effect that *this* is the procedure. Indeed, the main thrust of his position is precisely that much, if not all human action does not require propositional knowledge, let alone conscious affirmation of such procedures in order for them to be carried out. Knowing how to do something is very often a case of what is called 'tacit knowledge', which is, in one quite legitimate sense (see Chapter 7) understood as knowledge that is, *in principle*, non-articulable. This very fact means that admitting that *some* actions may be preceded by an avowal to the effect that the action should be done does not commit him to his own regress argument. However, while not explicitly, Ryle resists the idea that some action requires the exercise of judgement that draws on knowledge of procedures. The most he will acknowledge is that normative procedural knowledge is necessary to guide the practices of novices, like 'bannisters for toddlers'.[7] Mature action, although it requires judgement, does not need the support of explicit avowals. This, however, is not a conceptual matter, once one acknowledges that there is a non-regressive sense in which one can avow a proposition, but one of empirical investigation into different kinds of know-how.

Ryle, therefore, neither rejects third-person attributions of knowledge relevant to an action to individuals who successfully perform an action, nor does he discount the use of norms or rules as guides to action. However, he thinks the latter have limited value. First-person knowledge, either of procedures, or of propositions relevant to the carrying out of a procedure, are only reluctantly admissible as part of any account of knowing how to do something. Even a complex occupation like surgery seems to be partially exempt from a first-person explicit propositional knowledge requirement.

A man knowing little or nothing of medical science could not be a good surgeon, but excellence in surgery is not the same thing as knowledge of medical science; nor is it a simple product of it. The surgeon must indeed have learned from instruction, or by his own induction and observations, a great number of truths; but he must also have learned by practice a great number of aptitudes.[8]

This is a curious passage that bears further examination. First we are told that one needs to know some medical science in order to be a good surgeon. Few would dispute this. But we also learn that the surgeon may do this through induction and observation. This claim leaves us with a puzzle. One could take Ryle to be saying that it is logically possible for a surgeon to build up complete first-person discursive medical knowledge of his specialism through induction and observation. This is indeed a bare logical possibility, but to claim this is to make a somewhat shallow debating point, since it is something far removed from the realms of practical possibility in a mass health system, based on a scientific study of anatomy, physiology, biology and chemistry. No-one would contemplate abolishing medical education on the supposition that this logical possibility would be actualized.

On the other hand, if all Ryle is saying is that someone may build up a repertoire of successful surgical action through personal induction and observation, such that one could attribute *knowledge that* in the third person, without assuming that the surgeon would be able to successfully articulate such knowledge himself, then one is again in the realms of bare logical possibility rather than practical possibility. So it is far from clear what Ryle takes to be the need for knowledge that in successful know-how, let alone how it should be acquired.

The Relationship between Propositional Knowledge and Action

It has been argued in Chapter 2 that Ryle's claim that knowledge how to do something is a different attribute from knowledge that some proposition is the case is broadly right and that knowledge how to do something, F entails, broadly speaking, the ability to do F. We have also noted that nothing in Ryle's general anti-Cartesian approach need lead him to deny the fact, either that propositions are sometimes avowed 'inwardly' rather than asserted verbally, nor that the possibility of inward avowal leads to the regress that he argues the Cartesian is committed to. However, Ryle did not, within his own conceptual framework, provide the materials for showing how propositional knowledge might have a bearing on practice. It is now necessary to do so.

As a starting-point, we can reiterate the claim that there is no reason to suppose that someone's avowal of a proposition that describes a procedure that it is necessary to carry out in order to perform an action, need pose any logical problems in accounting for knowing how to do something, provided that we do not commit ourselves to the view that avowals always require knowledge of a relevant procedure. For example, an engine driver might note that an oil gauge shows low pressure, and after avowing to himself that the pressure is too low for safely continuing, he may shut off the engine. Subsequently, when asked why he did so, he may cite the pressure gauge reading as a reason for his action. Whether such a justification will constitute a *sufficient* justification for the action will depend on a variety of factors. These will include the degree of responsibility that is assigned to the driver or the extent and accuracy of his professional knowledge. In the first case, a knowledgeable technical operative might be expected to carry out further procedures to overcome or neutralize the problem. In the second case, it may be that the inference to shut-down was faulty. For example, if the inference-licence from pressure gauge reading to the need for engine shut-down was

> *Whenever an oil pressure gauge reading falls below X the engine is in danger of overheating (and hence of serious damage).*

And if this was thought by experts to be true only in limited cases, then the basis for the action's being necessary might be held to be questionable.

The Role of Knowledge in Practical Knowledge: *Kenntnis* and *Wissen*

It is worth returning now to a theme introduced in Chapter 1, namely the nature of subject knowledge. It was argued there, using the work of Paul Hirst as a guide, that organized knowledge (what Hirst calls 'Forms of Knowledge', and what were called in Chapter 1 'subjects') involves, not just the knowledge of propositions, but also of procedures. English does not explicitly distinguish between organized knowledge of this kind and singular knowledge of propositions with no particular systematic connection with each other, but German does. It is worthwhile looking at the distinction available in German in order to see if it is helpful to our present purpose. German distinguishes between two kinds of propositional knowledge: *Kenntnis*, which concerns contingent and discrete propositional knowledge, and *Wissen*, which is organized propositional knowledge including what in English would be called scientific and theoretical knowledge. *Wissen* is important for our inquiry as it is claimed, for example, within the German vocational system that mastery of a *Beruf* involves the application of *Wissen* to practice.[9] It might be possible to attribute *Kenntnis* and even a degree of *Wissen* to someone on the basis of observation of their actions in the workplace. However, a system of vocational education that explicitly develops a capacity for action on the basis, first of the acquisition of systematic knowledge and then its conscious application in judgement and action, presupposes that the agents themselves should be able to give an account of what they are doing. The premise of such a system of education is that it is *because* they apply systematically organized propositional knowledge that they are successful in action.[10] The possession of relevant systematically organized knowledge is not a by-product of the action, but a *prerequisite*. If this is so, there must be at least some cases where a judgement is made that involves moving from propositional premises to an action conclusion or to a judgement that such-and-such action is called for.

One further point about *Wissen* should be made. We saw in Chapter 1 that expertise in a subject matter that is organized in the manner of a Hirstian Form of Knowledge does not just entail knowledge of many propositions (although it undoubtedly does that), but also a mastery of inferential relationships between propositions, mastery of central concepts within the subject and practical knowledge of procedures for acquiring knowledge and testing knowledge claims. Such expertise itself often involves the ability to deploy propositional knowledge in practical procedures, for example, in checking whether a new knowledge claim is consistent with propositions that are already accepted within the subject, for example, in the construction of measuring or testing equipment. Thus, even if we are to account for subject expertise, let alone vocational action, we need an intelligible account of how propositional knowledge in general and deliberately utilized bodies of systematically organized knowledge can bear on practice in judgement.

What is Professional or Vocational Action?

We have a standard account of how to explain individual action, which can be found, for example, in the work of Hume.[11] This standard account suggests that action (and, by implication, judgement that a certain action is called for) consists, first of an element of desire or intention that such-and-such a state of affairs be brought about and, second, a belief that such-and-such an action will bring about the desired or intended state of affairs.[12] A combination of these two elements is sufficient, provided there are no intervening beliefs or desires, to bring about the relevant action. Some interpreters use this model *causally*, that is, the two elements, the doxastic and the conative are, other things being equal, sufficient to cause the action. Others interpret the model *inferentially*.[13] The two elements, desire and belief, provide a *prima facie* reason for why the action should be performed; they do not cause it. The model in its simplest form, in either causal or inferential formulation can be presented thus:

1. A desires or intends that p.
2. A believes that doing ψ will bring about p.
3. A does ψ.

It is easy to see that in this case 1 ascribes to a belief to A. If this belief is true the action is likely to be successful. In some sense, then, knowledge is required for successful action, and, by implication for the judgement that the relevant action is required. The model has to be complicated for the requirement that A needs to know how to ψ.[14]

1. A desires or intends that p.
2. A believes that doing ψ will bring about p.
3. A knows how to ψ.[15]
4. A does ψ.

Set out in this way, the formulation of a sufficient condition for action looks as if it does not need further explanation. However, once one gets down into the detail of the prerequisites for complex forms of action in complex situations, and, more importantly, the competence (in the sense of this term introduced in Chapter 4) required, it is far too sparse. Particular attention needs to be focused on condition 2.

There are undoubtedly many circumstances in which it is unproblematic for A to believe that a certain procedure will bring about the desired result. This would be the case for some well-established piece of contingent knowledge in a particular context, for example, when activating a siren sounds the alarm. However, there are other possibilities which we need to examine. In some cases, conceptual understanding of what is involved in acting in a certain way will be sufficient to suggest a procedure for bringing about the desired end.

For example, A wishes to act honestly having found a wallet in the street. A knows that handing the wallet into a police station will constitute acting honestly and A hands the wallet into the nearest police station. Apart from knowledge of the location of the police station, all that is required is a proper understanding of what it is to act honestly. However there are often cases where 2 needs to be elaborated:

5. A believes that either doing φ or doing ψ will bring about p.

In such cases it may well be necessary to come to a decision about which course of action is preferable. This may involve moral considerations, but the decision may also involve more technical ones concerning safety, speed, cost or efficacy. If the conclusion is

6. A does ψ.

Then it may need to be justified in terms of such technical considerations. And, in such circumstances it may well be the case that systematically organized knowledge will need to be brought to bear on the making of the decision. Even without the possibility of alternative procedures, it is often the case that the belief that a certain course of action is required cannot be arrived at except through a process of reasoning that leads to the judgement that such-and-such is the most appropriate course of action. Is there any philosophical problem about explaining this? We need two elements in the account: first an account of judgement that is not subject to the worries that Ryle had concerning the regressive implications of avowals and, second, an account of how reasoning can underpin judgement. Both these conditions can be met.

Geach's Account of Judgement

In one sense, there is nothing unproblematic about judgement. Ryle points out that doing something in a certain frame of mind, for example, paying attention to what one is doing is an occurrence and is therefore 'clockable'.[16] While it is true that very often we attribute episodes of judgement on the basis of observing that someone is paying attention to or is caring about what they are doing, and that in many circumstances we have sufficient reason to say that someone is exercising their judgement in such circumstances, it is nonetheless not sufficient for what we require here, which is an account of how someone may, as a *mental act* judge that something is the case or that a course of action is called for.

In the Cartesian conception of judgement, which is rightly criticized by Ryle, judgement is always a conscious avowal that something is the case or that an action is called for. As the activity of a *res cogitans* (thinking being) it takes place in a non-material medium and is only contingently articulated in an assertion. For reasons made familiar by Wittgenstein, on this account explaining how someone could ever come to make judgements in this *ab initio* solitary way is highly problematic. Geach instead assumes that our ability to judge is first manifested, not in an inner mental sanctum in principle accessible only to the subject, but in public activities such as making assertions.[17] Assertion of a proposition is the primary instance of judgement and as we acquire a growing mastery of language we are able to use it to soliloquize and then articulate it in 'inner speech' and, finally in forms which are *potentially articulable* on request, but not fully articulated within the act of judgement. Although these are episodes of judgement and hence loosely 'clockable' they are not precisely clockable in the sense that an act of assertion is. They are best understood as *analogies* of acts of assertion, and the ability to judge is one that develops out of the ability to use language to assert propositions.

What does this ability involve? First, in order to form a judgement one must believe that the proposition that one is judging is true.[18] In this sense, judging is unlike asserting, as one may assert a proposition that one believes to be false. Second, one is not constrained by public circumstances of appropriateness in making judgements. This kind of knowledge, very important in learning to take part in the practice of assertion does not usually, although it may, involve explicit knowledge. It is through our participation in normative activities that we learn when and when not to make assertions, without being able to formulate explicit rules for doing so.[19] However, one is not freed from the requirement for having good grounds for the judgements that one makes. People can be rightly criticized for their poor judgements because they lack good grounds for making them.

Learning how to make inner assertions will thus rely in the first instance on having good grounds, the second consideration of *social appropriateness* is not so relevant, if at all. Instead, one needs to be *situationally aware* that a judgement is required or is desirable or is possible at this time. However, there is nothing especially 'inner' about the learning of how to formulate good grounds for belief. This is learned as part of public practices of coming to justify one's assertions, criticizing those of others, responding to requests for clarifications, and so on. Learning to do this is to acquire practical knowledge of a certain kind and the criteria for mastery of this practical knowledge consists in ability to assert, justify, and so on in relevant situations so that one is understood. One is not required to give an account of how one is able to do these things and most individuals would be puzzled by what could be meant by such a request. The practical knowledge involved is, therefore, in an important sense, tacit knowledge and certainly does not require knowledge that there is such-and-such a procedure for asserting, thus avoiding the problems that beset Ryle's version of the Cartesian account. Avowing a proposition involves following a procedure but does not require avowable knowledge of the procedure. There is, therefore, no special knowledge needed to avow propositions in the relevant sense.[20] Such judgements may be asserted if the circumstances require and it may be expected that the agent can replicate the reasoning that led to the judgement in some circumstances as well. (Just as an assertion can have its analogical equivalent in an avowal, so also can a supposition – which might be part of the chain of reasoning.)

However, the requirement that there be good grounds for a judgement or an action is not removed by the absence of a need for articulation or by a soliloquizing of the relevant procedure. We appraise the quality of a judgement, whether verbally articulate or not, by the grounds for its asser- tion and its situational relevance. Likewise with the corresponding action, with the addition of an appraisal of how well it is executed. But the issue of having good grounds is an important one, as the simple case of singular contingent knowledge, as set out in the sequences above, is not a typical one in vocational and professional situations. In many cases, the element 2 (itself a judgement) in the underlying explanation or justification itself needs selection and justification either to the agent or to an interlocutor or to both. In the case of chains of reasoning of this kind, there are a series of connected judgements and suppositions which form the grounds for the final judgement that a course of action is required or the action itself.[21]

Arguments as Grounds for Judgement

Having established that a non-regressive account of judgement as some- thing that someone more or less consciously engages in is available, it is necessary to offer an account of the complex cases where a series of judge- ments and suppositions are linked together to form a justification for a course of action (or the action itself). Some vocational action depends on simple sequences of the kind outlined above. These often involve *Kenntnis* of facts or norms which serve as the second premises in judge- ment sequences. We are more interested, however, in inferences, usually in material rather than formal mode, which involve the agent drawing on systematically organized knowledge in order to form a judgement as to a course of action.[22]

In what follows, use will be made of Toulmin's account of reasoning in the material mode in *The Uses of Argument*.[23] According to Toulmin the transition from premise to conclusion, which characterizes what Levi calls 'pc argumentation' involves premises and conclusions and, implicitly, a *warrant* for the transition from premise to conclusion.[24]

P, so Q (using an accepted warrant W).

When an argument of this type is offered the warrant often remains implicit, because it is understood by all parties as an appropriate mode of transition from P to Q. This would most probably be due to acquaintance with the field of knowledge in which the inference is made (or subject if systematically organized knowledge is involved). However, it may be possible that the warrant is requested, in which case the person offering the argument would normally be expected to produce it.

In some cases, the applicability of the warrant may be questioned. In this kind of case, Toulmin argues, there would be a requirement for a *backing statement* or statement for the grounds for the applicability of the warrant in the original argument. If the argument is

Petersen is a Swede, so Petersen is a Protestant.

And the warrant is

All Swedes are Protestants.

An interlocutor may request the grounds for using that warrant. A justification might be a backing statement of the form:

All Swedes have recently been checked in the census and found to be protestants. (R)

In this case, one could substitute the backing statement for the warrant to derive a slightly different argument.[25]

P so Q because R.

The nature of R and the warrant that depends on it is going to itself depend on the nature of the subject from which it is drawn. In some cases it may refer to experimental evidence, in others to ethnographic, in others again to logical or mathematical proof and in others again to the existence of norms such as rules or laws. Ability to form judgements that are based on such action sequences relies on acquaintance with the relevant subject-dependent warrants in the first instance, on the ability to produce the relevant backing statement in the second and, in the third, to generate a backing statement through the appropriate procedures for knowledge generation within the relevant subject. Each successive ability suggests a deepening expertise within the subject, and is a constituent of a different degree of expertise in the area of occupational action to which it is applied.

It should be pointed out that expertise in an occupational area does not merely consist in expertise in the subject that provides its systematic underpinning knowledge, that is, the knowledge that informs judgement and action generally. Judgements have to be made and action performed in specific circumstances which have a bearing on the appropriateness of the actions concerned. These *Kenntnis* elements (which may involve a significant tacit element – see Chapter 7) need also to be brought to bear in the sequence of reasoning that precedes or, *post hoc*, justifies a particular course of action. This point however underlies the complexity of occupational judgement and action and serves to emphasize how simple sequences of reasoning are a very sketchy gesture towards much more complex sequences employed in operational situations.

Bringing the elements of occupational judgement together we can summarize as follows:

1. The ability to make judgements (or actions that embody judgement) does involve knowing how to follow procedures (of reasoning, of taking account of situational particularity) but need not involve first-person avowals that these are the procedures required. The ability to do so may be exercised in a solitary or non-verbal manner.
2. The chain of reasoning involved in arriving at such judgements is often complex and involves reasoning which justifies the choice of a particular procedure for undertaking an action.

Such chains of reasoning will most likely involve a further deliberation on whether or not application of the selected procedure is situationally appropriate.

It could be objected to the case for knowledge-based occupational expertise set out above that it is often not *necessary* that an agent consciously rehearses all or even part of such chains of reasoning in the course of occupational decision-making. Indeed, it might be said, it is the mark of experts precisely that they do not do so and do not need to do so. Such claims seem to be implicit in Ryle's examples and also in contemporary theories of expertise such as that of Dreyfus and Dreyfus.[26] Indeed, there are some forms of occupational action for which it is not possible to produce such justifications; not only are they not necessary, they are not possible. In order to deal with these points it must first be said that the account offered is not a general account of occupational know-how, let alone expertise. This deals with the last objection. To take the first, it can be easily acknowledged that in practice there is a very wide variety of cases, which range from the fully articulated explicit forming of chains of reasoning prior to action, to partially articulated to unarticulated ones. However, there is no compelling reason to suppose that all *expert* action that involves reasoning is located on the non-articulated end of the spectrum (see Chapter 8). However, it is not the case that such judgement formation is *only* relevant immediately prior to the choice of a course of action. There are many significant cases where, for example, a practitioner may be asked to justify a course of action *post hoc* by an examiner, an inspector or a board of enquiry. The quality of the overall structure of the judgement may then become highly relevant to an appraisal of the action that issued from such a judgement sequence. Such articulated sequences may also be highly relevant in teaching situations, in scenario exploration and in prior planning. Nor can we make the assumption that experts, although they will be acquainted with a wide variety of occupational situations, will always encounter the familiar. It is often in their ability to cope with the unfamiliar and the unexpected that they demonstrate their superiority and it is in situations like this that specialist knowledge, as well as tacit situational awareness, need to be brought into play.

The Variety of Theory

It is now appropriate to say more about the nature of the systematic knowledge that underpins many occupational practices in order to illustrate the varieties of subjects (theories, in many cases) that underlie action. In many cases more than one subject is drawn upon in an occupation and indeed some overlap and interlock with others, as examples below will illustrate. Sometimes again, subjects are reorganized specifically for occupational purposes. This can pose problems of its own, as we shall see in Chapter 10. The term 'theory' is here being used in a narrower sense than that proposed by Dreyfus and Dreyfus, which has the following features: it should be *explicit, universal in its application, abstract, context free in reference to human interests and institutions* and *systematic*.[27] A subject, although it may encompass a theory or theories, does not necessarily have these character-istics, except for the last. It is evident, for example, that there are implicit elements in the grasp of a subject, relating to the grasp of procedures and the presentation and defence of knowledge claims; some central proposi-tions of some subjects, like those of Mathematics, are universal while some, like those of Education, are not; some subjects deal with abstract know-ledge but others not; as a human institution a subject cannot be assumed to be independent of human interests and institutions. Subjects do, how-ever, have a systematic structure.

There are norms which govern knowledge acquisition, production and validation and there are traceable, identifiable and classifiable inferential relationships between concepts and propositions, including central pro-positions, within the subject. Evidently, then, the terms 'Subject' and 'Theory' are used in this study in a closely related way, and the key under-lying idea is that of the organized nature of the *propositional* knowledge concerned, that it is *Wissen* rather than *Kenntnis*. A theory, as a system-atic or organized body of knowledge concerning a subject matter, will be related to a subject or subjects or at least have aspirations to be such, since many theories aspire to the status of knowledge, but relatively few achieve it. Theories, unlike subjects, are taken to be bodies of systematically related propositions, rather than *both* procedures *and* propositions. The procedures employed in professional action are likely to derive from one or more subjects. A systematic account of subjects, will not be attempted here. However, for the purposes of understanding expertise in vocational and occupational contexts, broad distinctions will be made as follows:[28]

A Priori Theory. Primary examples are Logic and Mathematics. These are organized according to axioms and principles of inference, which give rise to theorems (statements that can be proved within the system).[29] The primary mode of inference in these disciplines is deduction understood in the Fregean sense as the derivation of theorems from axioms and rules of inference.[30] The construction of theories in the above sense is a char-acteristic activity of these disciplines. Theology is an *a priori* discipline of a somewhat different sort, based on revelation of central propositions through canonical texts or extraordinary events. Unlike logic and math-ematics, exegesis and interpretation play a significant role in its character-istic forms of reasoning.

Empirical Theories. Experience dependency is central to the nature of at least two broad areas of knowledge and many different academic subjects.

These rarely involve purely deductive reasoning, but often employ general statements which are testable, themselves derived through inductive procedures. As they are generalizations from particular cases, they are usually revisable, although it is often argued that there are both core and peripheral propositions and concepts, the former of which are much less likely to be readily subject to revision than the peripheral elements. Central parts of a theory are those which have a far-reaching relationship with other parts of theory and whose rejection entails rejection of large parts of the theory. These central parts of theory assume a normative or quasi-normative status and play an important role as warrants or what Moyal-Sharrock calls local hinge propositions.[31] Empirical theories often make use of the two other kinds of theory, partly as evidence, partly as technique in investigation. It is often possible in the case of some subject areas of the natural sciences to construct theories in Dreyfus and Dreyfus' sense, just as it is in Mathematics and Logic.

The so-called social sciences are in a different position as there is often widespread disagreement about their assumptions, methods, scope and even aims. Nevertheless, they are dependent on the gathering of knowledge about the world, in this case the social and personal, rather than the natural world. Although there have been attempts to construct theories in the narrower sense, these have been much less successful than they have in the *a priori* disciplines and in the natural sciences. *History* stands somewhat outside the family of the social sciences as, it aims for narrative truth rather than empirical generalizations. It does, however, rely on the gathering of evidence and the presentation of arguments according to publicly accepted standards of probity. It is thus systematic in the required sense.

Disciplines that are not one of the three above. They are, perhaps, marginal to occupational judgement and action but should, nevertheless, be mentioned. There are some areas of inquiry where it is a matter of dispute whether or not knowledge, as opposed to belief or opinion, could be available. Theology is, perhaps, one such. However, in areas like *literary criticism*, it is the interpretation of texts that is the crucial purpose of the inquiry, although it is clear that in order to do so, much knowledge of texts is necessary. A difficult case is *Philosophy*: the nature of the subject and its relationships with other subjects is widely disputed within the discipline itself. Its particular assumptions and methods are also philosophically contentious and there is much current debate about method: should it imitate the natural sciences? Should it involve connective or therapeutic conceptual analysis? Should its methods relate more to those involved in the study of

literature? What, again is the role of empirical considerations and examples
in philosophical argument? Philosophy clearly has its methods (although
these vary according to different currents within the discipline) but does
not yield knowledge in the way that other *a priori* theories do.

Although Philosophy seems marginal to the concerns of this book
it is not clear that this is necessarily the case. Philosophical issues crop
up within the other subjects mentioned above and also within the more
applied areas of occupationally oriented knowledge: practical ethics is one
obvious example, Philosophy of Education another.[32] It should, therefore,
be mentioned as one of the disciplines underpinning occupational activity,
even if it would be misleading to call it a body of organized knowledge, as
opposed to a systematic form(s) of inquiry.

Conclusion: How is Theory to be Used in Occupational Practice and Education?

The answer provided to this question has been general. Systematically
organized knowledge can be used to form professional judgements in occupational situations. How this occurs depends both on the level of expertise
within the subject of the user (see Chapter 1) and the particularities of the
subject utilized. This issue will receive further consideration in Chapter 9,
but at this point a few observations are in order.

1. Although the use of theory to inform practice is primarily a one-way
   relationship, the possibility of findings in the occupational field being
   used to inform theory should not be excluded, particularly once it is
   accepted that theory need not be universal or discrete in Dreyfus and
   Dreyfus' sense.
2. Access to theory should not merely be instrumental, but should serve a
   broader educational purpose for the individual involved. In this respect,
   it is desirable that any qualification structure that provides entry to or
   progression through an occupation should allow for *permeability* or progression to higher reaches of expertise, both within the occupational
   field and, where relevant, into expertise in the organized knowledge
   that informs the occupation. There is a good argument for saying that,
   even when taught with an occupational purpose in mind, the integrity
   of the subject should be maintained so that it is also an education into a
   culturally and politically valued body of knowledge and not just a body
   of knowledge with instrumental value.

3. The knowledge component of any form of vocational education should not just include the disciplines, subjects or forms relevant to successful operational practice, but should meet two further aims which will probably involve further organized knowledge. The first of these is the heightened understanding of the broader role that occupational practice plays in the society in which it operates. The second is the personal development of the individual concerned.

Notes

[1] White (1982), p. 29.

[2] 'A profound mistake is made in supposing that the best way to turn an apprentice into a master plumber is to instruct him in the complete theory of hydraulics, for the practical knowledge that the apprentice requires comes with initiation into and mastery of practical rather than theoretical discourse. The really good plumber, of course, is also physically skilful – but that's another story.' Carr, D. (1981) 'Knowledge in practice', *American Philosophical Quarterly*, 18, 1, pp. 53–61, p. 61.

[3] See also Malcolm, N. (1977) *Memory and Mind*, Ithaca, Cornell University Press. 'Suppose that Jones planted a dogwood tree in his garden, and that when he finished the job he leaned the shovel against the trunk of another tree. Later his wife wants to do some transplanting, and she asks her three boys, who are standing there, "Where did Daddy put the shovel?" The three boys (Tom, Dick, Jerry) had seen their father lean the shovel against that tree and they remembered that he had done so. This is surely an example of taking in and retaining information. In response to their mother's question, Tom replied, "Daddy leaned it against the tree by the dogwood"; Dick pointed at that tree; Jerry ran to the tree and fetched the shovel for his mother' (pp. 224–5).

[4] See for a more detailed development, Winch, C. (2009) 'Ryle on knowing how and the possibility of vocational education', *Journal of Applied Philosophy*, 26, 1, pp. 88–101.

[5] See Baker, G. P., Morris, K. (1996) *Descartes' Dualism*, London, Routledge, for an argument that many of the positions attributed to Descartes have been wrongly attributed.

[6] It is misguided to attack the premises of Ryle's regress argument on the grounds that they are false or mutually inconsistent, as a way of attacking Ryle's distinction, as Stanley and Williamson (2001) do, since this is precisely what Ryle himself was trying to show through the construction of the regress argument.

[7] For example, Ryle (1949), pp. 48–9, p. 59; (1946), pp. 218, 222.

[8] Ryle (1949), p. 49.

[9] This can be seen, for example, in the definition of a *Beruf* or occupation in Germany, in which the bringing together of theoretical and practical knowledge is made explicit, which is: 'a body of systematically related theoretical knowledge [*wissen*] and a set of practical skills [*können*], as well as the social identity of the

person who has acquired these'. Streeck, W. (1996) 'Lean production in the German automobile industry: a test case for convergence theory', in Berger, S., Dore, R. (eds) *National Diversity and Global Capitalism*, New York, Cornell University Press, pp. 138–70, p. 45.

[10] This is not to deny the importance of *Kenntnis* in successful action, but this is generally better developed in the workplace rather than the vocational college, the *Berufschule*. See Hanf (2007).

[11] This standard account is primarily concerned with the adoption of means to ends, not to the adoption of ends themselves. This, although important, is not the focus of the present discussion. Hume, D. [1739–40] (1978) *A Treatise of Human Nature*, 2nd edition, Oxford, Oxford University Press, p. 417.

[12] Cf. Brandom (2000), ch. 2 for a contemporary account.

[13] For the causal approach see, for example, Papineau, D. (1978) *For Science in Social Science*, Cambridge, Cambridge University Press.

[14] Cf. Carr (1981).

[15] ∃ is here interpreted as A has the ability to ψ, rather than just knowledge of a procedure of ψ-ing, which is taken to be a reliable way to bring about p.

[16] Ryle (1949), p. 140.

[17] Geach, P. (1958) *Mental Acts*, London, Routledge.

[18] One may, of course, run through a hypothetical course of reasoning mentally.

[19] The exception would be where there exist rules of etiquette which govern such behaviour in formal and hierarchical situations.

[20] See Toribio, J. (2008) 'How do we know how?' *Philosophical Explorations*, 11, 1, pp. 39–52 for a discussion of non-discursive procedural knowledge.

[21] Although Geach doesn't discuss it, one can assume that a similar account for supposition as for judgement is available.

[22] Brandom (2000), ch. 1 for a discussion of this distinction.

[23] Toulmin, S. (1958) *The Uses of Argument*, Cambridge, Cambridge University Press. Toulmin's view is that material inferences of the kind found in everyday argumentation cannot be recast in a formal mode without doing violence to their structure. I will assume that Toulmin's account works for inferences in vocational and professional situations without arguing for Toulmin's view, although I agree with it.

[24] Levi, D. (2000) *In Defence of Informal Logic*, Dordrecht, Kluwer.

[25] Toulmin argues that in this material mode, such inferences although they use the universal quantifier in both warrant and backing statement are, in fact, inductive inferences as the quantifier is not interpreted formally (1958, ch. 3).

[26] Dreyfus, H. L., Dreyfus, S. E. (1996) 'The relationship of theory and practice in the acquisition of skill', in Benner, P., Tanner, C. A., Chesla, C. A. (eds) *Expertise in Nursing Practice*, New York, Springer, pp. 29–47.

[27] Ibid. pp. 30–1.

[28] Theories in this sense may consist of elements from one or more subjects.

[29] Although Arithmetic is known to be incomplete in this sense.

[30] Toulmin adopts a narrower sense of 'deduction' see (1958), ch. 3.

[31] Moyal-Sharrock (2003), pp. 125–48.

[32] For example, Hutchinson, Read and Sharrock (2008).

Chapter 7

Tacit Knowledge

Tacit Knowledge: The Problem

Knowledge that is not articulated, or cannot be articulated, is often said to be *tacit*. 'Tacit knowledge' is an ambiguous phrase but is used to refer to least the following kinds of phenomena: knowledge (a) that we are not conscious that we possess; (b) that we exercise without being conscious that we are doing so; (c) that we could not be aware of; (d) whose exercise we cannot explain. The tacitness of knowledge is closely connected with our not bringing it forward for conscious inspection or our not being consciously aware of it. It is not always knowledge that we are necessarily not aware that we are exercising. Propositional knowledge, practical knowledge and knowledge by acquaintance can all be tacit in certain circumstances. The tacitness of *practical knowledge* is, however, of particular importance as it seems to point to an ineffability or inexplicability in accomplished or expert practical action which defies description or explanation. This is particularly the case with what is often called 'creativity'.[1] The corollary of this claim is that knowledge how, or at least certain highly prized forms of knowledge how, cannot be taught. It is even thought that knowledge of theory, so often considered to be one of the primary attributes of specialists or experts, is inimical to the development of expertise in certain kinds of practical knowledge. A misleading picture is thus built up of the mystery of creation and of expert performance which is sometimes thought to be the product of divine inspiration or genes rather than of the acquisition of propositional knowledge, hard thinking and constant practice.[2] It is the contention of this chapter that these claims are highly questionable and that, although being tacit is an important property of all three kinds of knowledge, it is neither mysterious nor does it make all practical knowledge, let alone expert practical knowledge, ineffable or inarticulable, nor is its acquisition beyond the reach of formal or semi-formal educational processes.

The Types of Tacit Knowledge

In order to begin to dispel the aura of mystery that can surround tacit knowledge it is best to begin by pointing to its most significant varieties and to show that we are not only familiar with but recognize, in their tacit nature, some of their most important characteristics as types of knowledge.

1. *I know that* p *(but am not consciously aware that* p*)*. This simple first-person knowledge claim does not entail that the person making the claim is conscious of the fact that *p* while knowing it. Knowing that such-and-such is the case is what Ryle called a multi-track disposition, manifested in all kinds of ways in circumstances not at all easy to pin down. To know that a proposition is the case is not to be aware of the contents of that proposition except in certain circumstances. Typically, these are circumstances in which some manifestation of the knowledge is called for. For example, I am aware that one drives on the left in Britain and this is manifested in my doing so (see Chapter 5). Only in certain circumstances would I said to be conscious of this fact when, for example, I am trying to make sure that I remain on the left and do not revert, out of habit, to driving on the right. This point applies just as well to second- and third-person attributions of knowledge. In this sense, ordinary propositional knowledge has a very significant and indispensable tacit element.

2. *I recognize/am aware of/notice A (but am not aware of or consciously aware of certain aspects of A)*. These cases of acquaintance knowledge, which very often form an important element in practical knowledge, do not, on the face of it, look likely candidates for tacit knowledge. To be aware of something, for example, seems to imply that one has it in one's consciousness, to notice something is to become aware of it, and to recognize something is to become aware of it *as* a something or *as* someone. How, then, could knowledge by acquaintance have a tacit element? In order to understand this we need to look beyond a range of limited cases.

In becoming aware of, say, an object or a person, we become aware of something complex. If Jones, whom I am aware of, has brown hair, a navy jacket and black shoes, it does not follow that I am aware of his brown hair, navy jacket and black shoes even though he is an object of my awareness and I am consciously aware that Jones is an object of my perception. Even if I perceive Jones, and Jones, as an object of my aware-ness, has these attributes, it does not follow that I am consciously aware of his black shoes, and so on. However, the claim that I am *tacitly aware* of these aspects of Jones, even though they are not brought to my own attention at the time, is not necessarily vacuous either. Jones may be a suspect for a crime and I may be a witness and careful questioning by the police may bring out an accurate recall of my having noticed these aspects of Jones's appearance. That this not mere *post hoc* invention may be ascertained by, for example, corroboration by other witnesses. We may note in passing that such ability to notice certain kinds of things may be trained in a person and that such a person may not be consciously aware of those heightened powers of observation while exercising them, nor necessarily aware of the things noticed while, at the same time, in some sense, noticing them.

In this connection there are a couple of logical points relevant to these observations that are worth making briefly. The first is that if P is an object of awareness and A perceives P to have certain properties a, b, c, . . . , it does not follow that in being aware of P, A is also consciously aware of a, b, c, ... The second point is that to be aware of something is not necessarily to be conscious of it – one may, for example, show one's awareness by reacting to an object in some way, without bringing it to mind or even noting it in one's perceptual field. Second- or third-person attributions of awareness may have this characteristic as when one points out to someone that they showed awareness of, say, the epaulettes on a captain's shoulder by saluting, even though they were not consciously aware of them at the time. A second point, closely related to the one just made about perception and awareness, is that it is often possible to attribute noticing, recognition or awareness to a third party without that third party being aware that they are noticing, and so on.

We will now turn to types of tacit knowledge that are more overtly prac-tical, although it is important to note that many types and instances of practical knowledge will involve knowledge by acquaintance and know-ledge that, including in tacit forms. These will initially be illustrated in the first person, as the most difficult case to understand, but will be under-stood to include second- and third-person cases as well.

3. *I F without being aware that I F.* Much of what we do is automatic, habitual or routine (these are not synonymous) and in acting in such ways we often pay limited conscious attention either to the action itself or to its com-ponents. This does not entail that we do not often exercise skill, care and

attention in relation to the activity in hand in cases like this, rather that conscious attention has a more limited role within our actions.

4. *I am aware of F-ing, but not consciously aware of every aspect of F-ing.* Indeed if we accept that any person's ability to devote their attention is limited, it must be the case that someone paying attention to their carrying out of a complex activity cannot be consciously paying attention to all components of that activity, including those that are themselves actions rather than processes. In general if A is aware of doing P and doing P consists of doing p, q, r, . . . it does not follow that A is consciously aware of doing p, q, r, ... This remains the case when A is consciously aware of doing A. This is unproblematic, well understood and is a grammatical point similar to that made about 2 above.

5. *I can F and know that I can F, but I cannot explain how I F.* Examples of this kind are of particular interest to this investigation and have received close attention from writers as diverse as Sturt, Polanyi and Oakeshott. In these cases, the first-person attribution is important because the claim to know-how is made without a claim also being made that I can fully articulate or even partially articulate what it is that I do when I F. It is also important for our purposes to note that these are cases of *action* involving *know-how* rather than processes internal to one's body, for example. At this point, the examples will be discussed and the problems that they pose recognized. Detailed discussion of how we are to understand them will follow in a further chapter. Sturt's example is drawn from his experience as a rural wheelwright at the end of the nineteenth and the beginning of the twentieth century.[3] A notable case involves a technique for placing the metal tyres on the wheel rims so that the carts for which they were designed could negotiate the muddy Kent lanes in which Sturt and his colleagues operated. Older workmen could practise this technique but could not explain what it was that they did. With the advent of the motor car the practice of the technique atrophied and so did the associated skills, as the only known mode of transmission was through experiment ('fumbling') observation and imitation. The second example comes from Polanyi, who is particularly interested in the ways in which the use of tools and instruments come to be regarded as extensions of our bodies.[4] Bodily awareness or proprioception is something we all exercise constantly but it is a condition of the exercise of our abilities and something of which we are usually not consciously aware. Our proprioceptive abilities are acquired without instruction and normally exercised without conscious awareness that we are doing so. An instrument, on the other hand, needs know-how for it to be successfully used. Our early attempts to master the use of an instrument,

be it a tool or a musical instrument, depend very much on conscious effort at mastery, as well as on imitation and practice. As we develop skill, we continue to be aware of what we are doing, pay a great deal of attention to our use of the instrument and continually try to expand our repertoire (if we wish to attain excellence). There comes a point, however, where, at a certain level of expertise, the instrument responds to our needs in the ways that our arms and legs do, through effortless, unconscious voluntary movement, usually in the service of some intention. At this point, we cannot explain the full details of our mastery any more than we can explain our mastery of our arms and legs in walking, lifting, and so on.

Oakeshott's treatment, already mentioned in Chapter 4, is somewhat different. He contrasts explicit procedural knowledge in the form of recipe-like rules (what he calls 'technical knowledge'), with the non-normatively bounded ability to act in a situationally aware manner in appropriate circumstances (what he calls 'practical knowledge'), for which no rules are available and which is to be acquired through participation in a practice or, in the case of an academic subject, in a *mode of experience.*[5] Since such knowledge is by its nature, according to Oakeshott, incapable of codification it is atheoretical, since theories need to be coded, and it also cannot be transmitted by discursive means for the same reason. *Participation in a practice* is, therefore, the only way in which to acquire such knowledge. But there is a more radical claim hidden within Oakeshott's account of participation in a practice. Just as Polanyi's extended kinaesthetic awareness of an instrument in use is something personal to the instrument user, so is the practical knowledge required for participation in a practice like politics. Each user of an instrument uses it in a personal way, unique to that individual, the use has its own 'signature' and that signature is, of course non-transferable. Thus although there is a type of know-how such as playing the piano or wielding a scalpel, each individual manifestation of that type of know-how is unique to the individual who practices it. The reader will, perhaps, have noticed the analogy between this type of tacit knowledge and the exercise of *phronesis* in know-how described in Chapter 4. For Oakeshott, this affinity would not be accidental, but two manifestations of the same kind of ineffable knowledge.

For Oakeshott, the practice of politics is a paradigmatic example of practical knowledge. Even within the study of politics one can distinguish between the study of the *language* of politics, which is constituted by the practice of politics and is concerned with the explanation of political activity and its *literature*, which is the distillation of precepts about political conduct which can be extracted from political practice as expressed in its language.[6] Oakeshott makes it clear that the literature is a much inferior form of knowledge to the language, which should itself ideally be learned in practice or at least within a university rather than a vocational environment. Oakeshott's concept of practical knowledge, with its roots in Aristotelian ideas about the acquisition and practice of virtue, together with Burkean reflections on the nature of politics, and, perhaps, a Herderian conception of community, has had an enormous influence, either direct or indirect, on current discussions of vocational education in Britain and America, primarily through the work of Jean Lave and Etienne Wenger.[7] The radical nature of the claims of these authors and their relevance for professional and vocational education will be discussed in the next section.

6. *I can do F, but the ability lies (necessarily) beyond my awareness.* The final notion of tacit knowledge to be considered is again highly influential, but has a different source, namely in the work of cognitivist writers such as Noam Chomsky and Jerry Fodor.[8] This is a complex but distinctive conception of ability which has the following features.[9]

It has a neurological basis. This means more than that there are neurologically necessary conditions for its possession, this being true of virtually every kind of know-how, but that the know-how is *representationally instantiated* in the central nervous system of the individual who possesses that know-how. The representational structure of neurologically encoded abilities is explanatory of the representational structure of actual personal abilities such as language use and conceptual mastery, as these are realized through a mapping from the representational neurological structure and sensory data on the one hand to the actual production of speech and writing on the other hand.

It is largely innate rather than acquired. According to Chomsky and Fodor, the basic syntactic and semantic elements of language are a genetic and evolutionary inheritance, whose applicability to linguistic and conceptual ability is guaranteed by exposure to some particular natural language in infancy. This is achieved by the mapping function from neurology and experience to output described above. The representational neurological structures, according to Chomsky, constitute the *competence* of the language and concept user. The outputs that result from the activated function constitute *performance*. It is a crucial part of the claim of these writers that *competence* can exist without any performance being possible. Competence, for writers such as Chomsky, is a categorical state encoded in an individual's nervous system, *not* merely a disposition to speak or write in appropriate circumstances.[10]

Such abilities are, and must be, situated beyond the possibility of conscious awareness. This claim follows from the nature of such abilities.[11] The contents of and processes within our central nervous systems are not subject to awareness, let alone kinaesthetic or conscious kinaesthetic awareness and, since these abilities are structures which are activated within the central nervous system they are inaccessible to their possessors *as neurological structures*, although they are of course accessible as abilities of which one can be aware of possessing through indirect means such as reading about them. Their tacit nature, therefore, lies in their ontological status as encoded neurological structures. Their usage must lie beyond our conscious control and hence beyond the possibility of their being transmitted through instruction or demonstration, although they must be activated through participation.

Both the latter two forms of tacit knowledge, 5 and 6 pose problems for our understanding of the nature and acquisition of certain important kinds of know-how. Cases 1–4 can all be explained as unproblematic features of our everyday understandings of knowledge, which presuppose that knowledge is deployed intentionally without our being necessarily aware that we are deploying it. Cases 1–4 also accounts for the *latency* of such assets, which merely means that they are possessed even when not being exercised. Neither do these features of knowledge compromise our understanding that it can be transmitted through social processes such as instruction, explanation, training and exemplification. Case 6 however seems to make the acquisition of such tacit knowledge the subject of innate capacities, while the accounts given of cases like 5 suggest that educational processes have little to contribute to the acquisition of this kind of know-how. These doubts, in their turn, threaten to give rise to a belief that education is not a necessary, or even a possible, prerequisite to the acquisition of such abilities. And, *a fortiori*, a doubt is cast on the claim that theory can inform certain kinds of practice and that instruction in theory is a necessary condition for the acquisition of certain kinds of ability. It is to this claim that the next section will turn.

Just How Ineffable is Tacit Knowledge?

As already noted, there is little that is mysterious in cases 1–4 above. But the cases to be considered under 5 pose distinct issues which require separate treatment. Case 5 itself encompasses three separate subcases which raise different, although related, issues.

The Wheel Planer

Sturt describes a familiar kind of situation, in which a manual skill, involving strength, dexterity and sensorimotor co-ordination, appears to involve a technique which, by its nature, cannot be explained in a comprehensive enough way for a would-be practitioner to acquire mastery. The wheelwright knows what configuration of wheel rims is required for negotiation of rutted Kent lanes. He also knows, in general terms, how one characterizes these configurations. What he is unable to do is to describe the subtle movements required to achieve the desired configuration. This is either because he is not consciously aware of the performance of these movements or because he lacks a vocabulary in which to describe them, or both. Thus the only way in which the technique can be transmitted is through a novice observing a master and then trying out the technique for himself until it is perfected, possibly with evaluative comment on the results from the master himself.

Note that Sturt is describing a particular *task* within the *occupation* of a wheelwright. He is not claiming that the totality of techniques of and skills practised in the wheelwright's trade are themselves ineffable, although it is clear that many of them are informally acquired and practiced. Indeed, the context-specific propositional knowledge necessary for the practice of the trade, for example, which copses contain wood that is 'foxy-hearted' and hence unsuitable for wheel-making, is transmitted verbally.[12] Neither do his claims exclude the possibility that a practitioner could, in principle, acquire the ability to give a more precise description of what he is doing when practising the technique. It is well-known, for example, through the work of Moshe Feldenkrais and his followers, that one can gain greater conscious awareness of voluntary muscular movements than one normally has, that one can come to describe these and even bring muscular movement that is not normally under voluntary control under voluntary control. There is no fixed barrier between those voluntary movements of which we are aware and those of which we are not, and, *a fortiori*, between those actions and skills of which we are aware and of which we are not. Neither does Sturt exclude the possibility that a wheelwright capable of practising the skill could be observed, recorded and an account of the technique that he uses be derived. Sturt's example is a fascinating and useful reminder of the non-discursive nature of many craft skills now unfortunately lost, and also a useful reminder that such methods for the acquisition of technique may continue to be indispensable, even in technical and professional occupations.

The wheelwright example can also be seen as an instance of the kind of personal knowledge that Polanyi identified. The woodwork plane is an extension of the skilled wheelwright's arms, his use of it guided by an extended kinaesthetic awareness of the possibilities and limitations of the instrument, together with a knowledge of the possibilities and limitations of the material that he is working with. In a sense, of course, that knowledge is personal and non-transmissible as the wheelwright has his own way of practicing the technique which depends on his own evolved physical constitution and the moral attitude that he brings to his work.[13] But in this sense, the skills and broader forms of know-how that we bring to bear on our work have this unique and personal quality stamped on them. One might say that it is precisely this capacity for effective work, together with the journey of self-discovery carried out, at least in part through work, together with the development of one's unique personality and 'signature' upon the world, developed at least partly within the workplace, that is a feature of a particular kind of education, namely the always-unfinished development of personality that goes under the name of *allgemeine Menschenbildung*.[14]

The Oakeshottian Politician

Oakeshott's examples are more problematic because the claims made for practical knowledge are more radical than those made by Sturt. They are also puzzling, because, while they rightly recognize the moral dimension in action, they also threaten to assimilate an intrinsic aspect of action, its moral dimension, into an account of action largely, if not solely, couched in moral terms themselves. We have already noted that Oakeshott dismissed technical knowledge in its pure form as the crude carrying out of a technique according to recipe-like prescriptions that were incapable of incorporating the subtleties described, for example, by Sturt. But practical knowledge is far broader in scope than the practice of a trade and encompasses what many philosophers have considered to be one of the highest forms of human activity, civic action or the practice of politics.[15] According to Oakeshott such a practice relies on the situated nature of morality as custom,[16] and socially evolving objectives based on a shared conception of the good. Following Burke, he argues that the complexity of human attitude and action cannot be captured in theory but rather through the kind of non-discursive awareness which Burke characterizes as *prejudice*.[17] It is not that we have not yet come up with such a theory but rather that we *could not* come up with one. The complexity, subtlety and situatedness of human activity makes such a theory impossible to develop, to which one might add that the reflexive nature of human life, taking account of the production of such theories, would render them rapidly obsolete. Such awareness is acquired through constant social action within the appropriate social *milieu* of politics. Since it involves the acquisition of non-transmissible virtues, attitudes and skills, such attributes, because they are personal and unique to the individual, can only be acquired through participation with others and the development of one's own unique 'signature' through such participation. Oakeshott does not, of course, exclude the existence of discourse within a practice and he would acknowledge that it did have an important role in acquainting a novice with the history and structure of the institutions in which politics is carried out, and also, presumably in aphorisms which encapsulate practical wisdom, which, of course, the novice must make use of in his own way.[18] However, the tenor of Oakeshott's account of such a practice and, by implication, of inculcation into it, is strongly suggestive of the idea that learning takes place almost solely through what Lave and Wenger have called 'legitimate peripheral participation' (LPP).

We need to ask, first, whether Oakeshott's own chosen example of politics will sustain his claims and, second, whether his general characterization of inculcation into a practice will withstand critical scrutiny.[19] The example of politics is persuasive to a large degree because it is evident that the ability to be effective in politics depends, to a large degree, on acquaintance with and awareness of the *milieu* in which the politician operates. This *milieu* includes an understanding of the nature of the relationships involved (the distinction between an opponent and an enemy, for example), the formal and informal normative structures of the polity in which one operates, an understanding of the relationship between civil and political society and of the ways in which power and influence are distributed. All of these understandings need to be grounded in a grasp, at least at an informal level, of the historical evolution of the polity. Oakeshott is on strong ground in suggesting that there is neither a theory nor an explicit recipe which can guide the experienced or even the novice politician in action and decision-making. However, he also seems to be making a stronger claim, namely that to be guided by a theory of political action or of the good is a mistake. 'Rationalism' is an error, not just of thinking that there is an empirical theory capable of guiding politicians, but of thinking that there could be a normative theory of, for example, equality, human rights or democracy that could provide the objectives for political action.

On this point, he is on less strong ground. Adopting a metaethic based on a Humean idea of custom he argues that morality is not grounded in principles as in Kantian moral philosophy, but in ideas of the right and good that exist within particular cultures, which are in turn enshrined in particular practices of everyday life.[20] While one may be sceptical about the power of normative moral theory to provide moral guidance in everyday life, it is also true that systematic normative moral theories, not to mention metaethical reconceptualizations of the nature of morality, have had a profound influence on first-order moral theory and on the everyday practice of morality, as the work of Alasdair MacIntyre has established.[21] Rousseau, Kant and Nietzsche are all key figures in these developments. In each case, a moral psychology and metaphysical stance informs a reconceptualization of morality and a set of more or less explicit prescriptions for action. It would be difficult to deny the influence, for good or ill, that such reconceptualizations of moral thought have had on the everyday understanding of moral action. Ironically, it is arguable that MacIntyre's own revival of Aristotelian ethics is beginning to have a similar effect, for example, in the development of professional ethics. It is also the case that empirical and normative theory is often intertwined in some at least of these thinkers. Rousseau is a good example in this respect. In *Emile* he develops a normative moral psychology based on what he takes to be empirical truths about the sources of human well-being. This account, which issues in further prescriptions about the necessity of certain kinds of child-rearing and educative practices, leads to an account of the psychological conditions necessary for the practice of democratic politics.[22] What in Rousseau were philosophical insights into the psychological effects of relative inequality have been much reinforced in contemporary times by empirical studies into the epidemiological, medical and psychological effects of such inequalities.[23] Such studies, if taken seriously, have profound normative implications for anyone concerned with politics. A supporter of Oakeshott may reply that such understandings are implicit in the different approaches of contending political parties and do not and cannot need articulation. This response, however, does not merit much scrutiny. A politician need not study Rousseau or the contemporary literature on health and inequality and may operate on the basis of tacit understandings in the sense of 1 above, namely knowing that *p* without being aware of knowing it, perhaps even implicitly knowing it in the sense that correct third-person attributions of such knowledge can be made without first-person attributions being possible. We might, charitably, describe such a politician as *intuitive* in his approach, but a less charitable description would be *stupid.*[24]

Indeed, Oakeshott's own preferred example of the dangers of rational-ism in politics, in which he closely follows Burke, provides ample evidence of the limitations of his own claims. Burke's own strictures against an *a priori* approach to political practice gained some plausibility through his prediction in 1790 of the execution of Louis XVI in 1793 and the advent of the Terror. However, in the short term, let alone in the longer term, even his prediction of the instability and eventual self-destruction of the French Revolution proved wrong. By 1796 in the *Regicide Peace* he railed against the strength and rootedness of the Revolution as it was clear that it was capable of dealing with its internal and external enemies.[25] In the longer term despite various monarchical restorations it remains the case that the French polity is republican and explicitly based on principles of *Liberte, Egalite et Fraternite* which derive, at least partly, from the political and edu-cational writings of Rousseau. It is ironic that the strictures of Burke and Oakeshott on the failure of 'rationalistic politics' in the example of the French Revolution are themselves rationalistic in the sense that they derive from *a priori* considerations of the nature of moral and political life influ-enced by the metaphysics, psychology and moral theory of empiricist writ-ers such as Hume.

A more profitable way of understanding the French Revolution would be to combine a study of its intellectual and moral influences with a detailed historical account of the events, such as is to be found in Carlyle's *The French Revolution*,[26] which also makes clear how events both in domestic and international politics provided the dynamic through which political and moral ideals were realized. In this case, a different kind of expertise, that of historical research and interpretation, carried out systematically and with due regard to the historical study of knowledge in the sense outlined in Chapter 1 can provide both scholarly understanding and a basis for understanding the politics of revolutionary situations. It is thus far from clear that Oakeshott's claims about the tacit nature of practical knowledge, in his chosen paradigmatic area of politics, will bear much scrutiny. To say this is not, of course, to deny the important and unavoid-able tacit elements in political practice in the senses of 1 to 4 above. It is to deny, however, that all forms of know-how, whether in the sense of Oakeshottian practical knowledge, or in other senses, must necessarily be wholly tacit in nature. Scepticism about the prevalence of Oakeshottian practical knowledge ought to lead to scepticism about the accounts of learning to be found in the work of Lave and Wenger, for example. While not denying that some Liberian tailors might learn their trade through LPP, there is no reason to suppose that these cases need be in any way typical of professional and vocational learning, as we shall see more clearly in Chapters 9 and 10.

The Chomskyan Linguist-Scientist

We now turn to the other major influence on current ideas about the tacit nature of know-how, namely the work of cognitive linguists and scientists influenced by Chomsky, Fodor and others. As already remarked, tacit knowledge in this sense is a system of neurologically encoded representations, activated by limited forms of experience, which although necessarily beyond conscious awareness, nevertheless give rise to action which is, in a sense, expert, in the sense that we are all experts in the syntax and semantics of our mother tongues. The Chomsky-Fodor approach rests on representational architecture-based conceptions of mind, as opposed to connectionist models.[27] Such approaches are explicitly *representationalist*, that is, the postulate a mechanism whereby representations of syntactic or conceptual structure are transposed into action. Some connectionist approaches, which explicitly deny the modularity, systematicity and innate nature of mental representation are also representationalist. The commentary that follows is directed at both computational and connectionist accounts of tacit knowledge deriving from representational structures.

As already stated, there are well-rehearsed objections to the concept of *ab initio* solitary mental representation when this is conceived of as *normative* as opposed to *nomological* structure. Indeed, the idea of a nomological representational structure only makes sense against the background of a normative one. It is possible, for example, to use computer technology to set up such structures which then fit in with our normative systems of representations. It is another matter to claim that representation is primarily nomological.[28] Furthermore, it is not possible to claim that a structure can be both normative and nomological in character, since physical laws only admit of exceptions in terms of *randomness*, while normative laws may be followed or not followed according to the intentions of the agent. Any nomological law that underpinned a putatively normative one could only do so as a necessary condition for the operation of the latter, not as being constitutive of it. For the latter to be the case the normative law would have to take on the characteristics of the nomological which, as we have seen, are incompatible with it. A cognitivist-representationalist account of tacit knowledge would have to be broadly deterministic in structure and hence radically revisionist in respect of our ideas about know-how as opposed to underlying physical capacities. The arguments against adopting such a stance are strong and persuasive.

The first of these, outlined in more detail in other places and by other authors, is that the notion of an *ab initio* solitary normative representational structure is not coherent.[29] Second, even if such a possibility is admitted, the idea that representational structures could exist in a physical organ like the brain is of doubtful coherence. Third, better explanations of language and concept acquisition are available than those provided by cognitivist theory.[30] Cognitivists have encountered significant problems in realizing their own programme and have retreated to minimalist accounts of the representational nature of syntactic structure and to doubts about whether either modular or connectionist accounts can make sense of the abductive nature of human abilities, that is, our ability to integrate knowledge and abilities from different sources in order to make a unified and integrated decision.[31] The limits of explanations in terms of neurological mechanisms must reside in their account of the neurological conditions necessary for the existence of know-how, not as sufficient explanations for the acquisition and exercise of know-how.[32] The temptation to sufficiently describe accomplished forms of know-how in terms of synaptic connection arises from this kind of conflation. Those who hold that know-how is primarily acquired rather than innate, as in, for example, the connectionist paradigm, will describe representational structures in terms of empirically developed synaptic connections. But these can no more do the job required than can innately developed ones. No more will be said about these points for the moment, but will be further developed in the discussion of the theories of expertise put forward by, for example, Dreyfus and Dreyfus in Chapter 9.

Postscript: Ryle on Knowing How Revisited

This study has proceeded on the basis of a defence of Ryle's epistemological distinction between knowing how and knowing that and an affirmation of its particular suitability to describe an essential feature of know-how, namely that it comes in degrees and is subject to normative evaluation (Chapters 1 and 2). Nevertheless, discussion of Ryle cannot pass by without looking more closely at his account of accomplished action. Ryle, like Oakeshott, describes the actions of the novice in terms of the unreflective following of recipes. For Ryle, such rules are 'bannisters for toddlers' which can be discarded as accomplishment develops. It should be emphasized that nothing that Ryle says explicitly discounts the claim that accomplished know-how is not wholly tacit, nor that theory may inform accomplished practice. In this respect, he is more careful than Oakeshott was. However, the rhetorical tendency of Ryle's writings on this subject tends strongly to discount the explicit and the theoretical in accomplished performance.[33] The tacit elements of performance are, in the examples presented, made salient and the invocation of theory is discounted. Thus, for example, the novice angler eventually grows out of 'The Compleat Angler' and Mrs Beaton is discarded as the cook's skills and knowledge develop. Even a surgeon need not have acquired anatomical and physiological theory in the classroom but might have done so in practice.[34] While formally legitimate, in practical terms the tenor of Ryle's remarks on the development of know-how beyond that of the novice are nevertheless misleading in discounting in particular the role of knowledge and especially of theoretical knowledge (*Wissen*) in accomplished performance. What Ryle claims about the tacit nature of performance can be adequately subsumed under senses 1 to 4 of tacitness outlined at the beginning of this chapter, that is as an affirmation of the implicit and dispositional nature of both propositional and practical knowledge and of the selectivity and directedness of attention. It should be noted, however, that although Ryle's discussion of *heed concepts* such as care, attention, and so on give a full account of the role of the agent's awareness in acting in an accomplished way, little attention is given to *conscious awareness* which, arguably, is a key feature of certain forms of judgement. Ryle's reluctance in this instance seems to rest on his concentration on his prime philosophical target in his writings on know-how, the Cartesian Myth or the Intellectualist Legend. According to this Legend, any form of *knowing that* involves the avowal of a proposition and hence an infinite regress of avowals before any action can take place (see the discussion in Chapter 2). We have already noted, however, that although the Cartesian may require that all forms of *knowing that p* involve avowal that *p*, there is no good reason for Ryle to do so and his caution about action that involves prior avowal in terms of consciously aware mental action, is unwarranted. One may wonder whether someone who can avow that *p* must know how to avow that *p*. The phrase 'knows how to avow that *p*' seems odd, but it is also clear that being able to avow that something is the case is a normatively based ability deriving from the ability to assert propositions, which has its own canons of accuracy, fluency, appropriateness, and so on. The ability to avow, as an internalized linguistic ability is part of our practical cognitive repertoire. The oddity of the phrase 'knows how to avow' derives from the fact that avowal is too generic a term for the kinds of cognitive processes envisaged,

like asserting on the basis of evidence or memory, or by drawing a conclusion from premises. In these cases it is not odd to say that, for example,
'A knows how to draw conclusions from evidence.' Even if, however, we
were to acknowledge the appropriateness of the locution 'A knows how
to avow that p', however, it would not follow that 'A knows that w is a way
to avow that p', is true, which would be required to get the regress going.
The abilities, either to assert or to avow internally are best seen as forms
of unproblematic tacit practical knowledge.

Conclusion: The Role of Tacit Knowledge in Knowing How

In this chapter the various principal senses in which knowledge, whether
it be propositional, acquaintance or practical knowledge can be described
as 'tacit' have been outlined. Four of these senses pose no problems for
anyone who wishes to claim that some forms of practical knowledge involve
a non-tacit element, either because they do not preclude such an element
or because they are perfectly coherent formulations of the concept of
tacit knowledge. Two senses of 'tacitness' were identified as being more
problematic, however. The first of these was the Oakeshottian claim that
the significant kind of know-how, what he calls 'practical knowledge', is
necessarily a largely tacit form of knowledge, as opposed to one that can
be considerably informed by theoretical considerations, whether these be
normative or empirical. The second is the claim that tacit knowledge is
representational neurological structure. The Oakeshottian claim can be
dismissed through the detailed discussion of examples that are apparently
favourable to Oakeshott's case, the cognitivist claim is both conceptually
unsustainable and empirically otiose as an account of the acquisition and
exercise of fundamental forms of know-how.

Notes

[1] Cf. Barrow, R., Woods, R. (2003) *An Introduction to Philosophy of Education*, London,
    Routledge, ch. 11; Best, D. (1992) *The Rationality of Feeling*, Brighton, Falmer
    Press; Bereiter, C., Scardamalia, M. (1993) *Surpassing Ourselves*, La Salle, IL, Open
    Court Publishing, ch. 4.
[2] Howe, M. (1990) *The Origin of Exceptional Abilities*, London, Routledge, for sus-
    tained empirical questioning of this claim, through the use of case studies.
[3] Sturt (1923), pp. 138–41.
[4] Polanyi, M. (1958) *Personal Knowledge*, London, Routledge, ch. 4.

⁵ Cf. Williams, K. (2007) *Education and the Voice of Michael Oakeshott*, Charlottesville, VA, Imprint-Academic.

⁶ Oakeshott, M. (1962b) 'The study of politics in a university', in *Rationalism in Politics*, London, Methuen, pp. 311–33.

⁷ Burke, E. (1790) *Reflections on the Revolution in France*, London, Penguin; Berlin, I. (1977) *Herder and Vico*, New York, Vintage Books; Lave, J., Wenger, E. (1991) *Legitimate Peripheral Participation*. Ryle's claims about know-how as set out in 1946 and 1949 have similarities with those of Oakeshott, particularly in Ryle's scepticism about the articulability of knowledge how, although again no direct influence is discernible.

⁸ For example, Chomsky, N. (1988) *Language and Problems of Knowledge*, Cambridge, MA, MIT Press; Fodor, J. (1975) *The Language of Thought*, Cambridge, MA, MIT Press.

⁹ It is necessary to point out that the ideas of these thinkers have undergone considerable modification over the years and are here described in the 'full-blooded' form, which, arguably is the form in which they have enjoyed the most influence. Cf. Chomsky, N. (2004) *The Generative Enterprise Revisited*, Berlin, Mouton de Gruyter; Fodor, J. (2001) *The Mind Doesn't Work That Way* (Cambridge, MA, MIT Press); (2003) *Hume Variations*, Oxford, Clarendon. It is fair to say, however, that neither have abandoned the representational project, but have become more cautious in the nature of the claims made for it.

¹⁰ It is arguable, however, that such an account needs a further, dispositional, competence/performance distinction to take account of the presence of structures that arise from the mapping function (i.e. natural language) and their manifestation in speech or writing.

¹¹ Whether they should be classified as abilities or as forms of know-how is a moot point. Chomsky and Fodor would claim that they are nomologically based norms which set out their representational structure. Whether such nomologically founded structures could also be genuinely representative and hence have a normative structure is beyond the scope of this discussion to elucidate. See Winch, C. (1998) *The Philosophy of Human Learning*, London, Routledge, ch. 6, for further treatment which argues that this cannot be the case.

¹² It is evident from Sturt's account that the occupation of the Wheelwright is a traditional craft, rather than a technically based trade. Such knowledge as is required is *Kenntnis* (as in the wood example above) rather than *Wissen*. In this sense, Sturt's examples have nothing to say about the application of theory to practice because the practice does not involve the use of theory in any obvious sense.

¹³ What Kerschensteiner would call his *burgerliche Tugenden*, or the practice of virtue within the practice of a technique. Kerschesteiner, G. (1964) in *Ausgewahlte Padagogische Texte*, Paderborn, Schöningh.

¹¹ See Benner, D. (2003) *Wilhelm von Humbold's Bildungstheorie*, Munich, Juventa, for further explanation.

¹⁵ For a modern example, see Arendt, H. (1958), *The Human Condition*, Chicago, Notre Dame Press.

¹⁶ 'The tower of Babel' in Oakeshott (1962a), pp 59–79.

¹⁷ Burke, E. (1790) *Reflections on the Revolution in France*, London, Penguin, p. 183.

[18] For example, the admonition to a novice parliamentarian that it is not his enemies, but his opponents that sit on the bench opposite. 'Your opponents are in front of you. Your enemies are behind you.'

[19] For Oakeshott, 'A Practice may be identified as a set of considerations, manners, uses, observances, customs, standards, canons, maxims, principles, rules and offices specifying useful procedures or denoting obligations or duties which relate to human actions and utterances.' Oakeshott, M. (1975) *On Human Conduct*, Oxford, Clarendon, p. 55. The practice of politics would encompass all of these.

[20] See Oakeshott (1975). 'The tower of Babel' in Oakeshott (1962a), for example, p. 62.

[21] MacIntyre, A. (1981) *After Virtue*, London, Duckworth.

[22] See Rousseau, J-J. [1762] (1968) *Emile ou l'Education*, Paris, Flammarion; [1754] (1968) *Discourse on Inequality, Social Contract*, London, Dent; also Dent, N. (1988) *Rousseau*, London, Routledge.

[23] For a good recent survey of this literature, see Wilkinson, R. (2005) *The Impact of Inequality*, London, Routledge. For a classical source see Plato (1975), p. 215.

[24] The characterization of the British Conservative Party as the 'stupid party' cleverly encapsulates both the possibilities and the limits of such an intuitive approach. Post 1975 it became enamoured of an empirical and normative theory of politics deriving from the works of writers such as Adam Smith, Friedrich von Hayek and Robert Nozick.

[25] Burke, E. (1790); (1796) *Thoughts on the Prospects of a Regicide Peace in a Series of Letters*, London, J. Owen.

[26] Carlyle, T. (1837) *History of the French Revolution*, New York, Modern Library.

[27] It should be noted, however, that Fodor has, for some time, expressed scepticism about the representational modularity project while still vigorously promoting an innatist-representationalist approach to the understanding and explanation of the mind, see, for example, Fodor (2001).

[28] See Winch (1998), ch. 6 for further discussion.

[29] See Winch 1998; Malcolm 1990; Verheggen 1995, for example. Representing can be done incorrectly or incorrectly; it is therefore a normatively guided ability, a form of know-how. But since it is a normative activity it must be subject to forms of appraisal. *Ex hypothesi* these are not available for the *ab initio* solitary. But the neural representationist is just such an individual. Such an individual cannot, therefore, engage in representation prior to interaction with a normatively guided community.

[30] Cf. Baker and Hacker (1984).

[31] See Chomsky (2004); Fodor (2001).

[32] Bennett and Hacker (2003).

[33] Winch, C. (2009) 'Ryle on knowing how and the possibility of vocational education', *Journal of Applied Philosophy*, 26, 1, pp. 88–101.

[34] See references to Ryle in Chapters 5 and 6.

Chapter 8

Can There be a Theory of Expertise?

Introduction

This chapter will examine some influential accounts of expertise which, it is fair to say, have aspirations to constitute *theories* of expertise in the sense that they purport to be empirical generalizations concerning the necessary conditions for the attribution of expertise to a person carrying out particular tasks or engaging in particular occupations. As such they commend to us *how* expertise should be developed and are thus also *normative* theories of expertise. In particular, the work of Hubert and Stuart Dreyfus, Donald Schön, Carl Bereiter and Marlene Scardamalia will be examined with a view to assessing their claims. The claim of the chapter is that, while these commentators have important insights to offer on expertise in particular areas and also, to an extent, on some fairly general features of expertise, their claims concerning the essential nature of expertise cannot be sustained. Indeed, given the variety of situations and types of agency to which the term 'expertise' and its cognates are applied and which have been outlined in this book, it is difficult to see how one could construct a general theory of expertise, as opposed to making a contribution to a greater understanding of it by pointing to some important features that may be found in a variety of different circumstances. A greater understanding of expertise will be arrived at by appreciating its variety rather than by looking for what is common to all cases.

The study of these theories suggests that a powerful picture of the nature of proficient and expert performance has taken hold in a wide variety of professional and vocational education contexts. This picture is itself, at least partially, a reaction against an equally influential theory which emphasized the importance of the possession of a systematic body of propositional knowledge as the necessary feature of expertise.[1] From the perspective of this book, it is easy to see why this would be inadequate. We can see, for example, that some activities and occupations do not rely, or rely on marginally, on the possession of such knowledge. Chapter 1 suggested that even the possession of systematic knowledge cannot be adequately conceptualized solely in terms of the grasp of propositions. Philosophical work by Polanyi, Oakeshott and Ryle has also cast doubt on whether know-how should even be considered to be discursively communicable, let alone propositional in character. Autobiographical work such as that of Sturt, together with empirical studies, cited in the works of Dreyfus and Dreyfus, for example, also emphasize the tacit nature of much know-how. We have now reached a position where it is fair to say that the dominant picture of expertise among many philosophical and educational commentators is that it is characterized essentially by fluent performance of a very high quality unmediated by the use of rules or by reference to theory. Even where *reflection* is thought to be a key feature of expert practitioners, as in the work of Schön, this has been conceptualized in such a way as to be part and parcel of ongoing action in operational circumstances. A new picture has come to hold the professional and vocational educator captive: that of the tacit expert.

This chapter will argue that the important issue in an examination of expertise is not the attainment of a general account, applicable to all cases of expertise, but rather a greater understanding of the enormous variety of what we call 'expertise' and 'experts', together with an understanding of the different conceptual dimensions in which we talk about expertise (see Chapter 9 for more on this). We cannot assume that a theory of expertise will be capable of doing this, particularly if it holds us in thrall to a picture which, while it may well fit some cases beautifully, fails to cover the variety of usage of the term.

What is a Theory of Expertise?

We saw in Chapter 6 that the term 'theory' can be understood in different ways, for example, Dreyfus and Dreyfus were cited as defining theory as *explicit, universal in its application, abstract, context free in reference to human interests and institutions* and *systematic*.[2] This, it was argued, was too narrow and it was suggested that the concept of theory should be related to that of a body of organized propositional knowledge as either that body itself or as a subset, or as a body of propositions and practice that had the aspiration of being accepted as an organized body of knowledge. Theories, it was argued, have a degree of generality, even if they are not context free in reference to human interests and institutions. Indeed, any theory of expertise, insofar as it refers and relates to human interests and institutions could not be a theory in that sense. A theory of expertise would have aspirations to provide the necessary conditions for the attribution of expertise to a person working in a particular task, job or occupation.

A theory of expertise, such as that offered by Dreyfus and Dreyfus or by Schön, appears to draw on a variety of subjects and to offer a reasonably general if not universal claim about the nature of expertise. Typically, such theories draw on Philosophy, the Science of Artificial Intelligence, Psychology, Anthropology, Sociology and even Neurology. They are, therefore, eclectic not just in respect of their mix of empirical and non-empirical elements, but also in the empirical disciplines on which they draw.

Before we go on to examine such theories it may be helpful to make a few grammatical distinctions. In doing so, we shall see that the use of the term 'expert' and its cognates is not systematic, although theories of expertise do try and regiment the use of the term in order to impart a high degree of generality to their accounts. First, to be an expert is to be an expert in something or other which requires know-how. But beyond this, the range of specification for an expert is not clearly settled. One can be an expert in a very specific task, like making a salad dressing, in an occupation like bricklaying or a profession like medicine. Even the range of expertise in an occupation may be subject to considerable variation in its nature, for example, in comparing English and German bricklayers, we can see that the *scope* of the occupation varies very widely between the two countries.[3] Neither is it entirely clear what expectations there are about the quality of an expert's performance. Is an expert's work always excellent? Not necessarily, because even if it is an essential feature of an expert that the expert aspires to excellence in their work (and this is highly debateable), we cannot expect that the work will always be excellent or even of a high quality. Is it the *activity* of the expert to which the attribution of excellence should be applied, or is it the *outcome* of the expert's activity? What frequency and what degree of excellence in either activity or outcome should we expect from an expert? Finally, it is not clear whether the activities of an expert should include the teaching, however, informal, of non-experts. Hoffman, for example, has suggested that the category of Master should be superimposed on that of an expert to reflect the fact that experts do not necessarily have the wish or the ability to promote excellence in non-experts within their field.[4] One might reasonably, however, include in a formal definition of an expert in a particular occupation, that they are able to teach non-experts. Such a stipulation would, for example, correspond to the highest title in the German vocational education system, that of the *Meister*.

The criteria for expertise, therefore, are fluid, and this fact vitiates against attempts to construct theories of expertise.

Fluency Theories 1: Dreyfus and Dreyfus, Benner, Ryle

Fluency theories make the claim that an essential, or almost essential, feature of expertise, which justifies the attribution 'is an expert on or in F' to someone, is the fact that their performance is not only of a very high quality in relation to the standards appropriate to that field, but that it is conducted without hesitation, with rapidity and in such a way that the expert is not able to give a full account of what it is that he or she does, such that a non-expert could become one through listening to and acting on such an account. It is generally assumed that an expert is capable of performances and/or activities that exceed those of the merely proficient. But can experts make mistakes, act in an inferior way and produce, on occasions, inferior outcomes? Fluency theories do not concentrate on the *outcome* of expertise, but rather on the characteristics of the expert *performance*. This is hardly surprising, since the outcomes are likely to be as varied as the types of activities in which experts engage. Nevertheless it is usually assumed that the outcome of an expert performance is an excellent artefact or action. This raises the question, to be discussed later, of the role of the outcomes of expert action and whether they could be achieved by performances which do not have the 'fluency' characteristics of expertise.

Ryle has been mentioned because his reservations about theory informing practice have already been discussed in Chapter 6. His ideas concerning the fluent nature of accomplished performance have become influential, but it would not be correct to say that he offers anything like a *theory* of expertise. This is the case, however, with Dreyfus and Dreyfus who, relying on a mixture of philosophical speculation and argument and empirical research, offer a theory which although owing a debt to Ryle, also differs in significant ways from anything which he would have endorsed. Their theory of expertise is based on a model of *skill acquisition*, which shows how expertise as a characteristic of action is related to less than expert performances. The choice to frame expertise in this way is itself significant in the light of the discussion in Chapter 4 of the relationship between skill and *competence* and will be discussed further. The model uses five stages:[5]

Novice. Adheres rigidly to rules or plans (this has echoes of Ryle's 'bannisters for toddlers'); has little situational awareness (due to lack of experience of relevant situations and differences between those situations); has no discretionary judgement (this follows from the other two points).

Advanced Beginner. Guidelines for action are based on limited appreciation of the properties of situations and/or aspects (global situational characteristics) recognizable after some experience. No discrimination is made between the relative importance of aspects and they are treated separately.

Competent Practitioner. Is able to cope with more complex and busy situations and can relate action to longer term goals; can engage in conscious deliberate planning (using schemata of the kind discussed in Chapter 6); can operate standardized and routine procedures.

Someone operating at any of these three levels can engage in *calculative rationality*, or the ability to initiate and carry through a sequence of reasoning that results in action. In the case of the novice, for example,

1. Situation A requires action B.
2. This is situation A.
3. Therefore, do B.

In the case of the competent practitioner, a sequence might involve a prior process of reasoning that involves relating a sequence of action to a goal:

1. Achieving G requires actions of type A (depending on the situation).
2. Achieving G requires action in a situation of type S.
3. S situations require type A actions.
4. This is a situation of type S (reaching this conclusion this could involve a variety of inference schemata).
5. Therefore, this requires an action of type A as a necessary condition for achieving G.

The competent practitioner may well have to iterate this reasoning, relating a medium term goal or goals to a longer term one.

Proficient Practitioner. Such an individual will be able to see situations as wholes, including under different possible aspects; will identify important features of a situation, deviations from a normal pattern; will generate situationally sensitive maxims for guidance; will engage in rapid decision-making.

Expert. No longer relies on rules (the novice), guidelines (the competent) or maxims (the proficient); has a tacit understanding of situations (based on the 'internalization' of the above); uses analytical approaches in novel or problematic situations; has a grasp of what is practically possible.[6] In the use of analytical approaches, when it is practically possible, the expert engages in *deliberative rationality*, which is detached and meditative, although it has the same general scope of inferential structures as that of the competent practitioner.

> Deliberative rationality stands at the intersection of theory and practice. It is detached, reasoned observation of one's intuitive behaviour with an eye to challenging, and perhaps improving intuition without replacing it by the purely theory-based action of the novice, advanced beginner or competent practitioner.[7]

The idea appears to be that the expert can reason about his or her own behaviour, and hence improve on intuition in doing so, by preventing tunnel vision. However, Dreyfus and Dreyfus have a particular view of the intuitive element of performance (which will be tacit in one or more of the senses outlined in Chapter 7). 'Rule based procedures are based on the synaptic modifications that make possible an intuitive response.'[8] Elsewhere, they claim that rules and principles are *replaced* by synapse-produced situational discrimination.[9] The claim seems to be that ultimately expertise is based on the physical structure of the brain through the establishment of new synaptic connections and that intuition can be explained as activity within these newly acquired synaptic connections.

Critique of the Dreyfus and Dreyfus' Model

This model is highly influential and has clear links with other accounts of practical knowledge, such as those of Ryle, Oakeshott, and Lave and Wenger, although it has been subjected to criticism (e.g. Eraut 1994). There is no doubt that it represents a serious and systematic attempt to give an account of the nature of expertise, particularly in professional situations, making use of both conceptual and empirical materials. Neither is there any doubt that it contains important insights into the nature of expertise. Nevertheless there are serious flaws, both with its status as a theory and with some of the specific claims made about the characteristics of expertise.

The first point of criticism is with the model as the basis for a theory. Ryle would have not hesitated to have pointed that many (if not all) activities do not necessarily require a theoretical basis for their successful, let alone expert practice and that consequently this model would not apply to them. Insofar as theories are meant to be general accounts this compromises the model as the basis of a general theory.

The second point is that the account focuses on skilled *action* rather than on the *outcome* of action involving skill. This point raises complex and important issues. On the one hand, one wants to be able to say that an excellent outcome is the result of expert action, so that an excellent outcome produced by a fluke or 'beginner's luck' is not the action of an expert. On the other hand, although one may want to admit that action by experts (or even expert action) does not always result in excellent results, one would not want to admit this for more than a small minority of cases. This again suggests that there is something mistaken in focusing only on process, just as sole focus on outcome also gives a distorted and restricted notion of expertise. It may well be that one has to settle for a loose conceptual connection between expert performance and product-ive excellence without either detaching them completely or tying them too closely together. In this regard, it should also be noted that it is not a necessary feature of an expert (for Dreyfus and Dreyfus or for anyone else) that experts have always to give expert performances or have excel-lent outcomes. There must remain a degree of vagueness about these relationships.

The third criticism is the most important and relates to a very pervasive contemporary tendency to identify action with activity and/or structural features of the brain. *Correlations*, either speculative or empirically arrived at, between features of human brains and the activity of the people whose brains possess these characteristics are subsumed into *identities*. This seems to be a trap that Dreyfus and Dreyfus fall into. Not only do synaptic con-nections of the right kind *enable* the use of rule-based procedures, but they actually *replace* them. The first claim concerns neurological necessary con-ditions (presumably speculative) for certain kinds of activity; the second is a claim that certain activities (human actions) are replaced by processes in the ontologically different category of brain processes (i.e. physical proc-esses). Such a claim seems confused. It makes sense to say that a particular action was carried out in an expert manner (using rule-based procedures), not that a particular synaptic connection was expert or carried out in an expert manner – that is simply nonsense. Nor can one say that a synaptic connection was used expertly, as that would imply that the synapses were used by the agent whose synapses they are and, of course, they cannot be used in the relevant sense since the agent has no control over them and neither are there any rules for their expert use.[10]

The mistake of applying psychological predicates to physical organs like the brain can be approached in another way that is highly relevant to the understanding of expertise. Mature action, including that of experts, depends on successfully taking into account all the relevant factors within a situation. Although expertise is relative to some particular field of activity within which the expert operates, expertise does not involve some specialized form of human agency, but rather human agency directed to a particular field of activity.[11] In most such fields of activity, even relatively simple tasks that require some degrees of judgement, knowledge, skill, perception, experience are brought to bear on the situation in order to determine a course of action. The situation will have relevant features which call for attention if intentions are to be carried out. For example, the state of a firm's bank balance may be relevant to whether a particular investment decision is made, even if it is not the only relevant factor. One needs to be able to assess which factors are relevant, to what extent and the ways in which they are related to each other. Even when one has specialist abilities, such as financial or linguistic ones, if there are multiple factors relevant to decision-making, one cannot rely on one of these, but on an appreciation of their relative importance *to this particular situation*. Describing expertise 'synaptically' is actually regressive, since the non-expert, on the Dreyfus and Dreyfus' account *does* actually apply rule-based procedures, seeing situations as a whole, under relevant aspects. This ability, known as 'abduction' is something we all need to acquire in order to operate in everyday situations where expertise is not required, but it is needed as well, and takes more time to develop, in situations where competence, proficiency and expertise are possible evaluations of actions.

Fodor (2001) criticizes modular accounts of the mind for their inability to account for abduction. Linguistic know-how, encoded in the modular architecture of a brain, cannot itself determine whether the linguistic expertise is necessary in any particular situation. The connectionist alternative (to which Dreyfus and Dreyfus appear to subscribe), whereby powers of judgement are built up through experience which leads to networks of synaptic connection, does not escape this critique. Judgements of situational salience and relevance require that situations need to be considered on their own merits, even if the appreciation of previous patterns is necessary for that consideration to take place. Synaptic connections, if they are to account for judgements of relevance cannot be invariant, since their relative importance within a decision-making network will vary according to the features of each situation, becoming more relevant in some situations and less so in others. But it is a physical feature of such connections that, once made, they are invariant. They may, presumably, become less relevant as they are becoming increasingly embedded in wider connective networks, but they could not become more relevant relative to the existing and growing networks. This disqualifies synaptic networks from assuming the role of carrying out abductive judgement.[12]

A fourth criticism of this account focuses on that feature of expertise which makes use of 'analytical approaches in novel or problematic situations'. This is a puzzling claim since we are told that analytical approaches, embodied in calculative rationality, are features of non-expert performance. Non-experts have to cope with such situations, and since they do not have intuition to fall back on, making use of analytical methods appropriate to the field of activity is what one would expect them to do. The expert, therefore, cannot be distinguished from the non-expert in this particular respect. What one would expect of the expert, as opposed to the competent or proficient practitioner, is that the expert would be *better* able to cope with such situations. They would, for example, have a *deeper* theoretical base on which to form maxims of judgement, or *greater* experience of cognate situations, *enlarged* perceptual awareness of relevant features, *greater* dexterity, and so on. This would not take the nature of their expertise into an ontologically distinct realm from that of the non-expert and also suggests that there is nothing *essentially different* about the performance of an expert apart from the criteria that we are inclined to apply relative to a particular field of activity in which the expertise is exercised, which is then used to distinguish the expert from the non-expert. These could be the informal attributions of a peer group or formal criteria necessary for official certification as an expert and one might not have a match between the two.[13]

A fifth criticism is one already alluded to, namely that expertise (and indeed levels of ability below those of an expert), and conceived of in terms of the character of the actions and judgements that the agent makes, rather than in what results from what they do. It is, of course, true that in many cases the actual activity and its outcome are inseparable. For example, the activity of playing music or ice-skating is manifested in actions and it is precisely those actions which are assessed for their quality. It may be this feature of expertise that has led some commentators to neglect outcomes as a separate category. Nevertheless, they very often are in, for example, craft production. In Chapter 2 it was argued that the general criterion for knowing how to do something should involve *ability to perform the relevant actions*, rather than an ability to give an account of what such actions would involve.[14] In normal circumstances, one would expect such actions to result in what they were intended to bring about. Someone with greater expertise than someone else will, then, be able either to bring about the intended consequences of actions involving relevant know-how *more frequently* than the other, or bring about *better or more effective* consequences than the other, or both.[15] One would, therefore, expect reference to outcomes to constitute at least an element of what is to be understood as expertise, either in a relative or an absolute sense. Process accounts, which focus on the ways in which actions are carried out alone, rather than in the results of those actions, cannot do this.

A sixth criticism relates to the classification of the field of action in which expertise is supposed to be exercised. One is thought to be good or expert at something like an occupation, like cooking, fishing or surgery to use three of Ryle's examples. So far, so good, but the problems begin when one subjects such occupation-like fields of agency to further scrutiny. An expert, as understood in English, if not in other languages, has greater skill than other practitioners in the same field. It makes sense to talk of a skilled, surgeon, cook or fisherman, but it also makes perfectly good sense to ask of someone who makes a claim that 'A is skilled as a so-and-so', what exactly his skills are. I cannot, for example, make the claim that A is a skilled carpenter and not be prepared to give an account of the skills he possesses and the ways in which he exercises them. In other words, although it makes sense to attribute skill to someone who practices an occupation, the primary attribution of skill is to *tasks* rather than to occupations. It is as if conceptually the occupation is conceived of as a bundle of related tasks to which the primary attribution of skill applies.

Why is this significant? After all, it is perfectly acceptable to ask of a German with the *Fähigkeit* of a carpenter what skills (*Fertigkeiten*) he or she possesses. However, listing the *Fertigkeiten* of a carpenter does not exhaust the description of the relevant *Fähigkeit*, which includes something like the abductive ability to see carpentry projects as a whole, taking into account the needs of customers, the firm and other interested parties, personal attributes such as ability to plan, control, co-ordinate and evaluate, and moral qualities of care, not only for the work, but also for the occupation and the wider society. The main point, however, of someone who is *Fähig* in this sense is that they have an integrated occupational capacity which cannot be fully understood by the enumeration of the skills which compose it. Relating expertise primarily to tasks (even if it is via occupational specification) cannot do this. Yet, it is an important feature of many kinds of expertise that it is applied to such integrated capacities.

This point perhaps sheds some light on a distinction that David Carr has tried to make between professions and trades and the circumstances in which we are inclined to attribute 'good' or some other evaluative term to a practitioner within an occupational category.[16] He maintained that although one could call a tradesman a good butcher, for example, even though he short-changed his customers, it would be mistaken to describe a financially unscrupulous, although technically skilled doctor in such terms. The point being made is that one needs to conceive of the practice of a profession holistically in terms of character and moral attributes as well as in terms of skills and knowledge. Although he does not say so, Carr is, in effect, pointing to a *Fähigkeit* conception of a profession as opposed to a trade. In terms of English usage, Carr's claim is recommendatory rather than descriptive of our usage, since it makes perfect sense, context set right, to talk about good, but unscrupulous doctors, for example. However, as a recommendation about usage it has some considerable merit, and not just for those occupations described as 'professions'. If we could reorient the axis of our concern about the practice of occupations as a whole, taking into account their concern with excellent outcomes and the wider consequences of their practice, we might be able to move away from a narrow and incessant focus on skill to a broader conception of know-how. Dreyfus and Dreyfus' account of expertise does not really enable us to do that.

A seventh and final point about Dreyfus and Dreyfus' account relates to the concept of *excellence*. They are right in not specifying *excellence of outcome* as a necessary feature of expertise. In terms of know-how and action, the account can be seen as attempting to provide a specification of an excellent performance, characteristic of what one would expect of an expert practitioner. Whatever the merits of this account it is debateable, as already argued, whether understanding action can be conceptually detached from understanding the intended outcome of action, although the nature of the link is not a precise one and is not easy to specify. Classical discussions of excellence have tended to focus attention on the nature of the outcomes of expert performances rather than on the actions that lead to them and, while this may distort our understanding somewhat, is, nevertheless, an important feature of what we understand by expertise.[17]

As a preliminary point, we attribute excellence to activities and outcomes that are considered to be worthwhile or unusual accomplishments. So many activities that are far from automatic are often not considered to possess criteria of excellence because they are not considered to be worthwhile.[18] Activities that were once considered unusual, like the ability to read, were thought to be done in a way that could be described as manifesting excellence in outcome. Such an attribution would sound odd in an age of mass literacy. So the attribution of excellence is related to our appreciation of the nature of the activity. It is also worth pointing out that we do not always associate expertise with excellence, particularly in those cases, for example, where there are criteria for the accomplishment of an action, but the action itself is not one to which it is appropriate to attribute excellence. An excellent action or outcome is attributed on the basis of criteria appropriate to that activity or outcome. This is not just a matter of personal judgement, but of criteria which are more or less held in common by the relevant community, which could consist of practitioners and those who use and consume what results from action. In many cases the recognition and application of such criteria is unproblematic, but this is not always the case. There are many cases, for example, where the aims of the activity are unclear or contested. Notoriously this is often the case in education and hence judgements about what constitutes excellence in teaching cannot be settled according to criteria that are agreed upon by all the relevant parties.[19] In relation to attributions of excellence to performance, the Dreyfus and Dreyfus account of expert performance is a case in point, insofar as expert performances are judged to be superior to every other kind, since it is precisely the attribution of criteria for the excellence of expert actions that is the matter in contention.

Excellence, is, then, a not entirely unproblematic concept to work with in understanding expertise. Its attribution consists of a mixture of *conceptual* criteria, which may themselves be contested and *empirical* ones concerning what the evidence is that such-and-such is an expert performance or that so-and-so is an expert in an area. But this does not mean that it can be ignored, particularly in relation to the ontologically distinct results of expert performances.

Fluency Theories 2: The Reflective Practitioner (Schön)

It is impossible to underestimate the influence that Schön's account of reflective practice as a characterization of the expert (and indeed, the merely accomplished) practitioner has had. Despite criticism, it still continues to hold considerable sway, not just in academic commentary but perhaps more importantly in the regulation of initial and continuing professional and vocational education.[20] The core of Schön's account is that the accomplished or proficient professional is *reflective*, both in the course of professional action (reflection in action) and after action has been completed (reflection on action), although Schön puts considerably more importance on the former than on the latter. The important point in understanding Schön is grasping what is the *basis* for reflection and also what is its *subject matter*. According to Schön the expert reflects on actions carried out in professional contexts using experience of previous professional situations, as well as the current situation, as a basis for that reflection. This claim immediately raises the question as to whether or not professional activity, where action is mandated by a body of theory, can be underpinned by reflection which is largely detached from the mandating theory. One reason why Schön is reluctant to incorporate theory as an ingredient in any reflective process is that he wishes to offer an account of professional practice that avoids what he calls *technical rationality*, or the use of theory to construct schemata for action through norms derived from the relevant body of theory. As do Oakeshott, Ryle, and Dreyfus and Dreyfus, he regards such procedures as more characteristic of non-expert rather than expert performances and therefore to be avoided in any account of proficient and expert professional performance. Once again, there are echoes here of Ryle's 'bannisters for toddlers'.

Critique

A critical difficulty, however, with this approach is that, although some professional or semi-professional activity is thought not to require a systematic theoretical underpinning (teaching and nursing being perhaps paradigm examples), this is not true of, for example, medicine, law, engineering and architecture, where initial professional education requires prolonged acquaintance with the theoretical basis of the occupation and prolonged experience in applying that theory to practice. An account like that of Dreyfus and Dreyfus deals with this issue by arguing in effect that the need to refer to theory in professional activity is largely, although not completely, sloughed off when one reaches the level of expert. Dreyfus and Dreyfus do not, however, suppose that an expert can reflect *in action* as claimed by Schön. But, as we have seen in our critique of the Dreyfusian conception of expertise and in the discussion of the theory-practice relationship in Chapter 6, it is far from clear that the role of the mandating theory of a profession can be dispensed with at the level of expert performance. The best way of seeing this is, perhaps, through the extended consideration of an example.

Let us suppose that a tunnel engineer, drawing on the discipline of Geology for assessing the characteristics of tunnelling through certain kinds of rock, discovers that he has to work within a formation of different rocks and soil whose combined characteristics mean that he can no longer rely on previous experience working with these particular permutations of rock and soil. Nor can he rely on known facts about the characteristics of the types of rock and soil with which he is concerned because the relevant theories do not tell him enough about the properties of these materials in the kinds of combination which he has currently encountered. However, his previous experience and his geological knowledge, when combined, present him with plausible avenues for working out a viable strategy. In doing so, he not only draws on experience and theory, but is also potentially capable of making a contribution to practical Geology. His own personal theory of tunnelling, built up by an amalgam of experience, learning from fellow engineers and the systematic knowledge that he acquired in initial formation and subsequently, has also been extended.[21] There is no dichotomy between reflection on experience and reflection on theory; both are brought to bear in combination in a search for a solution to a particular problem. Schön's account of reflection manages to cover only one side of a much more complex story.

Schön's prioritization of reflection *in* action is also debateable. In the example above, the engineer reflects during the course of the project, but it is unlikely that he does so while on site supervising tunnelling operations in a situation of what Beckett and Hager call 'hot action'. More likely, he does so in the tranquillity of his office where he can refer to notes, books, and so on and maybe consult with colleagues who are at a distance. In this sense, the engineer's reflections are 'on' rather than 'in' as they occur after the problem has been encountered, but before it is solved. Indeed, it is debateable whether or not it is possible, in a meaningful sense, to reflect in 'operational conditions' where one is immersed in action and preoccupied by the exigencies of the situation one is in, whether it be the battlefield, workshop, classroom, building site, operating theatre, courtroom or ward. It is characteristic of such situations that they have one or more of the following features: they are safety critical, time critical, decisions have serious and far-reaching circumstances and mistakes made cannot be easily unmade. It is necessary to act thoughtfully and with attention in such situations and one may well have to 'think on one's feet' at times, but to call such thoughtful action and moments of *ad hoc* problem-solving 'reflection' is stretching usage of the term to implausibility. At most, it will be possible to engage in 'calculative rationality' using something like the second and more elaborate scheme for the competent practitioner described in the account of Dreyfus and Dreyfus above, in such a way as to engage in the 'rapid decision-making' of the proficient performer. If reflection in action, where 'action' is understood as 'working in operational conditions' is, however, practically unlikely, what of 'reflection' after one has withdrawn from operational conditions? In discussing this, we will move from Schön to consider the work of Bereiter and Scardamalia.

Bereiter and Scardamalia – a Processual-Experiential Account

Bereiter and Scardamalia focus on two aspects of expertise which, it was argued, are insufficiently attended to by Dreyfus and Dreyfus, namely the ability to do something that is excellent in that particular area of activity and also on the characteristics of individuals who are required to reach a standard of excellence in their work. They suggest that excellence is not achieved merely through long experience, and counsel against confusing the experienced with the expert practitioner, because the former may not be capable of producing excellent work, while the latter is. This characteristic, they argue, is achieved through a constant process of self-questioning, even when one has attained the status of expert, because, they maintain, one may cease to be one when one ceases to be either willing or able to maintain the high standards of performance characteristic of the expert.

This process of self-questioning is voluntary and invariably occurs outside operational conditions and can accurately be described as reflection on action. In Bereiter and Scardamalia's account it is precisely this *post hoc* ability to reflect that is crucial in building up expertise. It thus poses a meaningful and substantive alternative to both Dreyfus and Dreyfus and Schön. It might be objected that many people acknowledged as experts do not meet the standards that Bereiter and Scardamalia set, or that someone can somehow achieve their expert status without going through this process,[22] but this is to miss their important point, which is the emphasis on excellence and how it is achieved, which is neglected by other commentators. They present us with a picture of experts as individuals who are continually striving to improve their performance by engaging in the kind of reflection involving both experience and the theoretical underpinning of the occupation (where one exists) as materials. Interesting and quite persuasive examples are given of how the expert teacher is marked out from the one who is merely proficient, both in terms of what they can do and how they arrive at the capability to do what they can do.[23] It is this unwillingness to be satisfied with 'good enough' or 'satisficing' action that marks the expert out as someone wishing to and capable of achieving expertise.

Critique

This is promising, but unfortunately Bereiter and Scardamalia harden their insight into dogma by claiming that we should redefine expertise not as an attribute of the expert, but as a *process* which experts or those striving to be experts engage in. However, there is little to be gained from a somewhat arbitrary piece of redefinition, given that their point can perfectly well be accommodated within established ways of looking at expertise and offers a new insight, by rotating our investigation around the axis of *excellent performance*, rather than *fluent performance* as in the case of the other commentators considered earlier.

Bereiter and Scardamalia are concerned with the fact that relatively few people are experts. Given that they have a criterion-led definition of expertise and believe that such a criterion can be met by many more people than it currently is, they think that many more people can become experts. Their solution is to suggest that this can be achieved by people becoming, as early as possible, *experts in learning*. In their own terms, this means people whose learning (in the task sense) results in excellence (in the achievement sense) in terms of the quality of the knowledge and skill acquired. Moving from a useful insight about the nature of some expertise via an arbitrary redefinition of the concept of expertise, they arrive at a characterization of a particular kind of expertise underlying other expertises which is the key to the generation of many more experts.

The problem with their suggestion is not that there may not be individuals who achieve such excellence in the way in which they go about learning, or even that achievement of this expertise may not be an important condition of attaining expertise for many people. It is rather that they have fallen into the trap of thinking that there is a sovereign remedy for learning a skill, or competence of 'learning how to learn', which is capable of covering all cases of learning.[24] Even the studies that they cite, however, suggest that the ability to learn varies from subject matter to subject matter and that individuals vary in the kinds of things that they are good at learning about and how to do. We should not be surprised at this. The ability to learn is the ability to learn something or other and needs a more or less particular specification of the kind of material learned or to be learned in order to be intelligibly applied to anyone. Their own account also suggests something important about effective learning, namely that the individual who strives for excellence must care deeply enough about what they are doing to be patient and persistent enough to strive for better performance. In other words, in order to become an expert, one must seriously want to become one. It is difficult to see how someone could care about learning *per se*, without caring about the matter or activity which is to be learned. If this is the case, and this seems to be a plausible claim, since caring about learning as such is not to care about anything specific, then it is not helpful to characterize the would-be expert as someone who cares about learning rather than someone who cares about carrying out the activity that they care about in an excellent way. The issue about increasing the number of experts in any given field then becomes one about getting more people to care about achieving standards of excellence in a field. They cannot just be the putative future experts, but those who already practice and control the selection and education of future practitioners, as well as the society in which they operate. If society does not care about such matters, it is less likely that the practitioners or those who would strive to be practitioners will do so as well.

There is another problem with their suggestion which is that if an expert in learning is someone whose expertise consists in successfully learning, then they are, by that token, an expert in what they have learned. In that case they become an expert in the more traditional sense of the term and Bereiter and Scardamalia's account adds nothing new. If, on the other hand, they are experts in the process of learning then it is not clear why the self-questioning attitude characteristic of the expert is to be valued if it does not result (at least for much of the time) in excellent outcomes. And, if this is the case it is hard again to see what new insight is being offered by Bereiter and Scardamalia.

Conclusion

Various influential accounts of expertise have been examined. Each contains important insights. However, to the extent that each of these accounts attempts to construct a theory of expertise that will cover all cases it fails. In the next chapter we will look more closely at why this is so by considering the different dimensions through which expertise can be approached, depending on the subject of activity concerned. Such an examination will show us why the generality required of a theory of expertise cannot be achieved in the face of so much complexity and variety of human activity.

Notes

[1] For discussion see, Eraut, M. (1994) *Developing Professional Knowledge and Competence*, Brighton, Falmer Press, pp. 142–8.

[2] Dreyfus and Dreyfus (1996), pp. 30–1.

[3] See Brockmann, M., Clarke, L., Winch, C. (2008a) *Crossnational Synthesis of Project on European Vocational Qualifications*: http://www.kcl.ac.uk/schools/sspp/education/research/projects/eurvoc.html, consulted 15 July 2009.

[4] Hoffman, R. R. (1998) 'How can expertise be defined? Implications of research from cognitive psychology', in Williams, R., Faulkner, W., Fleck, J. (eds) *Exploring Expertise: Issues and Perspectives*, Basingstoke, MacMillan.

[5] Dreyfus and Dreyfus (1996). A later work, Dreyfus, H. L. (2001) *On the Internet*, London, Routledge, proposes two further stages of learning beyond the acquisition of expertise. The first is *mastery*, which is concerned with the acquisition of an individual style. The second is *practical wisdom* or *phronesis* in the sense introduced in Chapter 4. I consider these to be important dimensions of expertise and do not wish to query Dreyfus' identification of these as important elements in expertise. My purpose here is to critique the stage account of expertise offered in Dreyfus and Dreyfus (1996) and in particular their account of expertise, which is largely preserved intact in Dreyfus (2001).

[6] See the exposition in Eraut (1994), p. 124 to which the above account is indebted.

[7] Dreyfus and Dreyfus (1996); Chesla, C. (1996) *Expertise in Nursing Practice; Caring, Clinical Judgment and Ethics*, New York, Springer, pp. 29–49, p. 44.

[8] Ibid. p. 45.

[9] Ibid. p. 41.

[10] For more on such confused talk, see Bennett and Hacker (2003) esp. ch. 3, esp. sections 3.3, 3.4. On the other hand, there is evidence that some professionals (e.g. consultants) tend to use deduction rather than intuition in the clarification of situational specificities. This point makes it clear that it is the nature of the thinking, rather than the configuration of synapses that it is important to get clear about in understanding how judgements are made and of what kind they are. See Boreham, N. (1987) 'Learning from experience in diagnostic problem solving', in Richardson, J. T. E., Michael W. E., Piper, D. W. (eds) *Student Learning: Research in Education and Cognitive Psychology*, Guildford, SRHE, pp. 89–97, cited in Eraut (1994), p. 141.

[11] It may, therefore, make some use of transferable abilities, such as the use of logical schemata in the application of theory to practice. See Boreham (1987).

[12] Fodor, J. (2001), *The Mind Doesn't Work That Way*, Cambridge, MA, MIT Press, pp. 50–1.

[13] Compare, for example, the attributions of expertise to a teacher by her colleagues and the possession of the official status of 'Advanced Skills Teacher' in England.

[14] While also noting that someone who knew how to do something could not be always expected to do it in the relevant circumstances.

[15] The first point would be particularly relevant to those actions where the action and its results are spatially and temporally identical.

[16] Carr (1999).

[17] See, for example, Plato (1950) *The Republic*, London, MacMillan.

[18] This is not, of course, to suggest that others may not think them worthwhile, or that at other times and in other places they may not be considered worthwhile.

[19] See the discussion of 'good practice' in Alexander, R. (1992) *Policy and Practice in the Primary School*, London, Routledge, ch. 11, pp. 174–91.

[20] For example, Eraut (1994); Beckett, D., Hager, P. (2002) *Life, Work and Learning*, London, Routledge, p. 21.

[21] That is, his own set of principles concerning how he integrates his own knowledge with his practice, as opposed to the way that the theory itself sets out guidance to the practice.

[22] Although as Howe, M. (1990) argues from case studies, this is unlikely – see his *The Origins of Exceptional Abilities*, London, Routledge.

[23] Similar examples can be found in the work of Tsui, A. (2002) *Understanding Expertise in Teaching*, Cambridge, Cambridge University Press, pp. 245–82.

[24] Winch, C. (2008) 'Learning how to learn: a critique', *Journal of Philosophy of Education*, 42, 3–4, pp. 649–65.

Chapter 9

Novice, Journeyman, Expert

Introduction – the Aim of This Chapter

This chapter explores the various dimensions, both work and activity related, and epistemological, of expertise. Following from the discussion in Chapter 8, theory-building is avoided. We begin by explaining the distinction between crafts, technical activities and professional activities. The question is posed:

> Can there be an overarching theory of skilfulness and/or expertise or just various accounts that deal to varying degrees with how skilfulness and expertise manifest themselves in a range of different contexts and activities?

The interplay of *knowing how* and *knowing that* in the development of expertise will be examined and the question of how the relationship differs in various kinds of work will be considered. This issue will be discussed through a range of cases, exemplifying crafts, techniques and professions. The importance of *Wahrnehmung* or knowledge by acquaintance in the development of expertise will also be argued for. Ryle's account of the novice-expert distinction will also be revisited. The conclusion will be drawn that the related concepts of skilfulness and expertise can only be understood in a variegated way. There is no account of expertise that adequately captures all our understandings of those concepts and, in order to understand them, we need to relate them to the activities in which they are manifested.

Novice, Journeyman, Expert

We established in the previous chapter that there is not and cannot be a generalized theory of expertise. Nonetheless, the distinction between novice, journeyman and expert is important in vocational contexts and there are important issues at stake in establishing who is what in different occupations. The 'novice-expert continuum' has a range of related purposes. First to establish a basic level of capability, second to identify those who have progressed in the mastery of their occupation, third to identify those who achieve excellence in their occupation. There will be no general guidelines for doing this, but we hope to map out the conceptual territory in order to help those whose job it is to delineate different degrees of expertise in particular areas, to make sense of the complexity of their task. In order to do this satisfactorily a considerable amount of surveying of the conceptual territory will need to be done, from the perspective of understanding the growth of proficiency.

Know-How and Normative Structure

Chapter 5 set out and defended the claim that know-how needs to be understood in the context of the normative structures and activities in which it is exercised. It was argued in that chapter that normative structure can be understood both formally and informally and that the informal nature of many normative phenomena must be appreciated before we can fully understand them. It was also argued that rules may be understood in two ways: rigidly, that is, admitting of no exception; or alternatively as standing in need of interpretation in certain contexts so that they are defeasible. Part of the grasp of the normative structure in such cases is precisely an understanding of when norms are defeasible and when they are not. These distinctions between formal and informal normative structures on the one hand and between defeasible and non-defeasible norms on the other hand, will give us a starting-point for understanding what it is to be a novice in an activity.[1]

A novice is someone who is newly initiated into an activity and is, by definition, not fully able to participate. A novice needs to learn enough to satisfy whatever may be the criteria of most basic competence necessary for that activity. It is possible to identify a number of approaches to the induction and development of novices, each of which postulates a slightly different form of inculcation into normative structure.

'Legitimate Peripheral Participation' (LPP)

Lave and Wenger identify LPP as a central case of human induction into practices, whether of work or of some other type of activity or institution.

The idea of LPP is, first, that the novice is *entitled* to participate, that is he or she has some recognized right to be present in the activities to be carried out. The principal method of learning, according to Lave and Wenger's empirical studies, is that of the novice initially taking responsibility for some of the marginal activities in the occupation, usually those for which know-how already exists or is easily acquired. The classic case would be 'making the tea' in a film studio as the first step to one's ascent to become a Welles or a Schlesinger. Gradually, the peripheral participant, by dint of observation and imitation, and through the consent, tacit or otherwise of those core members of the occupation or workshop who control its activities, gradually assumes more and more responsibility for activities nearer the core of the occupation. Induction into the normative order of the occupation, in its technical, moral and political aspects, proceeds through the implicit grant-ing of rights to further participation in more and more of the core activ-ities until the formerly peripheral participant is a fully fledged practitioner of all the relevant occupational activities in what they term a 'community of practice'. Lave and Wenger appear to make the strong claim that both the process of acceptance and induction and that of learning itself is tacit, involving a minimum of explicit communication, but a good deal of para-linguistic indication through facial expression, gesture and posture.[2]

It is not difficult to see in this scenario quite strong affinities with an Oakeshottian view of practical knowledge. Because such knowledge is neces-sarily tacit it cannot be transmitted verbally, but must be acquired *in situ* and through participation in the activity itself. It is not dependent on explicit rules but on implicit norms transmitted in the paralinguistic manner indi-cated above. While LPP is undoubtedly an aspect of novice learning, their account is a highly selective and arguably romanticized picture of what nov-icehood consists of, certainly as a general case beyond their very limited range of empirical studies. It is not even 'learning with Nellie' in the sense that Nellie might well be expected to issue instructions and admonitions in the course of inducting a novice. It cannot be accepted as an anthropolo-gically reliable account of the greater part of human occupational induction because of its restricted resources for describing initiation and participation and the restricted empirical base from which it is derived.

Recipe Following

Ryle's account of knowing how relies heavily on the contrast between the novice and the accomplished practitioner. The novice requires rules, usually explicit, for guidance. Such rules, formal and explicit, provide non-interpretative guidance in the basic aspects of the activity. Mrs Beeton's cookbooks and Isaac Walton's fishing manual provide examples of what is meant.[3] Ryle does not consider the presence of Mrs Beeton or Isaac Walton to the novice and the difference this might make to their initiation. The suggestion is that the novice takes the rule and applies it to the situation in a rigid manner at first, gradually gaining in fluency, proficiency, situational awareness and interpretative ability. Oakeshottian *technical knowledge* peculiar to the novice is gradually transformed into something more like *practical knowledge* in Oakeshott's sense by dint of practice and training. There are a couple of slightly puzzling aspects of Ryle's account which don't quite fit together. The first puzzle is to do with his tendency to characterize the normative structure of the activity in terms of principles that then become discarded, just as the toddler, who initially needed banisters, can now walk down the stairs without anything to guide her. It is as if toddling apparently requires a normative structure while walking does not. As we noted in Chapter 5, it is misguided to see such activities as walking and talking not being bounded by a normative structure. It is as if the transition from novicehood to proficiency is, at the same time, a transition from norm-guided to norm-free performance.

The second puzzling feature is Ryle's apparent tendency to ignore the role of knowing that in the acquisition of proficiency. Neither the cookbooks of Mrs Beeton, nor *The Compleat Angler* consist solely of prescriptions. They may not contain theoretical descriptions of the chemical properties of flour or eggs or of the hydrodynamics of piscine morphology, but they do say a great deal about the properties of ingredients and the habits of different species of fish that are relevant to the novice cook or angler. Part of what the novice is expected to do is not just to follow instructions but to gain some practical understanding of the properties of eggs and flower or the feeding habits of perch in order that he formulate his own principles for action relevant to his own circumstances.[4] These examples suggest that the novice is a solitary, in contrast to the LPP model, where the novice is necessarily part of a community. The model presented looks like one that a solitary might follow in teaching himself. Such a person, the *autodidact*, is often criticized for the lack of a nuanced understanding of the material that he has attempted to master. This is to no small extent because there has been no-one on hand to provide the interpretation necessary in order to develop the novice's situational awareness.

However, Ryle was also alive to the social nature of leaning and in other places this is made clear. Particularly helpful is his distinction between *training* and *drilling.*

> Training, on the other hand, though it embodies plenty of sheer drill, does not consist of drill. It involves the stimulation by criticism and example of the pupil's own judgment. He learns how to do things thinking what he is doing, so that every operation performed is itself a new lesson to him on how to perform better.[5]

Drilling is a process which involves the explicit and repetitive inculcation of patterns of behaviour until they become automatic. By itself, it does not involve the development of *judgement,* which training does. And, as Ryle makes clear, training involves a trainer as well as a trainee. It is not absurd to suggest that the trainer is also someone who can interpret the principles set out in recipe books, and so on in a way that is intelligible to the novice. Ryle does, then, provide the elements of a much richer concept of novicehood than the recipe-following examples might suggest.

Horizontal, Vertical and Scope Dimensions of Expertise

There are three ways in which expertise can be understood, which are not often clearly distinguished. The first way was drawn attention to in Recipe Following section, and it is based, as noted, on the academic conception of expertise as a growing acquaintance with and grasp of a subject. In more recent schemes of this kind, such as the EQF metaframework, a category of personal characteristics such as responsibility and autonomy are added to the hierarchy of expertise, although in the German system such personal characteristics are intrinsic to the concept of *berufliche Handlungsfähigkeit* or occupational action-competence (see Chapter 4 for more detailed treatment). The growth of expertise in this sense is linked to the growth of the use of systematic knowledge (*Wissen*), the application of this in problem-solving abilities and the growing capacity for autonomy and responsibility for other workers.[6] It is assumed that the development of expertise in each of these three categories will more or less match each other at each relevant level. This conception of expertise is linked with the growth of formal educational qualifications and progression in a managerial hierarchy. It will be looked at more closely in the next section. It is not, however, the only way in which expertise can be understood.

In order to understand this, it may be most helpful to take an activity like a traditional craft, in which initial formation does not take place through formal education or the acquisition of *Wissen* but rather through the application of contingent knowledge and perceptual discrimination to the application of know-how that involves dexterity together with co-ordination, or, in other words, to skill in the primary sense (see Chapter 3). The practice of a fisherman working in a traditional fishing community on a riverbank might conform to this model. We can assume that there are no formal qualifications attached to the practice of the activity, but that a novice fisherman is accepted into the community of fishers on the basis of an apprenticeship of some kind. At this point he or she is expected to be able to practice in such a way that he makes a productive contribution to the work of the fishing community, that is, he contributes to whatever surplus is made. Within this community there is little or no formal hierarchy of management or expertise, but those deemed to have high ability in the activities associated with fishing have informal authority and their advice is taken seriously. In addition, they may be taken to have a certain moral authority, especially in matters concerned with all aspects of the occupation. This model conforms quite well to the LPP model and the kind of account of practice given by writers such as Oakeshott and MacIntyre.

What does expertise consist in, in such a situation? It cannot be the same as the 'vertical' model described above because it lacks the basic features of academic expertise and managerial hierarchy characterized by that model of expertise. Nevertheless, it is not at all implausible to suppose that this would be the traditional form in which expertise was and is recognized in many craft occupations whose continued renewal does not depend on educational qualifications and whose structure is, to a large extent, informal. In order to understand the nature of what is going on here, we need to remind ourselves of a central feature of know-how that any satisfactory account needs to recognize, namely that know-how is subject to normative evaluation, that is, one performance may be considered to be better than another, either that of the same individual or different ones. This claim may or may not involve the deployment of academic knowledge, and Ryle, rightly in my view, makes the case that expertise in this sense (the ability to perform *skilfully*) does not require this. Instead, evaluative criteria internal to the practice (in the sense described above) are brought to bear on the exercise of know-how. Such evaluative criteria employ concepts that are particular to the practice itself (in this case to do with fish and their habits, together with the techniques and knowledge necessary for catching

them, for example), and also employ concepts which apply to many different activities (care, attention, cunning, patience, insight, intuition, quick-
ness of perception and of learning might all be examples). The expert in
this sense will be someone who has great experience of a large variety of
different situations, including unusual ones, who can perceive the salient
relevant features of a complex or unusual situation, who can quickly size up
what is required in a typical situation, whose local knowledge of relevant
conditions, habits, seasonal changes, and so on is very great,[7] and who can
pass on knowledge, skill and experience, not necessarily in a discursive
manner.[8]

It would be an exaggeration to claim that the 'horizontal' conception of
expertise, that is, the growth in ability within a particular category of activity or within an occupation has no affinities with a 'vertical' conception of
expertise. For example, the experienced fisherman will have more knowledge than the less experienced (even though this is likely to be *Kenntnis*
rather than *Wissen*), and may well have a position of responsibility for the
carrying out of work and for the supervision of less experienced practitioners. But in many cases, such knowledge and autonomy is informally recognized and is seen as a widening and deepening of the range of abilities
that are already required for successful practice. In addition, of course,
'horizontal' expertise involves factors that don't necessarily involve additional knowledge or independence, such as sureness of technique, grasp of
a range of techniques and ability to cope with change and unusual professional situations. Such abilities need not be preceded by formal learning,
nor be accompanied by an ability to explain what the agent is doing, but
can be observed by the excellence of the way in which the work is carried
out and the quality of what results from that work. Ryle's examples of the
growth of technique in activities such as fishing and cooking tend to fit well
with this pattern and his account makes a good match with the idea that
know-how is linked with evaluative 'intelligence concepts' whose application depends on the nature of the activity being evaluated. It is less well
suited to 'vertical expertise'.

One point, however, should not be neglected, namely that horizontal
expertise is closely linked, not just with the concept of *mastery* of the activity
concerned, which could consist in regular and reliable high-quality performance, but also with the idea of *excellence*, or the idea that one should
aim for the very best kind of performance possible. This is not to claim
that an expert must be a person who strives for excellence as Bereiter and
Scardamalia seem to do, but to say that there is a significant connection
between expertise and excellence in the sense that it is in the practitioner

whose work is widely admired that one may hope to find both excellent work and the striving for excellence in what is done.

The conception of 'horizontal' expertise then is not something peripheral or outdated, but is fundamental to our understanding of practical knowledge. Anyone wishing to attain mastery of a particular occupation or activity has to move along a path towards expertise in this sense. As commentators have noted, as the growth of mastery does not depend on the gaining of educational qualifications, the ways in which that mastery is to be attained are very much based on practice and experience of the activity or occupation itself, possibly, but not necessarily, under the more or less informal tutelage of experienced practitioners. Indeed, as we saw in Chapter 2, only some accounts of practical knowledge are able to provide a satisfactory account of what it might be to become an expert in this sense. We need to understand horizontal forms of expertise in terms of criteria of quality that are internal to the activity itself, bearing in mind that the activity itself is unlikely to be hermetically sealed from the larger culture and society in which is exists. What MacIntyre has called the 'internal goods' of the activity as well as some of the 'external goods' which Hager argues should be taken account of are both the result and the objective of activities that aim at expertise.[9] To understand expertise in this sense is to be acquainted with the activity, its traditions and the ways in which it relates to other activities and to the wider society and culture in which it exists. The work of MacIntyre and of Ryle are helpful in gaining an understanding of what this involves, despite some of the problems in the accounts of expertise that they offer.

The third sense of expertise relates to the *scope* of activity. Agency is related to action categories such as task, job and occupation and, as such, is connected with the range of activities that someone may undertake within such an action category. A task or, strictly a task-type, is a recurrent action to be performed which involves one or more acts of judgement usually connected with the carrying out of a limited project: sawing the plank, fixing the door, teaching the lesson, performing the operation – would all be examples of tasks. A job consists of the range of tasks which an individual is contracted to carry out. This might be within an occupational context (see below) or it might involve no more than a range of more or less related tasks. The most important category for our purposes is, however, the occupation, which itself has a different significance in different cultures. In its conceptually richest form it is a socially recognized action category connected with the production or carrying out of particular types of goods or services of recognized social and economic value. Traditional crafts, the German *Beruf,* the French *métier* and the English *profession* would all be examples of occupations in this sense. As such, it does not just involve a collection of tasks, but of their sequencing and integration, together with the co-ordination of a given occupation with other, related ones (e.g. the bricklayer with the carpenter, the railway manufacturer with the track engineer, the lawyer with the psychiatrist, to give but a few examples). It very often recognizes the necessity for certain distinct personal qualities including a degree of independence and discretion. Countries and economies differ greatly in the extent to which they conceptualize economic activity in terms of occupations or in terms that are more task-oriented. The latter are usually narrower in their sphere and co-ordination of operations than the former.

The Growth of Competence (Vertical)

We are probably more familiar with the 'vertical' concept of competence which is a product of two related phenomena: the impact of systematic knowledge on know-how and the growing involvement of formal educational institutions on the accreditation of suitability for occupations and jobs. This is hardly a new phenomenon, the mediaeval universities, for example, provided a formal education for entry into professions such as the law and medicine, while entry into crafts was regulated by the trade guilds through a system of apprenticeship with a career path towards becoming a master craftsman, although this progression was not necessarily connected with educational qualification and hence had more affinities with 'horizontal' progression towards expertise.[10]

With the involvement of educational institutions and the concept of an educational qualification has come the growth in the 'vertical' conception of expertise, based on the application of systematic knowledge to the practice of an occupation. Not that all occupations have become based on such knowledge, but there has been a strong tendency to organize occupational activity under the influence of a conception of action that involves the application of systematic knowledge to practice in complex operational conditions. This organization is, in turn, closely related to the development of academic and vocational educational qualifications that provide a guarantee, both of the possession of the relevant systematic knowledge and of the ability to apply it in practice. In what follows, I will set out schematically what such a conception of expertise involves, while noting that it will take different forms in different societies. However, the classification offered is implicitly hierarchical, both in the sense that it is related to the organization of knowledge in educational institutions and in the sense that it is also, to a certain extent, related to managerial responsibility.

Crafts

The traditional concept of a craft involved the production of a good or the provision of a service through the practice of *technique* or a way of doing something embodied in the skill and competence of the craftsman (or woman in some cases). Induction into crafts has traditionally occurred through some form of apprenticeship, with horizontal progression towards expertise as a master craftsman being the normal career route. Craft activities have traditionally been characterized by the practice of *skill* in its core sense, of the employment of manual and co-ordinative ability, typically in a wide range of occupational activities.

The practice of a craft involved propositional knowledge, usually of a local and implicit kind, to do with tacit grasp of the materials used, the needs of customers in local conditions, the peculiarities of the apparatus used, and so on. Such knowledge can often be acquired both through practice and conversation with other practitioners. The LPP is too abstract a model to really take full account of the complexity and variety of such processes and the role that conversations of various kinds play in the life of crafts.

Two important points should be noted about craft activity. First, that it is rarely just about the practice of *technique*, but about the practice of technique in a human and social context. Craft work in the traditional sense should be distinguished from the fragmented labour process to be found in industrial societies, whose work organization is based on a disassembling of the range of tasks associated with an occupation, together with the removal of personal control over the labour process. By the 'labour process' I mean the integrated and connected series of activities and tasks carried out by individuals serially, but usually within a co-operative social context which results in the creation of a service or product. The labour process in this sense is connected with the creation of something or other and describes the conception and planning, activities, social co-ordination and evaluation necessary to bring that something about. Some philosophers have remarked on the way in which this process of creation does, in an important sense, give voice to an important aspect of our humanity, our ability to conceive of, plan and to put into effect a project of some kind through an integrated series of intentional activities.[11] By contrast, the fragmentation of the labour process described by Adam Smith in *The Wealth of*

Nations, by Frederick Taylor in *The Principles of Scientific Management* and as 'Fordism' or the application of Taylor's principles to the use of machinery in a production-line, have restricted the role of the operative to the repetition of particular tasks (the 'work process') with an abstraction of conception, planning, co-ordination and evaluation from the work undertaken, as well as any role in invention, innovation and improvement. A significant part, but by no means the whole of the complaint against the dismantling of the labour process in conditions of industrial production, is that it also evacuates the social and moral context in which work is conducted: the relationships with fellow workers (see the quote from Weil in note 11), the customers and clients, the apprentices and other outside bodies. The point is that induction into a craft activity is not merely a matter of learning a technique, but also involves becoming a part of a moral community in which the development of character is important.

The second point worth making about crafts concerns the traditional nature of craft work, in which knowledge and skill is passed on through informal and tacit methods, suggesting that it is static and conservative. However, this has never really been the case. The context of crafts does not preclude either incremental innovation or invention or the impact of new technologies on the practice of the craft.[12] Indeed, there is some evidence that the practice of crafts was distrusted for this, among other reasons and that the crafts and their practitioners were closely regulated in, for example, Greek city states such as Athens, to prevent their abilities and techniques from threatening the aristocratic social order.[13] The striving for professional excellence, the mark of someone who has to earn their living through the practice of technique, is also thought by some to be inimical to a life of cultivated leisure and hence to be discouraged among the leisured classes.[14] The practice of traditional crafts has always had a tendency towards dynamism within the context of traditional practice and should not be necessarily seen as unable to change or to respond to changing circumstances.

Technical Occupations

It is common nowadays to distinguish crafts from technical occupations, not just in terms of nomenclature, but also in terms of the nature of the activities. This distinction is also commonly made in terms of the formal educational level required for practice. Once again it is necessary to emphasize that we are not dealing with sharp and clear distinctions in every case, but with similarities and differences between crafts and technical occupations. The key to understanding this difference lies in the nature of the knowledge that or propositional knowledge deployed in each case. In technical occupations, as opposed o crafts, a significant part of the knowledge required for practice is based on systematic propositional knowledge (*Wissen* as opposed to *Kenntnis*) either normative, or empirical, or a mixture of both. This has momentous consequences for vocational education and for the conceptualization of expertise.

Technicians[15]

At first sight, it might seem that a technical occupation is something that requires little ability, particularly if we think in terms of Oakeshott's category of *technical knowledge*. There, as we saw, the conception was of the putting into effect of rigid rules of practice, these rules being derived from a body of knowledge. To recall a schema set out in Chapter 6, the model of action to carry out a task proposed is

1. A desires or intends that p.
2. A believes that doing ψ will bring about p.
3. A does ψ.

And the claim that

4. *doing ψ will bring about* p

is not inferred by the agent, but by someone who has conducted enquiries into the matter and who can authoritatively determine that this is so through the presentation of evidence to the effect that, in the main

5. *doing ψ correctly does bring about* p *in the vast majority of instances.*

The consequence is that there is a division of labour between someone who has determined that 5 and has prescribed that 4, which, in turn, is all that the agent needs to know in order to bring about p. Someone operating in such a way I call an 'executive technician' as all they do is to execute a precept derived from someone else on the basis of interrogation of a body of systematic knowledge. Such a person, whose area of discretion is much less than that of a craft worker, is not a technician in the normally understood use of that term. Such a person in fact bears close affinities, if not identity, to the 'Taylorized' or 'Fordized' worker described above.

A technician in the sense in which that term is normally understood (an autonomous technician) is someone whose grasp of the relevant body of systematic knowledge is such as to allow them to infer 2 from belief in 5 and thus to use the body of systematic knowledge to devise a plan of action and to carry it out. Such a person will have some expertise in the body of knowledge that underpinning the technical occupation sufficient for him or her to work out a plan of action on the basis of (a) the systematic knowledge; (b) the aims of the activity; (c) the constraints of the situation in which the activity is to take place. Conditions b and c are of enormous importance to this enquiry as the claim that technical knowledge is the mere application of rules is a tendentious one. Rules normally have to have a context in which they are applied, and sometimes no interpretation is necessary in order to apply those rules. Consider, however, a situation in which an electrician has to devise and install electrical wiring in a house. What he can do is constrained by the amount and type of power available, together with the equipment at his disposal. These facts in turn impose normative as well as physical constraints on his action which have to be taken account of in planning. But they are not rules of the type:

6. *do X.*

But rather of the type:

7. *if you want to achieve X you must take account of Y.*

Such a rule is not an unconditional imperative but a hypothetical advisory constraint which does not directly prescribe action. In fact, since b and c as well as a have to be taken account of, it is not even in itself a hypothetical action prescription as it needs to be considered in terms of both the task (the wiring of the house) and the local conditions (budget, time, equipment, state of the building, electrical mains, etc.) which will themselves generate decision procedures like 7. It can, therefore, be seen that the type of means-ends reasoning characteristic of 'technical rationality' is of a highly complex kind, and involves repeated decision-making which relies not just on repeatedly using (implicitly or explicitly) structures of the general schematic form:

1. A desires or intends that p.
2. A believes that doing ψ correctly does bring about p in the vast majority of instances.

3. A believes that doing ψ (or some variant of it) in these particular circumstances will bring about p.
4. A does ψ.

but integrating them with each other in a sequence of action. The autonomous technician is someone who works like a craftsman in many respects, but who has also got to take into account a body of relevant systematic knowledge as part of the formulation and execution of action sequences. In order to do this, the technician must be introduced to the relevant systematic knowledge to such an extent that it can serve him as the basis for independent decision-making in operational situations. The basic 'threshold' competence of the technician must, then, depend on a certain level of academic education before even probationary, let alone controlled operational practice is possible, without the threat of failure or even of death and injury. The growth of expertise 'horizontally' (as an autonomous technician) will only occur partially, if at all, not through further instruction in the underpinning discipline or disciplines, but rather through increasing ability to apply the systematic (or theoretical) knowledge in a wide variety of demanding practical situations.[16] It may well also be the case that the technician will discover a range of cases where:

doing ψ correctly does bring about p in the vast majority of instances

does not apply and where some or maybe no variant of ψ is effective. Such discoveries are obviously relevant epistemic constraints on the kinds of decision that the technician is likely to make, and will inform action, maybe as additional *ad hoc* non-systematic knowledge that will constitute part of his expertise. However, such discoveries may also be seen as contributions to the underlying systematic theoretical basis of the occupation, in the sense that the theory requires a number of peripheral qualificatory propositions about the circumstances in which it is of general application. At the extreme, such technical discoveries may attack the core part of the theoretical basis of the activity and bring about revisions in the theory.[17] We may envisage a variety of kinds of autonomous technician, each with their own horizontal continuum of expertise, with different levels of engagement with underpinning systematic knowledge. Normally the technician is thought of as someone whose academic engagement with the relevant systematic knowledge is at level 3 in the national and European frameworks, roughly equivalent to A level, Baccalauréat or Realschule Abschluss. It is, however, possible and indeed required, to consider levels of technical know-how that depend on a higher level of academic knowledge such as are to be found in Higher Apprenticeships in the United Kingdom, for example, which issue in qualifications at level 4 or 5 or the lower tiers of higher education.

Technologists[18]

At some point, we may wish to describe the engagement of a worker with the underlying theory to be of such an extent that it is no longer appropriate to consider contribution to the application of theory in local conditions to be a peripheral, although perhaps important part of his work, but to acknowledge that the engagement with the theoretical side of the occupation has become a significant part of the labour process involved in the occupation. Such a person is a *technologist* rather than a *technician*. This is not to say that there is necessarily a sharp break between these two types of work, but there is at least a significant change of emphasis. The technologist will have one or more of the following characteristics:

1. A more thorough academic knowledge of the discipline than the technician, which would allow him or her to be able to access, assess and contribute to the systematic underpinning knowledge relating to the occupation.
2. Engagement with the development of techniques and equipment for technical application based at least in part on the systematic underpinning knowledge relating to the occupation. This would include what is often called 'invention', both incremental and radical.
3. Ability to cope with more complex and unusual technical problems than a technician, including those that involve interrogating and making use of advanced features of the systematic underpinning knowledge relating to the occupation.
4. Ability to plan, to co-ordinate and evaluate the work of teams of technicians, according to a large-scale project strategy that extends from initial specification to final evaluation.

The Researcher

Just as there is no clear cut-off point (except in formal terms) between a technician and a technologist, this is also true of the technologist and the researcher. Researchers, unlike technologists, will have a closer relationship to the underpinning systematic knowledge and a more distant relationship to occupational practice than will the technologist. However, research in this sense often results, like the work of the technologist, in innovation and invention. However, unlike the technologist, the primary focus of the researcher's efforts is the acquisition of knowledge in the area relevant to the occupation, and, in the case of applied research, this knowledge will be directed towards the creation of a product or a service. The role of research biochemists, pharmacists and others in the pharmaceutical industry are cases in point.

The transition from novice to expert, conceived of 'vertically' rather than 'horizontally', is thus largely a story of increasing involvement with the underpinning systematic or theoretical knowledge that is associated with the occupation. It is broadly true that horizontal and vertical forms of expertise can develop independently of each other and that a practitioner at a research or technologist level need not be a technician in order to acquire the competence necessary to become a technologist or researcher. The question of whether 'vertical ascent' from technician to researcher during the course of one's career is possible or desirable is, however, a very interesting question which will receive further attention in the next chapter. The issue here is not merely whether this is a good way of maintaining a supply of good technologists and researchers but is also to do with the value of qualifications, not merely as a condition of entry into the labour market but also as a marker of academic educational achievement and an instrument of social mobility. The term often used to describe the degree of 'vertical ascent' possible is 'permeability'. A qualification is permeable with respect to the relevant academic qualification above it in the vertical hierarchy if it is acceptable as an entry qualification to the pursuit of a programme leading to that (higher) qualification. The desirability of permeable qualifications and the possible barriers to their construction will be considered in Chapter 10.

The growth of competence and personal development: the cumulation of competence; self-discovery, the growth of individuality, civic growth
So far, the understanding of expertise has been set out in terms of the possession of know-how, either in terms of skills or more holistic abilities which may include some form of occupational competence, or in terms of the ability to apply systematic knowledge to an occupation. However, this treatment of expertise is open to a radical objection of incompleteness, which is indeed one of the themes of this book. The objection is this: the development from novice to expert, whether horizontally or vertically, is

not merely about ability to perform occupationally, but is also about personal and civic growth and, furthermore, all these factors are related to each other in one significant understanding of what it means to become an expert. The point is that progression from novice to expert is not just a matter of becoming better at the carrying out of the activities associated with an occupation, when considered under the aspect of the quality of the product or the service created, considered in isolation from its environment, but is also to do with the *process* by which it is brought into being as well as the individual social, political and moral context in which it is brought into being. In Chapter 4, the conceptualization of skill in morally neutral terms was criticized, using Kerschensteiner's concept of a 'bourgeois virtue', whose practice, although necessary to the pursuit of excellence, has within it the danger of turning individual practitioners into *banausai* or those whose primary motivation is greed or financial reward.[19] But acceptance of the concept of 'bourgeois' or 'technical' virtue in the practice of skill is not enough to describe the moral dimension of practice and the growth of expertise.

It is desirable, for the moral health of the individual, or the occupation or society in which it exists that experts are no *banausai*, even when they have achieved mastery of technical virtue in the practice of their technique. Anticipating this problem, Kerschensteiner, as we saw in Chapter 4, distinguished between bourgeois virtues (*bürgerliche Tugenden*) and civic virtues (*staatsbürgerliche Tugenden*) which are concerned with a person's relationships not just with his immediate work, but with his sociomoral environment and with the polity of which he is a member.[20] If we shift the focus of the growth of expertise away from the practice of skill to that of the growth of *occupational competence* or *berufliche Handlungsfähigkeit*, as suggested in Chapter 4, then the issue of personal development as part of the development from novice to expert comes to the fore. Growth towards expertise then takes place horizontally not just in terms of technical proficiency (even technical proficiency informed by 'bourgeois virtue'), but also in terms of growth as a human being with a growing individuality and presence in their society.[21]

This involves the growth of personal identification with the occupation that one is pursuing, with a commitment to its traditions, values and future well-being, not to mention its place within the society and culture. There are 'external goods' of intrinsic value to be pursued by the authentic worker-citizen, which remove the potential stigma of becoming a *banausos*, even in terms of pursuing excellence in a narrow sense of producing high-quality work for financial gain. Even a person who is not a *banausos* but who remains occupationally focused in a narrow sense is, according to some accounts, not fully human. Occupational consciousness, although it may be a necessary component of civic consciousness, is not the same thing.

Occupational consciousness, without a broader civic consciousness, implies a fractured society and limited people. Hölderlin's complaint, that on returning to Germany, he encountered not people, but occupations, captures something of the problem.[22]

But, just as important is the growth of individuality. This includes the development of oneself as a distinctive individual, even though one is the practitioner of an occupation. In Chapter 4, the point was made that the growth of one's character, partly achieved through the practice of the virtues in the broadest sense is one's growth as an individual, because, but not exclusively because, of the way in which one practises the virtues. The growth of unique individuality, partly through occupational engagement, is an important theme in Germanic culture, reflected both the literature and in educational theory and policy. The literary *Bildungsroman* tradition, emphasizes the hero's self-discovery through occupational engagement.[23] Learning to become and to develop as, a worker, then, may become a critical part of the completion of one's education in Humboldt's sense of *allgemeine Menschenbildung* in the course of which character is formed in a way that integrates the young worker into the society of which he is a part, while at the same time developing his individual uniqueness.[24] Unlike the educational experiences of the *Bildungsroman* tradition, this need not be a preliminary to a different sort of life, but to one which composes part of a worthwhile existence. Humboldt, for example, recognizes that paid employment is the fate of most citizens. It need be a demeaning fate, however, only if individuals lack the general education and character formation that allows themselves to develop in work in adult life.[25]

Excellence and Creativity

The previous chapter was quite critical of certain theories of expertise and the ways in which some commentators talk about *excellence* and *creativity* was commented on critically. In this section, I would like to say something about the roles that both of these concepts play in the understanding of expertise. While it is true to say that experts are generally excellent at what they do, it is not necessarily the case that they constantly strive for

excellence, as Bereiter and Scardamalia suggest. These authors do, however, draw attention to something important, namely that it is a central
feature of the work of many experts and expert practitioners that they
do strive for excellence in their work and, as a result themselves develop
as practitioners. We will not understand fully what this means, however,
unless we take into account the field of action in which the practitioner
is located. We have suggested that *occupation* rather than *task* or *job* be
taken as the central focus for our consideration and, paradigmatically, the
conception of *Beruf* with its associated conception of agency as *berufliche
Handlungsfähigkeit* which, as we have seen, encompasses more than the
purely technical aspects of performance. Taking this as a point of reference, excellence (and the attempt to reach it) can be seen as multifaceted,
involving a strong affective element of identification with internal criteria
of production but also with a concern for the reputation of the profession,
for the needs of the client, for the future generation of workers, for the
social and civic implications of professional activity as well as the excellent
performance of particular tasks, because these will be part of a larger
conceptualization of professional activity, to be understood in the context
of what the aims of the occupation are.[26]

We would not be surprised to find an expert in this sense of the term to
be someone who exercises powers of *imagination* which will be found in a
lesser degree in merely proficient performers. The expert will want to see
matters, not just from his or her own perspective of completing a series of
tasks to a high standard, but as possibilities of desired outcomes that may
concern clients, other interested parties, apprentices, and so on.[27] It may
involve, visual or audial imagery, but often the capacity to articulate what
is required in *this situation* for *this person*. It may also involve the increasing
discrimination of *perception*: the ability to notice features or even aspects of
a situation not available to the novice or non-professional, for example, and
to notice these in a way directed towards reaching for excellence in performance. As pointed out by Wittgenstein, this capacity to notice aspects
is connected, not just with sensory or cognitive ability, but also with the
use of the *will* and preparedness to see things in a certain way, which may
require an *effort* or a change in how one goes about matters.[28] The capacity for professional imagination is often developed through the desire to
improve and its growth is part of the character/vocational development of
the individual.[29]

Imaginative growth is then part of the growth of the person, not of
brain capacity (although changes may occur to the brain as a result of this
process).[30] The exercise of imagination in this sense of the envisaging of

possibilities that may result in the excellence of what is made or created is usually thought to be an important aspect of the exercise of *creativity*, another often claimed feature of the expert. This is not to say, of course, that all experts and all manifestations of expertise must involve the exercise of imagination, let alone of creativity. However, although not tight logical connections, the looser conceptual connections between *expertise, the striving for excellence, the development of imagination, originality* and *creativity* are significant ones, which both the vocational educator and the educatee would do well to keep in mind.

The envisaging of possibilities that are not routinely obvious often results in the solution to problems that are original in the sense that they would not be present to the mind at first consideration of the problem. When these possibilities are envisaged in the context of wishing to achieve a solution of the highest standard within the general normative structure of the occupation, it is fair to say that success does lead to activity that may be acknowledged as creative, in the sense that it involves work in a recognizable genre, achieves the highest standards and has elements of originality about it.[31] It is often said that creative individuals break with the normative structure of the occupation, profession, genre in which they are working and, consequently, their products and performances do as well. This claim has a large element of truth, but also needs to be treated with a necessary qualification. An important part of our grasp of norms is the ability to *interpret*, not merely in the sense of *seeing what is required in this circumstance*, but also in the sense of *this is another possibility for satisfying/following this normative structure* or even *this norm/rule/convention/way of operating* can be understood in this *different* way.[32] In other words, normative structure can provide a flexible field of operation for professional activity involving knowing how, both giving it a sense and also allowing for innovation.

Concluding Remarks

The main focus of concern has been expertise in the 'horizontal' sense, while acknowledging that the growth of systematic underpinning knowledge as a relevant factor in expertise has accentuated the tendency to think of expertise in 'vertical' terms as well. Expertise has many facets, not all of which are present in any given instance of an expert or of expertise. However, important features of expertise in professional contexts have been mentioned, namely the ability to deal with the non-routine and the notion of excellence as an occupational attribute.

Notes

[1] Here, as elsewhere, we assume the context of discussion is the richest form of occupational institution, the *Beruf*. Remarks, where relevant, also apply to professions, occupations, jobs and tasks.

[2] Lave and Wenger (1991), ch. 3, pp. 59–88.

[3] Ryle (1946), p. 222.

[4] Walton, I. [1653] (1982) *The Compleat Angler*, Oxford, Oxford University Press; Beeton, I. (1861) *Mrs Beeton's Book of Household Management*, London, S. O. Beeton Publishing.

[5] Ryle (1949), p. 43.

[6] European Union (2006) *Recommendation of the European Parliament and Council on the Establishment of a European Qualification Framework for Lifelong Learning*, pp. 18–20.

[7] See, for example, Smith [1776] (1981) on agricultural workers, Bk 1, section 10, p. 79. In a commercial activity, knowledge of customers and markets would also be important.

[8] See, for example, Sturt (1923), ch. 27.

[9] Hager, P. (2008) 'Refurbishing Macintyre's concept of a practice', unpublished ms.

[10] Clarke, L. (1999) 'The changing structure and significance of apprenticeship with special reference to construction', in Ainley, P., Helen Rainbird, H. (eds) *Apprenticeship: Towards a New Paradigm of Learning*, London, Kogan Page.

[11] See, for example, Marx (1970a) (1887); (1970b) *Economic and Philosophic Manuscripts of 1844*, London, Lawrence and Wishart. Kerschensteiner [1901] (1964), pp. 5–88; (1906), pp. 5–25. Another striking example, which brings out the social nature of the labour process can be found in Simone Weil: 'a team of workers on a production-line under the eye of a foreman is a sorry spectacle, whereas it is a fine sight to see a handful of workmen in the building trade, checked by some difficulty, ponder the problem each for himself, make various suggestions for dealing with it, and then apply unanimously the method conceived by one of them, who may or may not have any official authority over the remainder. At such moments the image of a free community appears almost in its purity.' Weil, S. (2001) *Oppression and Liberty*, London, Routledge, p. 95.

[12] See Sturt (1923), for examples.

[13] See, for example, Cuomo, S. (2007) *Technology and Culture in Greek and Roman Antiquity*, Cambridge, Cambridge University Press, ch. 1, pp. 7–40.

[14] See the comments of Aristotle on music education; Aristotle (1988) *The Politics*, Bk 7, section 13, in Everson edition, p. 179 on this point. See also Plato (1975), Bk 1, where training for excellence in trade is explicitly discounted as a form of education, Saunders edition, p. 73.

[15] The terms 'technician', 'technologist' and 'researcher' are here used in a generic way and include but are not exhausted by the usual use of the term to relate to 'technical' occupations which involve the application of knowledge from the natural sciences.

[16] This is not to exclude, for example, further updating work on new developments in the body of systematic knowledge as part of the growth of horizontal expertise.

17 For accounts of this type of process in the Philosophy of Science literature see Newton-Smith, W. H. (1991) *The Rationality of Science*, London, Routledge; Okasha, S. (2002) *Philosophy of Science*, Oxford, Oxford University Press; Lakatos, I. (1970) 'Falsification and the methodology of scientific research programmes', in Lakatos, I., Musgrave, A. (eds) *Criticism and the Growth of Knowledge*, Cambridge, Cambridge University Press.

18 See also the distinction made in classical Greece between the *cheirotechnoi* with an emphasis on physical work and master technicians or *architectones*, who have an understanding of underlying principles. Cuomo (2007), p. 13.

19 Cf. Cuomo (2007), p. 9. See also the discussion of orientation to reward in Lynch, T., Walsh, A. (2003) 'The Mandevillean conceit and the profit-motive', *Philosophy*, 78, pp. 43–62, for some fine-grained distinctions in this area. Interestingly, in the MacIntyrean schema of internal and external goods one can pursue excellence and still be 'banausic', presumably the possibility that most concerned Plato and Aristotle.

20 Arguably the distinction is a little simplistic since relationships with colleagues form a central part of one's participation in the labour process. For this reason, presumably, the official German characterization of competences distinguishes between technical, personal and social competences (see Hanf 2009, p. 21).

21 For MacIntyre, however, skills, however, remain means to ends, rather than having virtues intrinsically bound up in their practice. See MacIntyre, A. (1999) *Dependent Rational Animals*, London, Duckworth, p. 92.

22 '*ich kann kein Volk mir denken, das zerrissner wäre, wie die Deutschen. Handwerker siehst du, aber keine Menschen, Denker aber keine Menschen, Priester, aber keine Menschen . . . – ist das nicht, wie ein Schlachtfeld, wo Hände und Arme und alle Glieder zerstückelt untereinander liegen, indessen das vergossne Lebensblut im Sande zerrinnt?*' 'I can think of no people as torn as the Germans. Tradesmen but no humans, thinkers but no humans, priests but no humans . . . isn't it like a battlefield where dismembered hands, arms and limbs lie on top of each other, whose spilt lifeblood flows into the sand?' Hölderlin, F. (1797, 1799) *Hölderlin's Werke*, Band 2, Leipzig, Metzger und Wittig, p. 149.

23 See, for example, Keller, G. [1854–5] (1951) *Der grüne Heinrich*, Zurich, Atlantis Verlag; Goethe [1796] (1980). J. R. R. Tolkien's *The Hobbit* also follows the *Bildungsroman* pattern (London, Allen and Unwin, 1936).

24 Benner, D. (2003) *Wilhelm von Humboldt's* Bildungstheorie, Weinheim and Munich, Juventa, esp. ch. 1.

25 For Humboldt, therefore, general education, at least to primary level, is a pre-requisite of *Bildung*.

26 The fact that these may be contested does not alter the point. Experts, if they are focused on the broad range of occupational concerns will think deeply about these issues as well. For a contrasting view of trades rather than professions, see Carr, D. (1999).

27 See Rhees's remarks about the ramifications of activities across a culture in Rhees (1970), referred to in Chapter 5.

28 See Wittgenstein (1953); Baker, G. P. (2004) *Wittgenstein's Method: Neglected Aspects*, Oxford, Blackwell; Mulhall, S. (1990) *On Being in the World*, London, Routledge.

[29] The fervent wish to do better is often critical. See Keller's descriptions of the stasis of Henry Lee's abilities in his time working in a mass production artistic workshop in *Der Grüne Heinrich*.

[30] This account of the imagination owes much to Bennett and Hacker (2003), ch. 6, esp. pp. 180–7.

[31] This is not to offer a canonical, or even a paradigmatic, definition of *creativity*, a much misused term. It is to draw attention to core features of the use of the term in the context of the kind of activity under discussion here. For further discussion, see Barrow and Woods (2003); Gingell, J. (2001) 'Against creativity', *Irish Educational Studies*, 1747–4965, 20, 1, pp. 34–44; Best, D. (1992) *The Rationality of Feeling*, London, Routledge, for further discussion along these lines. For an appreciation of the effort involved in developing creativity, see Howe (1990).

[32] See the comments of Winch, P. (1958) *The Idea of a Social Science*, Oxford, Routledge, p. 87, for example.

Chapter 10

Vocational Education and the Development of Expertise

Introduction

This chapter will consider the implications of the preceding philosophical discussion of practical knowledge and expertise for vocational and professional education in the light of current discussions and speculation about the 'knowledge economy' and a 'high skills equilibrium'.[1] Vocational education, in common with the other aspects of national education systems, has distinctive national characteristics, formed by history, culture, society and economy. Even within an area like North Western Europe, the cultures of whose countries are closely linked and between which considerable interchange takes place, one can find highly distinctive systems of Vocational Education and Training (VET), reflecting different philosophical, cultural and economic assumptions.[2] It is not the purpose of this book to recommend one national approach or another, but rather to introduce to an English-speaking audience some relatively neglected aspects of the relationship between a particular conception of practical knowledge and both Initial Vocational Education and Training (IVET) and Continuing Vocational Education and Training (CVET).

It will be helpful to recall the main lines of argument first. The book defends a conception of practical knowledge which is both distinct from and closely related to propositional knowledge (Chapters 1, 2). At the same time, it would be misleading to think of action in this sense, solely in terms of *skill*. A fuller understanding of agency in vocational contexts requires that we take into account *occupational* as well as *task* contexts, with their own agentive, social, moral and civic dimensions. Skill is contrasted with *competence*, encompassing this wider conception of practical knowledge (itself subject to cultural variation) (Chapters 3, 4). This is of practical knowledge as action within a normative context (Chapter 5). Such a conception gives space to apply evaluative concepts to action and hence to develop conceptions of *degree of mastery* related to practical knowledge. This conception is filled out in relation to the connection between propositional and practical knowledge (Chapter 6) and tacit aspects of practical knowledge (Chapter 7). The concept of expertise is then looked at in more detail in Chapters 8 and 9.

The suggestion of the book is that we approach the development of practical knowledge in VET in a certain way. Rather than rotating it around the conceptual axis of *skill* and *task*, we do so in terms of *competence* and *occupation* in order to see what important aspects of practical knowledge have been neglected within the Anglo-American-Australian conception of practical knowledge in vocational contexts. The relevance of this project is underlined by the development of a pan-European framework for the comparison of different qualifications, which is itself based on an uneasy compromise between different national conceptions of skill, knowledge and competence.[3] Drawing out these implications is the principal task of this chapter.

What are the Implications of Prioritizing Competence and Occupation as Organizing Concepts?

Both 'competence' and 'occupation' are place-holding terms for a variety of *conceptions* of action on the one hand and employment on the other hand, (some mutually inconsistent) that go under these names. However, since the argument of the book has been to suggest that we should pay attention to conceptions that might prove to be particularly fruitful in understanding new and underexamined possibilities, we will suggest that particularly rich conceptions are the ones most worthy of our attention, that is, conceptions that express a multidimensional view of agency incorporating the integration of practical and theoretical knowledge together with a developed moral, social and civic sensibility. To this end, the German conception of occupation as *Beruf* will be adopted as a starting-point for the investigation. In the German context, *Beruf* has moral, social and political, as well as economic significance. Its conceptual analogue in the Anglo-American context should better be seen as *profession* rather than *trade*. The reason is that the concept of a profession has, like that of *Beruf*, an association with ethical commitment, social identity, defined legal status and personal agency. However, *Berufe* are to be found in areas of economic activity which would not be counted as professional in the Anglo-American context, such as carpentry, hairdressing, and many others. There are currently in Germany about 350 *Ausbildungsberufe* or *Berufe* for which IVET is explicitly provided.[4] We need to distinguish between a culturally and historically informed concept of *Beruf* which, for example, can be found in literary sources, from the official, legally defined conception which structures German VET, as is the case for the English concept of a profession.

In the latter sense, the link between *Beruf* and *Kompetenz* is a close one, but is to be understood in terms of distinctively German traditions of thinking about occupational agency, which received a fully developed formulation in the writings of Georg Kerschensteiner.[5] To be qualified to practice a *Beruf* one must satisfy competence criteria, which are encapsulated in the term *berufliche Handlungsfähigkeit* or 'occupational action capacity' in English. *Berufliche Handlungsfähigkeit* has a specific meaning as the ability to act competently in the workplace within one's occupational field. As noted in Chapter 4, the concept of a *Fähigkeit* is holistic; although one can describe the different facets of a *Fähigkeit* using the vocabulary of *Kompetenzen*, it is more than a bundle of skills, but is unified through a conception of agency which involves planning, control, co-ordination, self-monitoring and evaluation, as well as the performance of a variety of tasks requiring specific skills. It also includes the ability to appreciate the broader economic and civic implications of occupational action. In the third dimension of expertise outlined in Chapter 9 it is, therefore, broad in scope and an expert in a *Beruf* is master of a range of integrated and co-ordinated activities.

> According to the Vocational Training Act (*Berufsbildungsgesetz*) (last amended 23 March 2005; Fed. Law Gazette [BGBl.], Part I p. 931) any occupational training in line with the '*Berufskonzept*' must prepare for complex activities in accordance with a set of competences laid down in training standards, called '*Ausbildungsordnungen*', it must combine specialized and comprehensive skills and knowledge to obtain occupational capabilities and to create a sound basis to take up further studies independently, and it must also considerably contribute to the social integration and future social provision of the respective youths.[6]

The type of worker who has a *Beruf*, the *Facharbeiter*, who has undertaken a three-year IVET course, has qualifications at level 4 in the EQF, which put that worker in the category of someone who applies *Wissen* or systematically organized knowledge to their practice and who exercises a considerable degree of operational autonomy.[7] This is true to a lesser extent of those qualified after a two-year programme.[8] We have here two levels of vertical forms of expertise, each of which correspond to what in England would be called a 'skilled worker'.

For the sake of comparison, skilled workers in England would be classified at level 3 in terms of English qualifications and even this would be 'charitable', since some level 3 qualifications have little or no underpinning knowledge attached to them, let alone systematically organized knowledge.[9] Level 2 qualifications in the English context, which would identify someone as being able to practice some trades like bricklaying, would classify someone as skilled or semi-skilled. In the German system such workers would be classified as 'unskilled' or at most as 'semi-skilled' and there does not exist a qualification in Germany at the moment that takes account of this vertical level of expertise, which involves no more than 'basic factual knowledge of a field of work or study'. We can see here, that terms such as 'skilled' do not have an absolute, but a relative usage, depending on what set of criteria are used as a means of comparison.

Just as with professions, the expertise of a *Facharbeiter* does not rely on underpinning knowledge alone, nor on the observed ability to perform specific tasks in the workplace. Rather it depends on all the attributes which the individual has developed being deployed in effective action, including the putting to use of propositional and theoretical knowledge in practice within a context of autonomous agency and ethical judgement. What kind of IVET is best suited to the development of such a person? It should be noted that Germany, in common with most other countries, does not usually prescribe one single IVET route, even for the same *Ausbildungsberuf*. There is, however, one route that is of particular interest, namely the *Dual System*, which needs to be explained.

The Dual System

The Dual System, variants of which are to be found in Switzerland, Holland, Austria and Denmark as well as in Germany, is heavily influenced by the ideas and policy of Georg Kerschensteiner among others in the early years of the twentieth century.[10] These ideas, developed as a Philosophy of Education particularly concerned with the nature of learning and the development of *Bildung* for those who were not going to receive an academic upper secondary or higher education, were applied as a robust and successful form of vocational education, first in Munich and then in other areas of Germany. Kerschensteiner, like Marx, sees the characteristic form of human activity to be the forming of plans and their putting into effect.[11] This is also the characteristic form of much human learning. Through self-directed activity we acquire qualities of character, such as patience, persistence and attention to detail, the so-called bourgeois virtues (*bürgerliche Tugenden*).

It is a characteristic of Kerschensteiner's thinking that he considers activity in paid employment as well as in leisure and schooling situations, to be the proper sphere for the development of virtue as an honourable and worthwhile exercise of human capacities, in contrast to Aristotle, who discounts work, but prizes contemplation, leisure and civic engagement. It is precisely what Aristotle thought was disgraceful about work, namely the earning of one's living in operational conditions, that Kerschensteiner considers to be particularly fruitful for learning and for engagement in a worthwhile life. Through work, we learn what really matters to us and we learn it best when we have to do so in real, rather than simulated, conditions. Only in this way can excellence be achieved. However, such forms of learning carry their own dangers. Not only do modern crafts and industrial processes require the acquisition of scientific and technical knowledge to master them, a *citizen* (*Bürger*) in a modern industrial society, as opposed to a *subject* (*Untertan*) in a preindustrial autocracy, needs a continuing general, moral and civic education and needs, in particular, to acquire the 'civic virtues' (*staatsbürgerliche Tugenden*), which will allow him to act as a citizen and to continue his education. *Bildung*, it should be noted, is conceived in some parts of the Germanic conception of education as an incomplete process of developing one's unique individuality while taking part in productive activities, a conception of education sometimes known as *allgemeine Menschenbildung*.[12] For this to be the case, it is necessary to recognize that the practical working environment, although powerful for the learning of crafts and technical occupations, is inadequate. For some of the working week, therefore, apprentices, although employees, would be released from their firms to attend a vocational college in order to extend their technical and occupational knowledge as well as to receive a continuing academic and civic education.

There is another reason for this partial removal of the learner from the working environment, a danger that we have already alluded to and which Kerschensteiner was very conscious of, namely that of a narrow-minded, greedy and limited appreciation of what productive work has to offer, in terms of goods and satisfactions. In order that workers should not become *banausic* their education needed to give them a wider appreciation of what MacIntyre calls the 'external goods' that can result from practicing a craft or technical occupation, namely an awareness of its benefits and responsibilities within the society in which it is practiced. The Dual System aims, then, to give young people at work the basic materials for a continuation of the possibilities for *Bildung* beyond formal schooling.[13] This is an important point, not always fully appreciated. Kerschensteiner did not envisage *Bildung* in the academic sense as a realistic, or even desirable, possibility for all young people, but he did consider that the aim of vocational education was *Bildung* in the broader sense of an acquaintance with 'timeless values' and as a means of continuing personal development.[14] In this sense, he stands in the Humboldtian tradition of *allgemeine Menschenbilding*.

The Dual System is, therefore a means of developing competence in the sense of *berufliche Handlungsfähigkeit* as a form of wide-ranging agency in the workplace, coupled with a civic awareness of the consequences of one's economic activity and also, and by no means least, the equipping of a young person with the materials to progress further, both as a person and as a student. It is here, perhaps, that the greatest challenge to approaches like the Dual System can be found, although it should be said that the same or a similar challenge can be found in other systems. The development of expertise in the 'vertical' sense, described in Chapter 9, depends to a large degree on the availability of qualifications that are *permeable*; that is, qualifications that provide sufficient systematic and practical knowledge for their holders to progress to further qualifications that require more of the former at a more complex and abstract level. Currently the German Dual System enjoys only limited success in this endeavour, although there is a clearly established route from *Facharbeiter* at level 4 to the *Meister* qualification at level 6, formally equivalent to the Bachelor Degree. The *Meister* qualification allows and equips one to set up a business and to educate apprentices. However, any claim that vocational routes such as the Dual System can lead to further personal development through continuing participation in formal education through the gaining of higher qualifications is compromised to the extent that some vocational qualifications at EQF levels 3 and 4 do not equip young people for further study.

Initial and Continuing Vocational Education

If the relationship between initial and higher level continuing vocational education is problematic in systems like the German one, which place a considerable degree of emphasis on the academic part of vocational education, it is even more problematic for those countries, like England, which have a tendency, at least in some trades, to downplay this relationship and to emphasize instead the practical part of the occupation, the skills required to do the tasks prescribed. The NVQ qualification at levels 1–3 has these characteristics in a particularly strong form.[15] The contrast between the Dual System qualifications in Germany and the NVQ and Apprenticeship schemes in England is interesting as it exemplifies two different approaches to the role that systematic knowledge plays in vocational activity. The curricula in the Dual System assume that the systematic knowledge acquired in the *Berufschule* is learned in order to be deployed in economic activities in operational conditions. The pedagogical assumption is that the required level of expertise needed in the body of organized knowledge (the *Wissen* that underpins the *Beruf*) is best acquired in a systematic manner so that the relevant concepts, propositions and modes of evaluating knowledge claims are available in such a way that there are no critical gaps in the learner's knowledge. Such *Wissen* although it may no longer be directly linked to a traditional academic subject, or even a form of knowledge in the sense outlined in Chapter 1, should, however, be sufficiently systematic to enable self-directed learning in the relevant field to continue to take place post-IVET.[16] Intermediate and final examinations in the underlying theory of the occupation are an important part of the qualification.

However, further moves are needed in order for that knowledge to be deployed in practice. Since it is often difficult to do so in the workplace in operational conditions, where there are safety problems and the danger of damaging equipment and disrupting production, it is increasingly the case that the *Berufschule* or some other organization provides a simulatory environment for the safe practice of the knowledge-based skills (*Fertigkeiten*) that are necessary for vocational performance. It is only later that the apprentice is allowed to operate in the workplace in controlled conditions, initially of limited scope, but increasing as confidence and expertise grow. The characteristic final qualification in the Dual System is a global one, achieved by evidence of mastery of the relevant *Wissen* through examination and successful operational practice in which all the elements of the programme are integrated into action. For this reason, the qualification, because of its cumulative nature, guarantees a global ability and cannot be simply achieved through the successive addition of discrete modular units, as these would compromise the integrity of a single, integrated *Beruf*-oriented qualification.[17] Developments such as ECVET, or the European Credit Accumulation and Transfer System for Vocational Education and Training, have the potential to undermine such unified qualifications as they are explicitly designed to cumulate qualifications through the achievement of modules on a purely additive basis.

Apart from 'vertical' CVET, which allows, to an extent, progression to higher levels of qualification in terms of the deployment of more advanced and extensive systematic knowledge, the Dual System lays the foundations for 'horizontal' progression as well. One of the subcompetences in the specification for *berufliche Handlungsfähigkeit* is that of *Methodenkompetenz*, which enables employees to keep abreast of developments within their occupation through sufficient grasp of underlying principles and knowledge. The systematic nature of the knowledge gained in IVET makes this more possible.

Vocational Education and the 'Knowledge Economy'

The Dual System, with its strong emphasis on systematic underpinning knowledge and the development of high standards of work through controlled simulatory and operational practice, is suited to an economy run as a 'high-skill equilibrium', where high-specification goods and services are made and sold to comparatively highly paid consumers, who are also the producers of such goods and services.[18] It should be noted that the particular strength of this system lies in the technical and higher technical occupations classified at levels 3 and 4 in the EQF, and to a considerable extent in those available through vocationally oriented higher education for technologists at levels 5 and 6. Germany has relatively few young people in higher education compared with some other countries, 24 per cent of school leavers heading for higher education in 2004, of which 3 per cent went to universities of applied science.[19] This compares with 20 per cent more of British school leavers entering higher education at the time of writing (2009). Germany's 'knowledge economy' is, then, based on the development of technicians and technologists in the sense of those terms outlined in Chapter 9, rather than on generalist managers. It should also be noted that it is not uncommon for established *researchers* in the relevant areas to occupy senior management positions in enterprises in contrast to some other countries such as Great Britain.

A consequence of the relative autonomy afforded to the *Facharbeiter* due to his capacity for self-regulation and the broad scope of *Berufe* is a flatter management hierarchy than is to be found in countries such as the Great Britain and the United States. The system relies to a considerable extent on the 'horizontal' expertise of the *Facharbeiter* in promoting incremental product innovation, as well as the technologist and researcher roles for providing a more quality oriented innovation strategy. Although the Dual

System is not based on a partnership with higher education, the model is capable of extension to higher education so that technologists and future researchers could be employed and then developed through a combination of a rigorous programme of systematic knowledge linked to an operational role with an even stronger degree of autonomy and responsibility than that of the technician.

Learning Outcomes, Standards and the Acquisition of Vocational Knowledge

Despite its strengths, the kind of model that Germany represents, with a strongly collectivist ethos and a corporatist structure of interlocking institutions such as industrial democracy, employer associations and social partnership arrangements, is considered by some to be overly rigid and unresponsive to rapid market changes.[20] The most strongly contrasting system is that of England, in which more flexible forms of accreditation have been pioneered, and which has a more strongly hierarchical managerialist orientation than Germany. Although oversimplifications are dangerous, and there are considerable commonalities between the VET systems of North Western Europe and that of England, there are, nevertheless distinctive and influential features of the English system which are worth discussing, particularly as elements of them have been incorporated, to some extent into the proposed 'Lisbon process' of greater transparency in the education and labour markets of the European Union countries.

This alternative model is represented by National Vocational Qualifications (NVQs) which are seen as an important way of developing the English skill base. The NVQs are closely associated with the Apprenticeship programme which is considered to be a key means of ensuring the transition from school to work of an increasing number of school leavers in the future, particularly as the age of compulsory engagement with education is to be raised from 16 to 18 by 2013.

This model has a number of features which are distinctive.

1. Accreditation is based on the observed ability of the candidate to perform specified tasks.
2. This observed ability is characterized in terms of Learning Outcomes.
3. A Learning Outcome is conceptually distinct from any process that led to the ability to perform the tasks set out in the Learning Outcome.[21]

4. It follows from the above that accreditation based on satisfaction of a group of Learning Outcomes is not dependent on any particular model of prior learning, but on current satisfaction of the criteria laid out in Learning Outcomes.
5. Packages of Learning Outcomes define the range of tasks which characterize an occupation, which is itself an *ad hoc* construction based on current employer need.

One particularly important consequence follows from this characterization.[22] Whatever, theoretical or propositional knowledge systematic or contingent, that an individual may possess, which is relevant to the ability to manage the tasks concerned, it is not relevant to the assessment of ability to perform the task and hence to the achievement of accreditation. In the words of Gilbert Jessup, one of the designers of NVQs, 'Skills can only be demonstrated through their application in performance (doing something) while knowledge can be elicited through the more abstract means of conversation, questioning or talking.'[23] The conception of *skill* outlined in this quotation is one that is close to the 'paradigm case' described in Chapter 3 of a non-discursive manual or co-ordinative task ability. Can it have wider application? There are two issues of particular relevance to the discussion in this book, both of which bear on the way in which vocational expertise is characterized. The first of these concerns the need for and nature of the non-practical knowledge required for task performance. The second concerns the breadth of occupational operation.

To take the first, it might be argued, and Gilbert Ryle hinted at this, that relevant systematic knowledge could be accumulated through extended practice.[24] While this is a bare logical possibility, there are very good reasons for thinking that it is an unlikely scenario for any occupation of a reasonable degree of complexity. In order to appreciate this point, it is helpful to contrast two broad approaches to the acquisition of systematic underpinning knowledge (theory). The first is *deductive*, meaning that particular propositions and associated maxims for action are derived from a prior existing body of knowledge.[25] The second is *inductive* and involves the production of generalized propositions through the accumulation of conclusions derived from experience. Such a body of generalized propositions may then serve as the basis for future action. A system of qualification like NVQ could accommodate the latter, although it would not accredit the knowledge thus acquired. The former would simply be irrelevant. It is evident that approaches such as the Dual System or college-based approaches such as are found in the Netherlands and France are predicated on the deductive model. Could the inductive model work?

Let us work through the possibilities:

A relatively novice worker encounters a variety of situations in which measures are called for. A non-universal generalization of the relevant features of such situations is developed by induction from the range of experiences encountered. This process is iterated for different kinds of situations. The situation-measure model is also modified to take account of the specificities of particular contexts. Over time, the worker builds up a generalizable but contextually sensitive theory concerning action called for in different situations, based on the generalizations developed. He may also, to a limited extent, build up through observation and a combination of inductive and deductive methods, a working model of the systematic underpinning knowledge pertinent to his occupation. Could this be an effective substitute for the deductive approach? There are good reasons for thinking not. The main problem is that contingencies of work and operational constraint will expose the worker to a limited number of situations, thus limiting the inductive base on which any theory is going to be based. This is even more likely to be the case when the occupation is restricted in operational scope. One might add that the operative will not himself possess the particular competencies required by the researcher or technologist responsible for theory-building in the relevant area. Any theory built up through such methods will be vastly inferior to one that is developed through well-known, systematic and tested methods of theory construction and testing associated with a particular subject.

However, this is not the whole story because, as we saw in Chapter 8, it is not unusual and indeed is to be expected that any individual engaged with intensity and commitment with an occupation over a reasonable length of time will come to form a set of systematically related, experientially based propositions which serve as a *personal* theory guiding practice. One may reasonably expect that the inductive method will be capable of making a significant contribution to such a theory, which is a theory of *how that particular person*, with his abilities, limitations, personal character, should act in a professional context. In other words, it is a normative framework for the guidance of the individual rather than a general, non-individual – specific theory concerning occupational performance. However, the process of gaining expertise through personal theory construction for someone who does not possess underpinning systematic knowledge and that process for one who does is likely to be very different. In the latter case, any personal theory will involve the interaction between and possibly modification of the underpinning theory under the exigencies of the personal experience of the worker. The worker's own personal theory will be based, not only on experience, but on experience modulated through the previously acquired theory, which will affect the way in which situations are perceived and the kinds of conclusions drawn about them in ways unavailable to the former individual, relying solely on inductions from experience. Indeed, the broader the scope of occupational activity, the more difficult it will be to build a body of inductively based relevant generalizations.[26]

Thus one may expect successful theory-building to develop in an inductive way in cases where the scope of operations is relatively narrow and the range of experiences encountered relatively uniform. It is less likely to happen in those circumstances where operational scope is broad and a large variety of situations is likely to be encountered in the occupation taken as a whole, not necessarily within the experience of one individual. In such cases it will be necessary to provide the individual with the knowledge basis necessary for making judgements in situations not yet encountered. Indeed there is a further dimension of experiences that may not yet have been encountered *tout court* within the occupation, which may need to be taken account of in IVET.

In practice the shortcomings of NVQs in terms of underpinning knowledge are recognized through the institution of *Technical Certificates* or qualifications that provide the underpinning knowledge necessary for efficient task performance. Thus the government subsidized Apprenticeship scheme includes at level 3, the requirement, in many cases, to take a Technical Certificate as well as an NVQ. Unfortunately, there is no requirement as to the sequencing of these aspects of the Apprenticeship qualification. It is possible, therefore, to take the Technical Certificate part of the Apprenticeship *after* the NVQ. On the premise that underpinning knowledge is best acquired deductively in order that it may be effectively applied in operational situations, this is a nonsense. The point of an NVQ is to certificate task competence in operational conditions. If optimum performance of the task requires understanding and deployment of the underpinning systematic knowledge relevant to the task, it cannot be the case that a good (as opposed to a merely satisfactory) performance on the NVQ can be managed without having first grasped the matter examined by the Technical Certificate qualification.

Nevertheless, the Technical Certificate/NVQ duo contains the germs of an integrated qualification of the German type, if some reforming government were prepared to be more prescriptive about the sequencing of the qualifications within the Apprenticeship programme. For if Technical Certificates were to be assessed prior to the NVQ assessment, it would be possible in all cases to assess the NVQ according to a standard that *presupposed* relevant theoretical understanding integrated into operational capacity. Continuing unwillingness on the part of both employers and government to institute such a system indicates a lack of concern for operational competence that goes beyond a satisficing (just good enough) conception of skill performance to one that at least aspires to excellence.

The Relationship between Initial VET (IVET) and Continuing VET (CVET) in Developing Expertise

This brings us to an important and relatively neglected point, namely the movement from *competence* to *expertise*, whose general features were discussed in Chapters 8 and 9, and the role which vocational and professional education can play in such a transition. It is the aim of IVET to develop practitioners who are at least competent under supervision in occupational contexts. This may be the ability to practice a fairly narrow skill in some cases, such as a bricklaying apprentice who has left his course once he can lay bricks in a straight line and can gain employment. As the context of our current discussion is someone who possesses a developed capacity for occupational action, it will mean something different. Such people, as we noted, will already have a broad scope of operations at their disposal and will be able to exercise a considerable degree of autonomy and responsibility in their work. They will also have enough grasp of the underpinning theory of the occupation to be able to take account of new technical developments.

How, then, does expertise develop from this point? Here it is useful to remind ourselves of Bereiter and Scardamalia's distinction between an experienced and an expert practitioner.[27] There is no doubt that experience brings with it the development of increasingly efficient means to respond to frequently occurring types of situation as well at the encountering of less usual ones and the ability to form courses of action to deal with these as well. The practice of the experienced practitioner in this sense is likely to be *satisficing* rather than moving beyond minimal criteria for successful performance. This means that practice will be at least 'good enough' or 'competent' in the sense that it will not lead to complaint from clients and supervisors and may elicit a degree of approbation. Someone practicing at this level may well develop a range of effective repertoires for dealing with a wide range of situations, may be able to take account of new technical developments and take responsibility for some vocational education activities like mentoring. What will they lack?

The desire for and the pursuit of excellence is not a necessary condition of someone's being an expert according to the official criteria of expertise in most occupations. On the other hand, someone who successfully pursues excellence is likely to be considered as an expert, but furthermore someone who is capable of achieving unusually good results, far beyond the satisficing performances of the competent or experienced practitioner, is also likely to be so called. The achievement of performances beyond the satisficing is likely to depend first of all on a wish to do so and second, on much experience of practice and reflection on mistakes and successes, frequently in conversation with other practitioners. In this sense, continual vocational education includes practicing the occupation, maybe moving to less close supervision and to engagement with a variety of increasingly more challenging situations. There are good reasons to believe that careful attention needs to be paid to the needs of novice, but initially qualified, practitioners in order that they are not discouraged and disillusioned by being put in situations with which they find it difficult to cope. They are not there to make the life of the experienced more easy, but to become proficient and confident themselves.

There are different forms of CVET that are organized around the idea of updating and strengthening existing abilities and, alternatively, of introducing experienced practitioners to new tasks and processes. We can also understand clearly enough forms of CVET which enable a practitioner to make a vertical ascent to a more theoretically informed level of practice (e.g. from technician to technologist) through the acquisition of further qualifications at a higher academic level. Is it possible, however, to become more expert in what one is *already* doing by gaining further theoretical knowledge relevant to the practice that one is already carrying out? This does seem to be possible, for example, where an area of activity is complex and specialist knowledge in depth may shed light on issues and enable the development of techniques that would otherwise be difficult to acquire, for reasons already mentioned. For example, advanced qualifications in Applied Linguistics may well enable an experienced primary school teacher to increase her expertise in the teaching of reading and writing by equipping her with an advanced understanding of the *linguistic* issues with which she is concerned which can be applied to her already developed proficiency with diagnosis and assessment. Indeed, such a person, by gaining enhanced understanding of what she is doing through further study, may come to assume a position of advice to colleagues and a role in the curriculum and pedagogical development of the school in which she works. In such a case, the distinction between horizontal and vertical forms of expertise is not so clearly demarcated anymore. Such a person will develop her expertise horizontally and will, where the structure of the occupation and its qualification system makes this possible, become more technologically and managerially proficient, as well as becoming more independent in judgement, thus moving vertically in the occupational and educational hierarchy.[28]

In the Anglo-American context, this possibility needs to be borne in mind, particularly in relation to the organization of work. Individuals who possess expertise in an occupation have the possibility of guiding the work of others *because of* the breadth and depth of their practical knowledge concerning the operations within the occupation. They use that expertise to co-ordinate and guide others, as well as continuing to set an example as practitioners. At the same time, in a broadly configured occupation, they will also be guiding and co-ordinating workers whose initial vocational education endows them with a considerable degree of discretion in their work. It is worth pointing out that in Britain at any rate there has been a tendency to move in the opposite direction even with those occupations which require level 6 and above qualifications, for example, in schools, colleges and universities, with the putting in place of a 'low-trust' system of accountability and reporting on every aspect of work. The reasons for this are complex, but reflect a model of autonomy in the workplace which broadly reflects the idea that workers are not capable of taking *civic* responsibility for what they do, whatever moral commitment they have to their work is conceived of individualistically rather than with reference to the society as a whole.[29]

Implications for the Design of Educational Qualifications – the Case of the European Qualification Framework (EQF)[30]

The EQF represents an attempt to classify qualifications vertically as well as horizontally. The idea is that by specifying the propositional knowledge, practical knowledge and autonomy and responsibility that are exercised at each of eight ordered levels, ranging from upper primary to doctoral level, one will be able to arrive at a 'vertical' classification of expertise, primarily but not exclusively in terms of the degree of propositional knowledge that is available at each level. I say 'primarily' because the level of propositional knowledge required is understood to determine what practical operations are possible and hence what level of autonomy and responsibility may be expected. The EQF is organized around a concept of *competence* which encompasses both theoretical and practical knowledge, together with the exercise, by the agent, of autonomy and responsibility. In this sense it resembles the German concept of *occupational action capacity* or *berufliche Handlungsfähigkeit* discussed in Chapter 4 and elsewhere. Thus the framework could be seen to provide a hierarchy of levels of occupational action capacity in this sense.

The EQF does, therefore, go some way towards a reorientation away from the Anglo-American idea of skill related to the performance of tasks as a way of conceptualizing practical knowledge in work contexts, towards a conception of an integrated capacity related to an occupational field. Unfortunately, as a framework which has to take into account the different traditions of different European Union countries, there is no such absolute clarity of vision. The third subcategory of EQF, confusingly also called 'competence', is separated out from practical knowledge which, in occupational terms, in, for example, Germany, includes the ability to plan, monitor and evaluate one's own work and those for whom one is responsible. In terms of an occupational capacity, 'autonomy' and 'responsibility' are what one is expected to exercise as part of one's occupational practical knowledge (see Chapter 4), not an additional extra which might also be seen in managerial terms as the ability to give orders and to see that they are carried out. A framework which more faithfully represented such a conception of competence would not separate these two categories but would integrate them in the category of practical knowledge. The practical knowledge necessary to exercise responsibility within a hierarchy would then be specified in terms of the practical knowledge required for competence at a particular level.

However, the EQF does not include a necessary third dimension necessary for comparison and assessment of qualifications, namely that of *scope*, introduced as the third dimension of expertise in Chapter 9. A bricklayer in Germany and a bricklayer in England belong nominally to the same occupation. However, in certain firms and in certain jobs the expertise of a qualified bricklayer in England may only relate to a specific task-type such as laying walls. A bricklayer at nominally the same EQF level in Germany would, on the other hand, be required to engage in formwork, use concreting techniques, install insulation materials and mount plastering, screed and construction elements.[31] These differences in scope are not captured by EQF thus severely limiting its use as a way of comparing qualifications, let alone the expertise that may be embodied in them.

It can be seen, therefore, that EQF represents a compromise between different conceptions of *competence*, one rooted in the context of skill performance in relation to narrowly defined tasks, the other related to an integrated occupational capacity with the occupation being conceived of broadly. These two conceptions are in tension with each other. At the higher levels, and particularly in some occupations where a broad specification of operational scope is accepted, such as in nursing and software engineering, this tension does not emerge too strongly, although it may in terms of different ways of developing CVET. It will, however, emerge in those unregulated occupations whose national variations are quite strong and which exemplify in different countries, quite different ways of conceptualizing the occupation, for example, in bricklaying.[32] At the time of writing these tensions have still to emerge in the practice of the mutual recognition of qualifications, but to some extent EQF will constitute a battleground for the differing conceptions of competence in play within Europe. The thrust of the argument of this book, however, together with that of many other commentators, is that the development of economies that rely, not on 'symbolic analysis' alone, that is, expertise in mathematics and other technical disciplines in areas such as financial services, but on the production of high-quality, high-specification goods and services, relies on the development of expert workers with advanced technical capacities, with a regard for the standards of their work and the possibility, not only of control over what they do, but of advancement to more responsible roles within their sphere of operations. All the signs are at the present time that Britain, far from moving towards such a configuration of its economy, is moving away from it.

We have seen that expertise is multifaceted and its concrete instantiation relates closely to the action category to which practical knowledge is related within particular cultural, social and economic contexts. These action categories should be taken seriously in coming to an understanding of what expertise involves in particular instances. The danger in Britain lies in our failure, not only to appreciate the multiple dimensions of expertise in many different occupations, but also in our lack of appreciation of its importance and of the role of individual workers in ensuring excellence in activity, whether economic or non-economic. Such neglect runs the risk of impoverishing the spiritual as well as the material life of those societies which practice it.

Notes

[1] For a recent semi-official discussion which raises awkward questions for the United Kingdom, see *Ambition 2020: World Class Skills and Jobs for the UK* (2009), London, UK Commission for Employment and Skills, esp. pp. 124–37.

[2] Clarke, L. M., Winch, C. (eds) (2007) *Vocational Education: International Approaches, Developments and Systems*, Abingdon, Routledge.

[3] European Union (2006); Winterton, J., le Deist, F., Stringfellow, E. (2005) *Clarification of Knowledge, Skills and Competences: Clarification of the Concept and Prototype*, Centre for European Research on Employment and Human Resources, Group ESG Toulouse; Brockmann, M., Clarke, L., Winch, C. (2008a).

[4] Hanf (2009).

[5] For further details see Winch, C. (2006a) 'Georg Kerschensteiner: founding the German dual system', *Oxford Review of Education*, 32, 3, pp. 381–96.

[6] Hanf, G. (2007) *German VET Quick-scan*, http://www.kcl.ac.uk/schools/sspp/education/research/projects/eurvoc.html, p. 3.

[7] See Appendix 1, the EQF Grid.

[8] Level 3 is equivalent to the upper secondary exit qualification in the United Kingdom the 'A' level and level 4 to the standard reached after one year in higher education.

[9] Some recruiters for initial nursing education, for example, prefer level 2 qualifications if they are GCSEs rather than level 3 NVQs, even those these latter are nominally at a higher level in the qualifications hierarchy. However, current indications are that English level 2 qualifications have been deemed to be equivalent to EQF level 3. Whether this claim will be accepted on the labour market is, however, a moot point.

[10] Kerschensteiner, G. [1901] (1964) *Ausgewählte Pädagogische Texte*, Band 1, Paderborn, Ferdinand Schöningh; (1925) (1968) Band 2, Paderborn, Ferdinand Schöningh. Kerschensteiner was part of a broader movement to improve vocational education in Germany at the time, see Greinert (2007) for details.

[11] Kerschensteiner (1906), Band 2.

[12] For more on this, see Benner, D. (2003) *Wilhelm von Humboldt's Bildungstheorie*, Munich, Juventa.

[13] Kerschensteiner also thought that the lower secondary school, needed to provide young people with practical activities in workshops and gardens (as well as on the playing field) in order to promote learning and character development, which can only be done to a limited extent through academic education. See (1908) 'Die Schulwerkstatt als Grundlage der Fortbildungsschule', Band 1, pp. 116–29, in Kerschensteiner (1964).

[14] See Greinert, W-D. (2007) 'The German philosophy of vocational education', in Clarke and Winch (eds) for the view of Kerschensteiner as not primarily concerned with *Bildung* in vocational education. See also Kerschensteiner's own

(1925) 'Sitten, Gebräuche, Kulte als Wertträger im Bildungsverfahren', in 1968, pp. 63–9 in Band 2.

[15] Germany is not the only country to emphasize academic education as part of vocational education. Scandinavia, Belgium, Holland and France all do this, although a greater part of their post-school vocational education is conducted through colleges, where young people are not employees but students who are seconded to the workplace for supervised practical experience. It should also be noted that by no means all young Germans who take part in vocational education do so through the Dual System (only about 52 per cent of 15–21 year olds do so). See Hanf (2009) for more detail.

[16] However, the substitution of traditional subjects for fields of learning *Lernfelder* can plausibly be suggested both to be an academically regressive step in terms of the quality of knowledge acquired and also, just as seriously, a degradation of the civic and academic element of the *Bildung* that is supposed to be offered to students within the Dual System. See Wheelahan, L. (2007) 'How competency-based training locks the working class out of powerful knowledge: a modified Bernsteinian analysis', *British Journal of Sociology of Education*, 1465–3346, 28, 5, pp. 637–51, for further discussion of this issue.

[17] Cf. Ertl, H. (2002): 'The concept of modularisation in vocational education and training: the debate in Germany and its implication', *Oxford Review of Education*, 28, 1, pp. 53–73.

[18] See UKCES (2009); Culpepper, P. D. (1999), 'The future of the high-skill equilibrium in Germany', *Oxford Review of Economic Policy*, 15, 1, pp. 43–59. This model should be contrasted with the Reichian model of a knowledge economy based on a small number of 'symbolic analysts' operating in a global market. The upper reaches of the financial sector of the City of London, would be a good example of this type of 'Knowledge Economy'.

[19] Hanf (2007), p. 1.

[20] For a good account of the institutional basis of the German system, see Streeck (1992). It should also be noted that there are alternative approaches to developing strength at the technical level, relying on College rather than the workplace as the primary locus of IVET. See, for example, Géhin, J-P. (2007) 'Vocational education in France: a turbulent history and peripheral role', in Clarke and Winch (eds) (2007), pp. 34–48; Méhaut, P. (2006) *Key Concepts and Debates in the French VET System and Labour Market*, http://www.kcl.ac.uk/content/1/c6/01/57/15/FranceQuickScanNov071.pdf, consulted 19 July 2009.

[21] This is not the only way in which the term 'Learning Outcome' is ever used, but it is the conception adopted by the NVQ scheme and the EQF.

[22] For a discussion of the others, see Brockmann, Clarke and Winch (2007), pp. 99–113. These problems relate to an implicit contradiction in the design of such qualifications. On the one hand, they attempt to consider achievement *in isolation* from any other type or degree of achievement; on the other hand, as they are in an educational hierarchy of levels of vertical expertise, they *implicitly* presuppose the achievement of competence at the levels below the one actually being assessed.

[23] Jessup, G. (1991) 'Implications for individuals: the autonomous learner', in Jessup, G. (ed.) *Outcomes: NVQs and the Emerging Model of Education and Training*, Brighton, Falmer Press, p. 121.

[24] 'A man knowing little or nothing of medical science could not be a good surgeon, but excellence in surgery is not the same thing as knowledge of medical science; nor is it a simple product of it. The surgeon must indeed have learned from instruction, or by his own induction and observations, a great number of truths; but he must also have learned by practice a great number of aptitudes' (Ryle 1949, p. 49).

[25] This is not to suggest that the inference is necessarily *formally deductive* but rather that it involves inference from a body of knowledge to a particular case. See also, Clarke, L., Winch, C. (2004) 'Apprenticeship and applied theoretical knowledge', *Educational Philosophy and Theory*, 36, 5, pp. 509–21.

[26] See Eraut (1994), p. 141, which reinforces the importance of the application of the discipline-based theory to the specifics of a local situation.

[27] This is a useful analytical distinction, although ordinary usage is more fluid.

[28] It cannot be pointed out too strongly that the learning outcomes philosophy which guides both NVQs and the EQF undermines the idea of vertical progression by detaching assessment from prior achievement (see Brockmann, Clarke and Winch 2007).

[29] See Alexander, R. (1992) *Policy and Practice in the Primary School*, London, Routledge, ch. 11, for a discussion of 'good practice' in the sense of what authority, rather than the evidence would suggest.

[30] EQF is a very complex initiative. For a fuller discussion of English, German and Dutch conceptions of competence, see Brockmann, Clarke and Winch (2008b).

[31] BIBB (2009) *Leonardo Bricklaying Qualifications Project – Country Report, Germany*, BIBB, Bonn, pp. 5–6.

[32] See Brockmann, Clarke and Winch (2008a) for more detail.

Bibliography

Alexander, R. (1992) *Policy and Practice in the Primary School*, London, Routledge.

Aristotle (1925) *The Nichomachean Ethics*, edited by Ross, D., London, Dent.

— (1988) *The Politics*, edited by Everson, S., Cambridge, Cambridge University Press.

Baker, G. P. (2004) *Wittgenstein's Method: Neglected Aspects*, Oxford, Blackwell.

Baker, G. P., Hacker, P. M. S. (1984) *Language, Sense and Nonsense*, Oxford Blackwell.

— (1985) *Rules, Grammar and Necessity*, Oxford, Blackwell.

Baker, G. P., Morris, K. (1996) *Descartes' Dualism*, London, Routledge.

Barrow, R., Woods, R. (2003) *An Introduction to Philosophy of Education*, London Routledge, 4th edition.

Beckett, D., Hager, P. (2002) *Life, Work and Learning*, London, Routledge.

Beeton, I. (1861) *Mrs Beeton's Book of Household Management*, London, S. O. Beeton Publishing.

Bengson, J., Moffett, M. A. (2007) 'Know-how and concept possession', *Philosophical Studies*, 136, pp. 31–57.

Benner, D. (2003) *Wilhelm von Humbold's Bildungstheorie*, Munich, Juventa.

Bennett, J. (1964) *Rationality*, London, Routledge.

Bennett, M., Hacker, P. M. S. (2003) *The Philosophical Foundations of Neuroscience*, Oxford, Blackwell.

Bereiter, C., Scardamalia, M. (1993) *Surpassing Ourselves*, La Salle, IL, Open Court Publishing.

Berlin, I. (1977) *Herder and Vico*, New York, Vintage Books.

Best, D. (1992) *The Rationality of Feeling*, Brighton, Falmer Press.

BIBB (2009) *Leonardo Bricklaying Qualifications Project – Country Report, Germany*, BIBB, Bonn, pp. 5–6.

Boreham, N. (1987) 'Learning from experience in diagnostic problem solving', in Richardson, J. T. E., Michael W. E., Piper, D. W. (eds) *Student Learning: Research in Education and Cognitive Psychology*, Guildford, SRHE, pp. 89–97.

Brandom, R. B. (2000) *Articulating Reasons*, Cambridge, MA, Harvard University Press.

Brockmann, M., Clarke, L., Winch, C. (2007) 'Can performance-related outcomes have standards?' *Journal of European Industrial Training*, 32, 2/3, pp. 99–113.

— (2008a) *Crossnational Synthesis of Project on European Vocational Qualifications*: http://www.kcl.ac.uk/schools/sspp/education/research/projects/eurvoc.html, consulted 15 July 2009.

— (2008b) 'Knowledge, skill, competences: European divergences in Vocational Education and Training (VET) – The English, German and Dutch cases', *Oxford Review of Education*, 34, 5, pp. 547–67.

Brockmann, M., Clarke, L., Méhaut, P., Winch, C. (2008) 'Competence-based Vocational Education and Training (VET): the cases of England and France in a European perspective', *Vocations and Learning*, 1, pp. 227–44.

Burke, E. (1790) *Reflections on the Revolution in France*, London, Penguin.

— (1796) *Thoughts on the Prospects of a Regicide Peace in a Series of Letters*, London, J. Owen.

Carlyle, T. (1837) *History of the French Revolution*, New York, Modern Library.

Carr, D. (1979) 'The logic of knowing how and ability', *Mind*, 88, pp. 394–409.

— (1980) 'What place has the notion of a basic action in the theory of action?' *Ratio*, pp. 39–51.

— (1981) 'Knowledge in practice', *American Philosophical Quarterly*, 18, pp. 53–61.

— (1999) 'Professional education and professional ethics', *Journal of Applied Philosophy*, 16, 1, pp. 33–6.

Chomsky, N. (1988) *Language and Problems of Knowledge*, Cambridge, MA, MIT Press.

— (2004) *The Generative Enterprise Revisited*, Berlin, Mouton de Gruyter.

Clarke, L. (1999) 'The changing structure and significance of apprenticeship with special reference to construction', in Ainley, P., Rainbird, H. (eds) *Apprenticeship: Towards a New Paradigm of Learning*, London, Kogan Page.

Clarke, L., Winch, C. (2004) 'Apprenticeship and applied theoretical knowledge', *Educational Philosophy and Theory*, 36, 5, pp. 509–21.

— (2007) (eds) *Vocational Education: International Systems and Perspectives*, Abingdon, Routledge.

Cottingham, J. (1986) *Descartes*, Oxford, Blackwell.

Culpepper, P. D. (1999) 'The future of the high-skill equilibrium in Germany', *Oxford Review of Economic Policy*, 15, 1, pp. 43–59.

Cuomo, S. (2007) *Technology and Culture in Greek and Roman Antiquity*, Cambridge, Cambridge University Press.

Dent, N. (1988) *Rousseau*, London, Routledge.

Dreyfus, H. L. (2001) *On the Internet*, London, Routledge.

Dreyfus, H. L., Dreyfus, S. E. (1996) 'The relationship of theory and practice in the acquisition of skill', in Benner, P., Tanner, C. A., Chesla, C. A. (eds) *Expertise in Nursing Practice*, New York, Springer.

Eraut, M. (1994) *Developing Professional Knowledge and Competence*, Brighton, Falmer Press.

Ertl, H. (2002) 'The concept of modularisation in vocational education and training: the debate in Germany and its implication', *Oxford Review of Education*, 28, 1, pp. 53–73.

European Union (2006) *Recommendation of the European Parliament and Council on the Establishment of a European Qualification Framework for Lifelong Learning*, Brussels, European Union.

Fodor, J. (1975) *The Language of Thought*, Cambridge, MA, MIT Press.

— (2001) *The Mind Doesn't Work That Way*, Cambridge, MA, MIT Press.

— (2003) *Hume Variations*, Oxford, Clarendon.

Frake, C. O. (1964) 'How to ask for a cup of tea Subanun', in Giglioli, P-P. (1972) *Language and Social Context*, London, Penguin, pp. 87–94.

Geach, P. (1958) *Mental Acts*, London, Routledge.

Géhin, J-P. (2007) 'Vocational education in France: a turbulent history and peripheral role', in Clarke and Winch (eds) (2007), pp. 34–48.

Gingell, J. (2001) 'Against creativity', *Irish Educational Studies*, 1747–4965, 20, 1, pp. 34–44.

Glüer, K. (2001) 'Dreams and nightmares: conventions, norms and meaning in Davidson's Philosophy of Language', pp. 1–22, p. 20, http://people.su.se/~kgl/Nightmares.pdf, consulted 28 May 2008.

Goethe, J. [1796] (1980) *Wilhelm Meister's Lehrjahre*, Frankfurt am Main, Fischer Verlag.

Greinert, W-D. (2007) 'The German philosophy of vocational education', in Clarke and Winch (eds) (2007), pp. 49–61.

Hacker, P. M. S. (2008) *Human Beings: The Categorical Concepts*, Oxford, Blackwell.

Hager, P. (2008) 'Refurbishing MacIntyre's account of practice', unpublished ms.

Hanf, G. (2007) *German VET Quick-Scan*, http://www.kcl.ac.uk/schools/sspp/education/research/projects/eurvoc.html

— (2009) 'National report on German vocational education', unpublished report to Nuffield Foundation.

Hanfling, O. (2000) *Ordinary Language and Philosophy*, London, Routledge.

Higgins, C. (2003) 'MacIntyre's moral theory and the possibility of an aretaic ethics of teaching', *Journal of Philosophy of Education*, 37, 2, pp. 279–92.

Hirst, P. H. (1965) 'Liberal education and the nature of knowledge', in Archamabult, R. (ed.) *Philosophical Analysis and Education*, London, Routledge.

— (1993) 'Education, knowledge and practices', in Barrow, R., White, P. (eds) *Beyond Liberal Education*, London, Routledge.

Hoffman, R. R. (1998) 'How can expertise be defined? Implications of research from cognitive psychology', in Williams, R., Faulkner, W., Fleck, J. (eds) *Exploring Expertise: Issues and Perspectives*, Basingstoke, MacMillan.

Hölderlin, F. (1797, 1799) *Hölderlin's Werke*, Band 2, Leipzig, Metzger und Wittig.

Howe, M. (1990) *The Origin of Exceptional Abilities*, London, Routledge.

Hutchinson, P., Read, R., Sharrock, W. (2008) *There is no Such Thing as Social Science*, Aldershot, Ashgate.

Hyland, T. (1993) 'Competence, knowledge and education', *Journal of Philosophy of Education*, 27, 1, pp. 57–68.

Jessup, G. (1991) 'Implications for individuals: the autonomous learner', in Jessup, G. (ed.) *Outcomes: NVQs and the Emerging Model of Education and Training*, Brighton, Falmer Press, p. 121.

Keller, G. [1854–5] (1951) *Der grüne Heinrich*, Zurich, Atlantis Verlag.

Kenny, A. (1968) *Descartes*, New York, Random House.

Kerschensteiner, G. [1901] (1964) 'Staatsbürgerliche Erziehung der deutschen Jugend', in *Ausgewählte Pädagogische Texte*, Band 1, Paderborn, Ferdinand Schöningh, pp. 5–88.

— (1906) Produktiver Arbeit und ihr Erziehungswert', in *Ausgewählte Pädagogische Texte*, Band 1, Paderborn, Ferdinand Schöningh, pp. 5–25.

— (1908) 'Die Schulwerkstatt als Grundlage der Fortbildungsschule', in 1964, pp. 116–29.

— (1925) 'Sitten, Gebräuche, Kulte als Wertträger im Bildungsverfahren', in 1968, pp. 63–69 in Band 2.

Koethe, J. (2002) 'Stanley and Williamson on knowing how', *Journal of Philosophy*, 99, 6, June, pp. 325–8.

Kraus, K. (2008) 'Does employability put the German vocational order at risk?' in Gonon, P., Kraus, K., Oelkers, J., Stolz, S. (eds) *Work, Education and Employability*, Bern, Peter Lang.

Lakatos, I. (1970) 'Falsification and the methodology of scientific research programmes', in Lakatos, I., Musgrave, A. (eds) *Criticism and the Growth of Knowledge*, Cambridge, Cambridge University Press.

Lave, J., Wenger, E. (1991) *Situated Learning: Legitimate Peripheral Participation*, Cambridge, Cambridge University Press.

Levi, D. (2000) *In Defence of Informal Logic*, Dordrecht, Kluwer.

Lynch, T., Walsh, A. (2003) 'The Mandevillean conceit and the profit-motive', *Philosophy*, 78, pp. 43–62.

Lyons, J. (1969) *Introduction to Theoretical Linguistics*, Cambridge, Cambridge University Press.

MacIntyre, A. (1981) *After Virtue*, London, Duckworth.

— (1994) 'A partial response to my critics', in Horton, J., Mendus, S. (eds) *After MacIntyre: Critical Perspectives on the Work of Alasdair MacIntyre*, Cambridge, Polity Press in association with Basil Blackwell Publishers, Oxford, pp. 283–304.

— (1999) *Dependent Rational Animals*, London, Duckworth.

MacIntyre, A., Bell, D. R. (1967) 'Symposium: the idea of a social science', *Proceedings of the Aristotelian Society, Supplementary Volumes*, 41, pp. 95–132.

MacIntyre, A., Dunne, J. (2002) 'Alasdair MacIntyre on education: in conversation with Joseph Dunne', *Journal of Philosophy of Education*, 36, 1, pp. 1–19.

Mackenzie, J. (1998) 'Forms of knowledge and forms of discussion', *Educational Philosophy and Theory*, 30, 1, pp. 27–50.

McNaughton, D. (1988) *Moral Vision*, Oxford, Blackwell.

Malcolm, N. (1977) *Memory and Mind*, Ithaca, Cornell University Press.

— (1990) 'Wittgenstein on language and rules', *Philosophy*, 64, pp. 5–28.

Marquand, D. (2004) *The Decline of the Public: The Hollowing Out of Citizenship*, London, Polity Press.

Marx, K. (1964) (1858) *Precapitalist Economic Formations*, London, Lawrence and Wishart.

— (1970a) (1887) *Capital*, London, Lawrence and Wishart.

— (1970b) *Economic and Philosophic Manuscripts of 1844*, edited with an introduction by Dirk Struik and translated by Martin Milligan, London, Lawrence and Wishart.

Méhaut, P. (2006) *Key Concepts and Debates in the French VET System and Labour Market*, http://www.kcl.ac.uk/content/1/c6/01/57/15/FranceQuickScanNov071.pdf, consulted 19 July 2009.

Moyal-Sharrock, D. (2003) 'Logic in action: Wittgenstein's *Logical Pragmatism* and the impotence of scepticism', *Philosophical Investigations*, 26, 2, pp. 125–48.

Mulhall, S. (1990) *On Being in the World*, London, Routledge.

Newton, P., Driver, R., Osborne, J. (1999) 'The place of argumentation in the pedagogy of school science', *International Journal of Science Education, 21*, 5, pp. 553–76.

Newton-Smith, W. H. (1991) *The Rationality of Science*, London, Routledge.

Noë, A. (2005) 'Against intellectualism', *Analysis*, 65, 4, pp. 278–90.

Oakeshott, M. (1933) *Experience and Its Modes*, Cambridge, Cambridge University Press.

— (1962a) 'Rationalism in politics', in *Rationalism in Politics*, London, Methuen, pp. 1–36.

— (1962b) 'The study of politics in a university', in *Rationalism in Politics*, London, Methuen, pp. 311–33.

— (1975) *On Human Conduct*, Oxford, Clarendon.

Okasha, S. (2002) *Philosophy of Science*, Oxford, Oxford University Press.

Papineau, D. (1978) *For Science in Social Science*, Cambridge, Cambridge University Press.

Phenix, P. (1964) *Realms of Meaning*, New York, McGraw Hill.

Plato (1950) *The Republic*, London, MacMillan.

— (1975) *The Laws*, London, Penguin.

Polanyi, M. (1958) *Personal Knowledge*, London, Routledge.

Prais, S. J. (1991) 'Vocational qualifications in Britain and Europe: theory and practice', *National Institute Economic Review*, 136, May, pp. 86–9.

Raz, J. (2003) *Engaging Reason*, Oxford, Clarendon Press.

Rhees, R. (1970) 'Wittgenstein's Builders', in *Discussions of Wittgenstein*, London, Routledge, pp. 71–84.

— (1998) *Wittgenstein and the Possibility of Discourse*, Cambridge, Cambridge University Press.

Rosefeldt, T. (2004) 'Is knowing-how simply a case of knowing-that?' *Philosophical Investigations*, 27, 4, pp. 370–9.

Rousseau, J-J. [1754] (1968) *Discourse on Inequality, Social Contract*, London, Dent.

— [1762] (1968) *Emile ou l'Education*, Paris, Flammarion.

Rowbottom, D. P. (2007) 'Demystifying threshold concepts', *Journal of Philosophy of Education*, 41, 2, pp. 263–70.

Rumfitt, I. (2003) 'Savoir faire', *Journal of Philosophy*, 100, 3, pp. 158–66.

Ryle, G. (1946) 'Knowing how and knowing that', *Proceedings of the Aristotelian Society*, 56, pp. 212–25.

— (1949) *The Concept of Mind*, London, Hutchinson.

— (1974) 'Intelligence and the logic of the nature-nurture issue: reply to J. P. White', *Proceedings of the Philosophy of Education Society of Great Britain*, 8, 1, pp. 52–60.

Searle, J. R. (1995) *The Construction of Social Reality*, London, Penguin.

Schön, D. A. (1987) *Educating the Reflective Practitioner*, San Francisco, Jossey-Bass.

Siegel, H. (2010) *Reply to Johnson* in Winch, C. (ed.) *Teaching Thinking Skills*, London, Continuum.

Smith, A. [1776] (1981) *An Inquiry into the Causes of the Wealth of Nations*, Indianapolis, Liberty Fund.

Smith, P., Jones, O. R. (1997) *Philosophy of Mind*, Cambridge, Cambridge University Press.

Snowdon, P. (2003) 'Knowing how and knowing that: a distinction reconsidered', address delivered to the Aristotelian Society, 13 October 2003, pp. 1–29.

Stanley, J., Williamson, T. (2001) 'Knowing how', *Journal of Philosophy*, 48, 8, August, pp. 411–44.

Straka, G. A. (2002) 'Empirical comparisons between the English national vocational qualifications and the educational and training goals of the German dual system – an analysis for the banking sector', in Achtenhagen, F., Thång, P.-O. (eds) *Transferability, Flexibility and Mobility as Targets of Vocational Education and Training.* Proceedings of the final conference of the COST action A11, Gothenburg, 13–16 June 2002. Göttingen: Seminar für Wirtschaftspädagogik der Georg-August-Universität. pp. 227–40.

Streeck, W. (1996) 'Lean production in the German automobile industry: a test case for convergence theory', in Berger, S., Dore, R. (eds) *National Diversity and Global Capitalism*, New York: Cornell University Press, pp. 138–70.

Sturt, G. (1923, 1976) *The Wheelwright's Shop*, Cambridge, Cambridge University Press.

Taylor, C. (1964) *The Explanation of Behaviour*, London, Routledge.

Taylor, F. (1911) *The Principles of Scientific Management*, New York, Norton.

Tolkien, J. R. R. (1937) *The Hobbit*, London, Allen and Unwin.

Toribio, J. (2008) 'How do we know how?' *Philosophical Explorations*, 11, 1, pp. 39–52.

Toulmin, S. (1958) *The Uses of Argument*, Cambridge, Cambridge University Press.

Tsui, A. (2002) *Understanding Expertise in Teaching*, Cambridge, Cambridge University Press.

UK Commission for Employment and Skills (2009) *Ambition 2020: World Class Skills and Jobs for the UK*, London, UK Commission for Employment and Skills.

Verheggen, C. (1995), 'Wittgenstein and "solitary" languages', *Philosophical Investigations*, 18, 4, pp. 329–47.

Wallis, C. (2008) 'Consciousness, context, and know-how', *Synthèse*, 160, pp. 123–53.

Walton, I. [1653] (1982) *The Compleat Angler*, Oxford, Oxford University Press.

Weil, S. (1949) *L'Enracinement*, Paris, Gallimard. Translated into English as *The Need for Roots* (2001) London, Routledge.

— (2001) *Oppression and Liberty*, London, Routledge.

Wheelahan, L. (2007) 'How competency-based training locks the working class out of powerful knowledge: a modified Bernsteinian analysis', *British Journal of Sociology of Education*, 1465–3346, 28, 5, pp. 637–51.

White, A. (1982) *The Nature of Knowledge*, Totowa, Rowan and Littlefield, ch. 2.

Wilkinson, R. (2005) *The Impact of Inequality: How to Make Sick Societies Healthier*, London, Routledge.

Williams, K. (2007) *Education and the Voice of Michael Oakeshott*, Charlottesville VA, Imprint-Academic.

Winch, C. (1998) *The Philosophy of Human Learning*, London, Routledge.

— (2002) 'Work, well-being and vocational education', *Journal of Applied Philosophy*, 19, 3, pp. 261–71.

— (2006a) 'Georg Kerschensteiner. Founding the German Dual System', *Oxford Review of Education*, 32, 3, pp. 381–96.

— (2006b) Rules, technique and practical knowledge', *Educational Theory*, 56, 4, pp. 407–22.

— (2008) 'Learning how to learn: a critique', *Journal of Philosophy of Education*, 42, 3–4, pp. 649–65.

— (2009) 'Ryle on knowing how and the possibility of vocational education', *Journal of Applied Philosophy*, 26, 1, pp. 88–101.

Winch, P. (1958) *The Idea of a Social Science*, London, Routledge.

Winterton, J., le Deist, F., Stringfellow, E. (2005) *Clarification of Knowledge, Skills and Competences: Clarification of the Concept and Prototype*, Centre for European Research on Employment and Human Resources, Group ESG Toulouse.

Wittgenstein, L. (1953) *Philosophical Investigations*, Oxford, Blackwell.

— (1958) *Blue and Brown Books*, Oxford, Blackwell.

— (1969) *On Certainty*, Oxford, Blackwell.

— (1974) *Philosophical Grammar*, Oxford, Blackwell, p. 188.

Wolfe, T. (1987) *The Bonfire of the Vanities*, New York, Picador.

Index